If Walls Could Talk

If Walls Could Talk

An Intimate History of the Home

LUCY WORSLEY

First published in 2011
by Faber and Faber Limited
Bloomsbury House
74–77 Great Russell Street
London WC1B 3DA

Typeset by Faber and Faber Limited
Printed in England by TJ International Ltd, Padstow, Cornwall

A CIP record for this book
is available from the British Library

ISBN 978–0–571–25952–6

2 4 6 8 10 9 7 5 3 1

What I want to know is, in the Middle Ages, did they do anything for Housemaid's Knee? What did they put in their hot baths after jousting?

H. G. Wells, *Tono-Bungay*, 1909

Contents

Illustrations

TEXT ILLUSTRATIONS

Introduction

Why did the flushing toilet take two centuries to catch on? Why did strangers share their beds? And why did rich people fear fruit? These are the kinds of question I want to address in this intimate history of home life.

Moving through the four main rooms of a house – bedroom, bathroom, living room and kitchen – I've explored what people *actually did* in bed, in the bath, at the table and at the stove. This has taken me from sauce-stirring to breastfeeding, teeth-cleaning to masturbation, getting dressed to getting married.

Along my way, I was intrigued to discover that bedrooms in the past were rather crowded, semi-public places, and that only in the nineteenth century did they become reserved purely for sleep and sex. The bathroom didn't even exist as a separate room until late in the Victorian age, and it surprised me that people's attitudes towards personal hygiene, rather than technological innovation, determined the pace of its development. The living room emerged once people had the leisure time and spare money to spend in and on it, and I've learned to think of it as a sort of stage-set where homeowners acted out an idealised version of their lives for the benefit of guests. Meanwhile, the story of the kitchen is also the story of food safety, transport, technology and gender relations. Once I realised this, I saw my own kitchen in an entirely new light.

There are lots of tiny, quirky and seemingly trivial details in this book, but through them I think we can chart great, over-arching, revolutionary changes in society. A person's home makes an excellent starting point for assessing their time, place and life. 'I've a great respect for *things*!' says Madame Merle in Henry James's *The Portrait of a Lady* (1881). 'We're each of us made up of some cluster of appurtenances . . . one's house, one's furniture, one's garments, the books one reads, the company one keeps – these things are all expressive.' 'Look around this room of yours and what do you see?' asked John Ruskin in 1853. The answer, of course, is the same even today: you see yourself. That's why, now as then, people lavish so much time, effort and money on their houses.

What else have I learned from writing this history of domestic life? It's been brought home to me that biology has always been destiny. Many major social upheavals come back, in the end, to little changes in the way that people think about and look after their bodies. I also think it's interesting and instructive to find that the put-upon and down-and-out in the past weren't always worse off than they are today. Industrialisation was a Bad Thing for many people; to be rich placed certain social obligations upon a person in the past that are now far from familiar. But this is a very old-fashioned history book in that generally, over the centuries, we see living conditions improve. Seemingly iron laws about behaviour eventually relax; amazing inventions remove problems at a stroke; there is hope for the future. My conclusion is that we have some distance yet to travel on this journey towards the good life, but that history can help to show us the way.

Most agreeably of all, I feel that I've encountered some real people from the past, from all ranks in society, peasants to kings. If we reach out a hand across the centuries, we find that our ancestors are very much like us in the ways they lived, loved and died. 'Of all histories', wrote John Beadle in 1656, 'the history of men's lives is the most pleasant: such history . . . can call back times, and give life to those that are dead.'

In researching this book, I've had two sources of extra help from beyond the walls of the library. Firstly, working at Historic Royal Palaces, as I do, I am surrounded by people whose job it is to bring the past back to life for our visitors. We talk about the topics covered here every day. Secondly, I've had the privilege of presenting a BBC TV series on the history of the home. For that project I tried out for myself many of the processes and rituals described here. I blackened a Victorian kitchen range, lugged the hot water to fill an unplumbed bathtub, ignited a gas streetlight, waded through nineteenth-century sewers, slept in a Tudor bed, drank a Georgian medicine made out of seawater, coaxed a dog into turning a roasting-spit, and even used urine as a stain-remover. Each time we recreated some lost part of domestic life I learned something new about why and how houses developed.

Many of these humdrum tasks were so familiar to people in the past that they were hardly worth thinking about. 'I was talking about ideals, nobility, principles,' cries one of the characters in Marilyn French's classic feminist novel *The Women's Room* (1978). 'Why do you always have to bring us down to the level of the mundane, the ordinary, the stinking, f---ing refrigerator?' But I would argue that every single object in your home has its own important story to tell. Your relationship with your refrigerator reveals a great deal about who you really are. Is it full or empty? Do you share it? Clean it yourself? Have someone to clean it for you? The answers to these questions define your place in the world. As Dr Johnson put it:

Sir, there is nothing too little for so little a creature as man. It is by studying little things that we attain the great knowledge of having as little misery and as much happiness as possible.

PART ONE

An Intimate History of the Bedroom

Nearly a third of history is missing. You very rarely hear about the hours when people were asleep, or on the borders of it, and it's worth trying to fill that gap.

Today your bedroom is the backstage area where you prepare for your performance in the theatre of the world. For us it's a private place, and it's rude to barge into someone else's bedroom without knocking.

But this is a relatively new phenomenon. Medieval people didn't have special rooms for sleeping. They simply had a living space in which they happened to rest – or eat, or read, or party – and they used the same room for everything. The idea that you might sleep by yourself, in your own bed, in your own separate room, is really rather modern.

The functions of bedroom and living room eventually became separate, yet the bedroom remained a social space for a surprisingly long time. Guests were received in bedrooms as a mark of favour, courtship and marriage were played out here, and even childbirth was for centuries a communal experience. Only in the nineteenth century did the bedroom become secluded, set aside for sleep, sex, birth and death. In the twentieth century, even the last two left the bedroom behind and went off to the hospital.

Because the room in which you slept was so much more than just a place of rest, the history of the bedroom is a vital strand in the history of society itself.

1 – A History of the Bed

There are few nicer things than sitting up in bed, drinking strong tea, and reading.

Alan Clark, 27 January 1977

Once upon a time, life's great questions were: would you be warm tonight and would you get something to eat? Under these circumstances, the central great hall of a medieval house was a wonderful place to be: safe, even if smoky, stinking and crowded. Perhaps its floor was made only of earth, but no one cared if the hall was full of company, warmth and food. Many people, then, were glad to doss down here. At night the medieval great hall became a bedroom.

A medieval great household was rather like a boarding school in which most of the pupils were grown up. They came from humble homes to live and learn at a centre of culture and security for the surrounding area. They served their lord by day, and slept on his floor by night. If you had a particular job in the household, you perhaps slept in your daytime place of work: we hear of laundry-maids sleeping in the laundry, porters sleeping in their lodges, and kitchen staff bedding down near the fireplaces where they worked all day. A Tudor inventory made at Sutton Place in Surrey shows that the 'lads' of the kitchen slept in the same room as the household's fool. The one place you didn't sleep was a bedroom.

So nearly everyone shared their sleeping space with numerous other people. You'll often read that medieval people had no notion of privacy. Certainly it should not be assumed that it exists in every culture. In modern Japan, for example, privacy is much less important than in the West. Lacking their own word for the concept, the Japanese have adopted an English one, 'praibashii'.

Medieval lives were much more communal than those of today, but that's not to say that they contained no notion of privacy at all. People still took the trouble to seek out private moments, such as the times when lord and lady lay curtained off in their four-poster bed, or when a courting couple walked out into the woods in merry Maytime, or when a person knelt in prayer in an oratory. The private book, the locked and private box containing personal treasures, or the private oratory were private places indeed, even if smaller or less accessible than a modern person might expect.

On the other hand, there was, indeed, less 'private life'. Society was structured so that one's position in the hierarchy was obvious and explicit. There was a 'Great Chain of Being' extending down from God, through his angels, to the Archbishop of Canterbury and other notables such as dukes, before normal people got a look-in. But at least we lesser mortals could take comfort from being placed above the animals, the plants, and finally, the stones. Such a chain inevitably restricted people's hopes of bettering their social position, but it also comforted them. Those higher up adopted airs of superiority, but they also had clear and pressing responsibilities towards those lower down.

In this communal but strictly hierarchical world, literacy was rare; so, therefore, was diary-writing and introspection; so was time free from getting and making food. God, not the self, was the centre of the world. Understanding what it might have been like to inhabit such a mental world is the ultimate aim of historians' efforts in researching and constructing medieval furniture and the rooms it stood in.

Medieval beds for most people consisted of hay or straw ('hitting the hay' had a literal meaning) stuffed into a sack. These sacks might be made out of 'ticking', the rough striped cloth still used to cover mattresses today. A mattress might also be known as a 'palliasse', from *'paille'*, the French word for straw. John Russell in *c.*1452 gives instructions for making a bed for several sleepers, 9 ft long by 7 ft wide. He says you should collect 'litter' (presumably leaves, not crisp packets) to 'stuff' the mattress. Then the stuffing should be distributed evenly to remove the worst lumps. Each simple mattress should be 'craftily trod . . . with wisps drawn out at feet and side'.

It sounds rather uncomfortable, but presumably it was softer than the floor.

And snuggling up together in a big bed was normal, indeed desirable, for warmth and security. A French phrase book for use by medieval travellers included the following useful expressions: 'you are an ill bed-fellow', 'you pull all the bed clothes' and 'you do nothing but kick about'. The sixteenth-century poet Andrew Barclay describes the horrible sounds that could be expected in a roomful of sleepers:

> Some buck and some babble, some cometh drunk to bed,
> Some brawl and some jangle, when they be beastly fed;
> Some laugh and some cry, each man will have his will,
> Some spew and some piss, not one of them is still.
> Never be they still till middle of the night,
> And then some brawleth, and for their beds fight.

Because it was so easy to annoy or inconvenience your bedfellows, custom and etiquette developed about how to take your position in a communal bed. An observer of life in early-nineteenth-century rural Ireland noted that families lay down 'in order, the eldest daughter next the wall farthest from the door, then all the sisters according to their ages, next the mother,

5

father and sons in succession, then the strangers, whether the travelling pedlar or tailor or beggar'. Thus the unmarried girls were wisely kept as far as possible from the unmarried men, while husband and wife lay together in the middle.

William Harrison's is the best-known description of servants' beds in the Elizabethan age: 'if they had any sheets above them, it was well, for seldom had they any under their bodies, to keep them from the pricking straws that ran oft through the canvas'. Yet his comments must be taken with a pinch of salt because Harrison actually thought that a bit of discomfort was good for you. Like conservative commentators in all periods, he was bemoaning the fact that Englishmen had turned into softies, wanting all kinds of unmanly luxuries. Pillows, he said, were formerly 'thought meet only for women in childbed'; how times had changed when even *men* wanted pillows, instead of making do with 'a good round log under their heads'.

But sleeping in the great hall wasn't good enough for the actual blood family who owned the medieval manor house. The lord and lady might retire from the company of hoi polloi into an upstairs room adjoining the hall. Often it was called simply 'the chamber', sometimes the 'bower' or 'solar'. (The 'chamber' was overseen by a special servant called the 'chamberlain'.) In the chamber at Penshurst Place in Kent, one of Britain's most complete surviving medieval houses, a peephole or squint gives a view down into the hall below so that the boss could see what his employees were getting up to. He literally 'looked down' upon his servants.

The lord and lady's chamber was a multifunctional place: home office, library, living room and bedroom combined. But it almost certainly contained a proper wooden bed. It's quite hard to work out exactly what these beds looked like because medieval artists usually ran into difficulties with the proportion or the scale. When we made a reconstruction of Edward I's bed for the Medieval Palace at the Tower of London, our evidence included documents recording payment for its green posts painted with stars, and for chains to link the various parts together (plate 2). The contemporary illustration showing 'The Conception of Merlin' (plate 3) gave us a good idea about how to proceed. The bed was demountable because Edward I was constantly travelling round the country. His servants took it apart in order to transport it from castle to castle, and the chains held the whole thing together when it was re-erected.

We have another glimpse of the colour and grandeur of a late-medieval bed from Geoffrey Chaucer, who, at one stage in his career, was 'Yeoman Valet to the King's Chamber'. In this position he was responsible for bed-making, so he knew what he was talking about when he described a luxurious gold-and-black bed:

> . . . of downe of pure dovis white
> I wol yeve him a fethir bed,
> Rayid with gold, and right well cled
> In fine black satin *d'outremere* [from overseas].

Even towards the end of the medieval period, though, grand beds carved in wood were still few and far between. A 'pallet bed' was most people's accustomed lot. It was essentially a wooden box, perhaps with short legs, that could be easily carried from room to room as the number of servants or guests requiring accommodation ebbed and flowed. Pallet beds were so simple and practical they endured for centuries. At the Elizabethan Hardwick Hall in Derbyshire, an inventory from 1601 shows that a folding bed was kept on the landing of the stairs for some poor soul, and that there was a pallet even in the scullery. The memoirs of a valet who worked at an Irish country house in the 1860s record similar sleeping arrangements, though by then they must have been exceedingly old-fashioned: 'There were three or four beds in a room. Many of the men had folding or press beds here and there in the pantry and the hall.'

But the Tudor age also saw one of Europe's greatest inventions take on a fixed form. The four-poster bed was often the most expensive item in a house, and was an essential purchase upon marriage. (If you were lucky, you inherited yours from your parents.) Its canopy protected you from twigs or feathers falling from a roof which might lack a plaster ceiling. Its woollen curtains provided warmth, and also *some* privacy. It's very likely that even in a middle-ranking Tudor household the master and mistress would be sharing their bedroom with children or privileged servants using pallet beds or even wheeled truckle beds that lived underneath the four-poster during the daytime.

On a Tudor four-poster, the mattress lay upon bed-strings made up of a rope threaded from top to bottom and side to side. This rope inevitably sagged under the sleeper's weight and required regular tightening up, hence the expression 'Night, night, sleep tight'.

Pictures of pre-modern people in bed often show them in a curious half-sitting position. Propped up against pillows and bolsters, they look rather uncomfortable, and one wonders if they actually slept like that. Perhaps the answer is that art did not mirror reality, and that artists always positioned their models to get the best possible view of their faces. (Also it isn't likely, as so many contemporary images seem to suggest, that medieval kings slept in their crowns.) But I think the explanation for the pose is that beds strung with rope cannot fail to dip in the middle and feel rather like hammocks. In fact, sleeping on one's front is well-nigh impossible in a rope-strung bed, as I discovered when I spent the night in the medieval farmhouse at the Weald and Downland Museum.

On into the seventeenth century people were still accustomed to share their beds. When the daughter of Lady Anne Clifford was nearly three, her maturity was measured with three changes in her daily life: she was put into a whalebone bodice, left free to walk without leading strings, and allowed to sleep in her

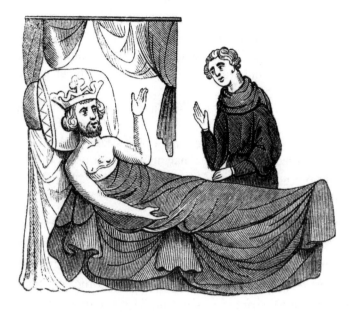

Did kings really wear their crowns in bed? And did medieval people sleep sitting up?

mother's bed. Sharing a bed was the action of a grown-up, not (as now) of a child.

Indeed, if you'd slept all by yourself in the 'Great Bed of Ware', now in the Victoria and Albert Museum, you might well have felt a little lost and lonely. It's a massive 10 ft 8½ ins wide. Dating from between 1575 and 1600, and once the property of the Crown Inn in Ware, it could accommodate a considerable number of sleepers. No less than twelve people once spent the night in it together (although that was 'for a frolick').

For people rich enough to possess a four-poster and all the appropriate sheets, hangings and linen, the ceremony of getting into bed involved a certain amount of ritual and help from their servants. A foreign phrase book for visitors to England published in 1589 includes a section on what an overseas tourist might expect to say to his hotel chambermaid as she prepared him for sleep:

My shee frinde, is my bed made? Is it good?

Yea, Sir, it is a good feder bed, the scheetes be very cleane.

I shake as a leafe upon the tree. Bryng my pillow and cover me well: pull off my hosen and warme my bed. Where is the chamber pot? Where is the privie?

At the right hand. If you see them not you shall smell them well enough.

My shee friende, kisse me once, and I shall sleape the better.

I had rather die than to kisse a man in his bed, or in any other place. Take your rest in God's name.

I thank you, fayre mayden.

Samuel Pepys, merely a prosperous seventeenth-century civil servant, nevertheless had servants to help him at bedtime: one day he wrote that he'd 'had the boy up tonight for his sister to teach him to put me to bed'. A man of his time, his bedroom hours were not restricted to sleeping: in his diaries, he may also be found using the room for playing his lute, reading, singing duets, discussing music with a friend, hearing his serving boy's Latin translation, arguing and teaching his wife astronomy.

Pepys's bed would have been made with a feather mattress placed on top of the one stuffed with straw. A feather bed was a prized possession: no wonder, as fifty pounds of feathers had to be saved from the plucking of numerous geese. Sometimes female servants in the kitchen were allowed to keep the feathers of the birds they'd plucked for the table as a kind of dowry, and saved them up for a marital feather bed. Such a bed needs constant punching, turning and shaking to keep it fresh and to disperse the lumps, and a new one was not necessarily more desirable than an old one because of the farmyard scent it would emit.

Efficient housewives would try to amass a large amount of bedlinen so that they only needed to do a big load of laundry once a month. When James Boswell and Samuel Johnson visited the Isle of Skye in 1773, the latter slept in the actual bed at Flora Macdonald's house in which Bonnie Prince Charlie had spent the night when he was on the run from the English a few years previously. Mrs Macdonald even had the Bonnie Prince's own dirty sheets kept safe and reverently unwashed, and was rather ghoulishly saving them for the wrapping of her own corpse.

Boswell noted that on this remote Scottish island people continually came barging into his bedroom. 'During the day, the bedrooms were common to all . . . children and dogs not excepted.' He was rather surprised by this because, by the Georgian age, the wealthy urban classes had begun for the first time to expect to be left alone in their bedrooms.

The conventional design of a middling seventeenth-century house – perhaps a farmer's, or a tradesman's – had an upper floor with the bedrooms leading off each other. This meant that the users of the second room could only access it through the first. In the eighteenth-century townhouse, though, an increasing demand for privacy meant that space was now being given over purely to circulation. The classic tall, thin, terraced townhouse had a landing on each floor, with two separate bedrooms opening off it. Now the people occupying the smaller, back bedroom could reach their room directly from the stairs, *without* passing through someone else's room first.

The next step, in larger houses, would be the corridor: its appearance at the very end of the seventeenth century allowed every bedroom to become completely independent and private. Cassandra Willoughby, an interested poker-about in other people's houses, thought it worth noting with approval in 1697 that one Mr Arthington's new house had an arrangement of balconies which allowed 'a very convenient passage from one room to another without making any of the Bed Chambers a thorough fair'.

So the Georgians began to treat their bedrooms as more exclusive, private spaces than the Tudors had done. It became customary to hang a bedroom door so that it opened inwards, towards the bed. 'The idea behind this is that the person entering shall not be able to take in the whole room at a glance as he opens the first crack of the door,' explained Hermann Muthesius, a German commentator on British homes, in 1904. Instead, a visitor must circumnavigate the door 'to enter the room, by which time the person seated in the room will have been able to prepare himself suitably for his entry'.

But bedrooms were still to some extent social, used for cards or tea or gatherings of friends, or else for writing or business or study. In William Hogarth's picture *The Countess's Levee* (1743), the countess in question has no less than ten people in attendance to help her dress: hairdresser, flautist, singer, priest, female friend, black page; even a boy from a toy shop has visited to offer his wares. But the countess is a flighty character, and her male guests are clearly undesirable, unmanly figures. Oliver Goldsmith in 1765 described such a bedchamber party:

> Fair to be seen, she kept a bevy
> Of powdered Coxcombs at her levy.

His disapproval shows that this kind of bedchamber socialising was beginning to be thought inappropriate. The next stage in the bedroom's development occurred in the Victorian age, where separation and privacy became not only desirable, but essential, and its achievement a source of paranoid anxiety. Men and women were to be kept apart, as were menservants and maids, and bed-making became an ever more time-consuming and expensive ritual.

For the Victorian upper classes, it would be unthinkable for a husband and wife with a large house to share a bedroom. This was an age in which shame and scruple grew up around sex, with ladies knowing less about it and fearing it more, and their husbands shielding them from carnal knowledge. The activities of the bedroom were now limited to sex and sleeping alone, and the other social purposes of the room fell away. *The Architect* magazine was very strict on the matter, stating that using a bedroom for *anything* other than sleeping was 'unwholesome, immoral and contrary to the well-understood principle that every important function in life requires a separate room'.

His dressing room was the place where a well-off gentleman often slept, perhaps slipping in late after an evening spent smoking with his male friends. A lady's own dressing room might be called her *boudoir*, a room which takes its name from the French verb '*bouder*', to sulk. This ideal of separation, once it became established in the homes of the rich, looked modern and desirable and was something to aspire to for the middle classes. The early twentieth century saw them emulating it in a small way by sleeping happily in twin beds in their semi-detached homes.

The beds in the Victorian home were more elaborately made than ever. Nineteenth-century household manuals devote much attention to the need to keep beds fresh, aired and layered with a multitude of sheets and blankets. They seem almost to fetishise bed-making, but then again a damp bed could be extremely dangerous in an age of tuberculosis.

In 1826, coiled metal springs began to replace the old rope bed strings. Now too the wool and linen of earlier beds were replaced with a new wonder product whose profits powered Britain into the industrial age. The nineteenth century was an age of cotton: half of the value of Britain's exports lay, by the 1830s, in cotton textiles alone. It was first India, and then America, that supplied the raw cotton spun and woven in the mills of Lancashire. The number of mills in Manchester (or 'Cottonopolis') peaked in 1853, when there were no less than 108 of them.

The products of these mills were jealously hoarded by Victorian housewives who prided themselves on their well-stocked linen cupboards and carefully husbanded their sheets by reusing the top sheet as the bottom one after a fortnight's use. Victorian bed-making was tight with tension, and Mrs Panton, author of *From Kitchen to Garrett* (1887), confided her fears that no servant could ever make a bed to her obsessively high standards. 'I have never yet found in all my experience a servant who can be really and truly trusted to properly air the bed,' she complained. Inevitably a servant's 'first idea is to cover it up and get it made', leaving it 'stuffy and disagreeable'.

All very well – but just imagine the labour involved in 'properly airing' a Victorian bed. It consisted of a bedstead, a sheet of thick brown Holland fabric to cover the metal springs, then a horsehair mattress, feather mattress, underblanket, undersheet, bottom sheet, top sheet, three or four blankets, eiderdown and pillow covers. Mrs Panton recommended stripping all this off, every day: 'there is not one single thing that should be left on the bed once one is out of it. Do not be content with turning all the bed-clothes over the rail; see they are all pulled out from under the mattress, separated, and hung up.' She then advised that her unfortunate servant should 'pull off the mattress, placing it as close to the window as it will go'. She also advocated that the frilled pillow cases decorating the pillows during the day be removed every night, 'and replaced by plain ones, from motives of economy'. At Tatton Old Hall in Cheshire I had a go at making a Victorian bed according to her instructions. It took half an hour, and I simply wasn't strong enough to turn the horsehair mattress without help. No wonder Mrs Panton's servants skimped.

Frilled pillow cases would not have made an appearance in Mrs Panton's servants' bedrooms. These, Victorian household manuals insisted, were to be kept as scrupulously simple as possible. 'A servant's bed-room should have as few articles in it as are consistent with comfort,' recommended *Cassell's Household Guide* (1880s). 'A bed and bedstead . . . unbleached sheets . . . inexpensive coloured counterpane, a chest of drawers, a looking-glass, wash-stand . . . and a chair, are all that is needed.' It sounds more than a little prison-like.

Mrs Panton also agreed that servants' rooms should not be 'unduly luxurious', though she did concede that each individual should have a separate bed. She treated her maids rather like animals, expecting little from them in terms of taste or care. Curtains should be forbidden, and 'neither should their own boxes be kept in their rooms . . . they cannot refrain somehow from hoarding all sorts of rubbish in them'. Given that their trunks, brought from home, were the only private space that the servants possessed in their employer's house, it seems more than mean of Mrs Panton to take them away.

The growing awareness of the existence of germs and the subsequent Sanitary Reform Movement brought an end to the most extravagant frills and furbelows of the heavily draped Victorian bedroom. Edwin Chadwick's report on *The Sanitary Condition of the Labouring Population* (1842) stressed the economic value of preserving workers from disease by keeping houses clean. Sanitary reformers favoured iron for bedsteads because, unlike timber, it failed to harbour lice and other nefarious pests. The only really certain way of getting rid of the bugs from a wooden bed was to burn it. So iron became the material of choice.

Yet the bed layered with sheets, blankets and eiderdowns persisted into the 1900s, and the labour of making it was still faithfully performed. The duties of a housemaid from the early twentieth century show that the occupant of a bedroom in even an only moderately grand house might by now have slept alone, but still shared the use of the space with at least one other very busy person:

Rise 6.30 am / Open windows, etc / Prepare early tea / Take hot water to the bedrooms / Prepare baths / Sweep and dust hall, clean doorstep / Lay and light fires / After breakfast, make beds, empty slops and tidy bedrooms / Prepare rooms for sweeping, clean them thoroughly / Be dressed [in uniform] by 3pm / Take hot water to bedrooms before dinner / Light fires and gas, draw curtains / If needed assist with toilet of younger ladies or guests / Help wait at table if needed / Turn down beds and prepare bedroom for the night.

It wasn't until the 1970s that the greatest revolution yet in bed-making occurred. This was the decade during which the duvet arrived from Scandinavia. With it the use of top sheet, blankets and bedspread would almost disappear, or at the very least, would come to appear deliberately nostalgic.

Terence Conran deserves the credit for introducing what was initially known as the 'Slumberdown', or by the alternative name which reveals its origins, the 'continental quilt'. Only a little later, after the French had enthusiastically adopted its use, did it become known by the French word for 'down': *duvet.*

Duvets were associated with liberation from the drudgery of bed-making, but also with liberation of other kinds: 'sleep with a Swede' was an early advertising slogan in this newly permissive age. Duvets and their covers were sold in Conran's new chain of Habitat shops, and Patricia Whittington-Farrell was one of the demonstrators employed to show customers just how quick and easy they were to use. She spent her days taking the covers on and off, and demonstrating the art of making the 'ten-second bed'. When I met and talked to her, she could no longer quite meet her ten-second standard, but she was still hugely enthusiastic about Habitat and the life-affirming qualities it represented to the young 1970s housewife.

The 'ten-second bed', put to rights with the flick of a wrist, also made a proud appearance in Habitat catalogues. The fabrics pictured were boldly coloured or patterned, as far distant from the pristine white of Victorian bed linen as possible. Modern and striking, they were navy, magenta, mustard, striped or flow-ered. People experimented by buying duvets for their children first, and those born in the 1970s – myself included – grew up knowing nothing else (though I remember overhearing the res-ervations of my grandmother and her friends: 'Isn't it heavy? Isn't it hot?').

But few people, once they'd tried duvets, went back to sheets and blankets. In fact, anyone still found sleeping under many layers of bedding is actually indulging in conspicuous consumption: they, or their staff, have the time to put such a bed back together in the morning, and to clean the component sheets, blankets, eiderdowns and throws according to their various complicated requirements.

The simplicity of most modern beds – just one mattress, just one covering – takes us back in a strange kind of circle to the medieval period, when a sack full of straw and a cloak were all one needed.

2 – Being Born

Grant we beseech thee to all infants yet unborn, that
knit together with their due veins and members, they
may come forth into this world sound and perfect
without fault or deformity.

Thomas Bentley, a prayer for pregnant women, 1582

Until lying-in hospitals began to appear in the eighteenth century, nearly everyone was born at home. Life began in a bedchamber, and more often than not it ended there too, perhaps in
the very same family bed. Until these great events were shuffled
off to hospitals, this room was the first and last sight a person
saw.

Any expectant mother today feels some sense of trepidation,
but in the past the stakes were much higher. Childbirth was
the biggest risk to life for young women, and the bedchambers
to which they retired as their time drew near were frightening,
daunting places. The medieval death rate was one in every fifty
pregnancies. Considering that it wasn't unusual for a woman
to give birth a dozen times, the odds quickly mounted up for
reproductive wives. Many pregnant Tudor ladies had their
portraits painted for the poignant reason that they might well
have been saying goodbye to their husbands for ever when
they disappeared into confinement. If so, their families would

at least have had a final image of a lost loved one (plate 9).

The Tudors knew what proponents of natural birth still know today: gravity helps. Sixteenth-century queens sat in a seat-less throne called the 'groaning chair', upholstered in gold cloth and complete with a copper bowl to catch the afterbirth. Cruder, seat-less stools were in the possession of midwives serving all ranks of society. Some had fancier features such as leather seats, ratcheted backs or handles for the woman to grip as she pushed.

The final few weeks of their pregnancies were filled with elaborate rituals for Tudor and Stuart women of high status. A well-prepared woman would have entered her marriage already equipped with her set of 'childbed linen', of both ceremonial as well as practical purpose. Now the various cloths and sheets lovingly prepared and stored in a chest would be brought out for use. The effort spent upon their preparation showed that a woman was ready to become a mother both physically and psychologically.

During the later stages of her pregnancy, a Tudor or Stuart woman would literally withdraw from the world. Sixteenth-century households sealed their pregnant women into darkened, well-furnished rooms for a whole month before the birth to minimise the risks of a miscarriage-inducing fall or fright. The darkness and stuffiness was to reduce the entry of bad 'airs', which, according to contemporary medicine, carried disease.

This theory that an evil 'miasma' carried illness through the ether was terribly important in the history of house-planning, and we will hear much more about it. It also caused great attention to be paid to the aspect of a house; a dangerously damp or valley site would have bad air, and therefore disease. You can understand why people thought like this. Malaria, for example, was common in the swamps of Tudor England. But it was spread by mosquitoes, not an imaginary 'miasma'.

Even after the great event, the new Tudor mother was not allowed to escape from her birthing chamber. She would be revived there with 'caudle', a sort of alcoholic porridge. Only two weeks later was she washed, her soiled straw mattress changed and she herself allowed to sit up. The 'upsitting' and the 'footing' a fortnight later when she got out of bed were celebrated by the women of the household with all-female parties. These rituals were taken over to New England as well: Mary Holyoke of Salem's eighteenth-century diary records how she 'kept chamber' before being 'brought to bed', hosting a party for five female friends two weeks later.

Being locked up for a period of enforced rest after giving birth may sound rather horrible, but it took women through the really dangerous days during which so many of them died from loss of blood or from puerperal fever (septicaemia; basically caused by dirty hands, and incurable). Lying-in continued until the conclusive ceremony of 'churching' a month after the birth, when the woman left the house to return to church (and came home to return to her husband's bed).

The gathering of the women, the gossiping, the pleasure they took in their shared experience made giving birth a much more sociable event than it is today, when it's chiefly an individual drama. In fact, the bonding nature of childbirth explains why the users of the 'molly-houses' (male brothels) of early eighteenth-century London replicated its rituals: homosexual men pretended to give birth, and celebrated with the traditional party afterwards. The first known piece of printed gay porn was entitled *A Lying-In Conversation with a Curious Adventure* (1748), and it describes a man in drag infiltrating a lying-in chamber. Fetishising childbirth is not common in modern male gay society, and that's probably because lying in bed alone in a hospital is not nearly so much fun.

Babies made their first appearance amid a world of women, with males being kept out of the birthing chamber until deep into the eighteenth century. 'My wife's mother came to me with tears in her eyes,' wrote Nicholas Gilman in 1740. 'O, says she, I don't know how it will fare with your poor wife, hinting withal her extreme danger.' Mr Gilman was entirely in the hands of his mother-in-law for information about the life or death of his spouse, and childbirth was the one part of household life over which men had no control.

Even expectant husbands paid due respect to the wise women called in to advise upon such occasions. Midwives were figures of enormous and mysterious power, well able to diagnose difficulties through years of practical experience. Because of the hold they held over the emotions of hopeful parents, they were able to use 'magic' to predict and to protect in a manner at which science would scoff. For aristocrats, the gender of the baby was of huge significance, and a male heir for the estates was always desperately sought after. A seventeenth-century midwife would try to win a bigger fee by predicting a boy rather than a girl. Clues would be provided by the condition of the mother's breasts: 'ye Nipple red, rising like a strawberry' was a good sign.

While childbirth was often a communal experience, sometimes harrowing, sometimes joyful, there could be other people present in the birthing room for reasons of surveillance rather than support. For example, events that took place in the bedchamber of Mary of Modena, the wife of the unpopular King James II, led to a revolution. James II had long been annoying his subjects with his despotic and Catholic policies, and when his young Italian wife gave birth in 1688 to a healthy baby boy, the king's enemies were chagrined that his position had been so strengthened. To discredit him, they put it about that Mary's baby had in fact died and that an imposter had instead been smuggled into her bed in a warming pan.

The rumour grew into a long-lasting and damaging smear against James II, and the baby would never be king. James II was overthrown soon afterwards, and his son grew up to be the 'Pretender', a rival, Catholic and unsuccessful bidder for the throne now seized instead by James II's firmly Protestant daughters.

There are two reasons for mistrusting the story of the warming pan, which is said to have taken place in the velvet bed now standing in the Queen's Bedchamber at Kensington Palace (plate 6). Firstly, a warming pan itself, a kind of frying pan containing hot coals to warm cold sheets, is hardly big enough to hold a baby. Secondly, to avoid any such monkey business a royal confinement was attended by many members of the court and church acting as witnesses. Mary of Modena gave birth with at least fifty-one other people present, plus 'pages of the backstairs and priests', and it seems unlikely that such a large number could have maintained a conspiracy with success.

This concern about the birth of a true heir to the British monarchy persisted into the twentieth century. When the Queen Mother gave birth to our current queen in 1926, the Home Secretary came to the house to wait and watch (though he wasn't actually in the room itself). This undignified custom was only suspended by George VI, who thought it 'archaic'.

At lower levels in society, the midwife could spill the secrets of her clients, and feminine betrayal took place in some bedchambers. A midwife could detect a woman's adultery, infanticide or pre-marital sex. A 'monstrous' birth or malformed foetus would suggest that immoral behaviour had taken place: the seventeenth-century governor of New England, Sir Henry Vane, for example, had two women servants in his household; 'he debauched both, & both were delivered of monsters'.

During the course of the seventeenth century, men finally began to penetrate the birthing chamber and its mysteries. They brought with them a healthy dose of scepticism about many of the ancient customs surrounding childbirth, and they also introduced a new and important piece of birthing-chamber equipment: the forceps. These iron tongs were invented around 1600 by one Peter Chamberlen, but he kept them as a family secret, thereby building up an extremely impressive reputation for the dynasty of doctors that he founded. But it's William Smellie of

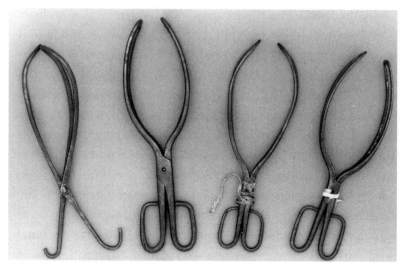

The forceps which revolutionised childbirth: the original set belonging to the Chamberlen family

Scotland (1697–1763) who's usually given credit for bringing the forceps into wider use.

There's no doubt that using them saved many lives. Previously, an iron hook had been used to drag out babies reluctant to emerge, which inevitably killed them. Yet midwives had misgivings about the forceps. *The Ladies Dispensatory, or Every Women Her Own Physician* (1739) recommended they be employed only in extreme circumstances, defined as cases where labour had lasted for *four or five* days.

The male physician began steadily to usurp the midwife's ground, even if he had much less practical experience, and gradually took control over childbirth away from women. A minister named Hugh Adams, of Durham, New Hampshire, claimed to have sorted out a very difficult confinement in 1724. He was called in after a midwife had despaired of a three-and-a-half-day labour, even though he had never delivered a child before. He performed his miracle only with some 'strong Hysterick medicines' and the knowledge he had gleaned from reading a few books.

Circumstances like these caused 'Old Wives' Tales' to begin to take on their modern reputation for inaccuracy and fallibility. Yet the male midwife would remain a figure of much suspicion throughout the Georgian period. The idea that another man would see his wife's private parts was troubling to many husbands. In satirical caricatures, the male midwife was often depicted with his ranks of medicine bottles, many of them containing sedatives which he used to knock out women in order to have his wicked way with them (plate 8).

As male doctors gradually took over more of the responsibility for delivering babies from the midwife, the design of the birthing chair began to change. A lower chair is better for a woman giving birth, as she can brace her feet against the floor. Its drawback is that the midwife has to bend down low, 'always leaning forward and bent over, with hands stretched out, watching for the foetus to appear'. But from around 1700, when doctors began to take over, birth chairs started to have longer legs. These higher chairs meant the physicians didn't need to stoop, but they were less comfortable for the woman. Eventually mothers were encouraged to lie down flat on their beds and push, instead of to sit and use gravity. It strikes one as being more to the benefit of doctor than patient.

A seventeenth-century birthing chair from the Wellcome Collection, London

Pain relief in Tudor times lay in the power of

prayer. Westminster Abbey's 'Girdle of Our Lady' was sometimes lent by its abbot to ladies in labour, such as Henry VIII's
sister Mary Tudor. They might also turn to recipes such as John
Partridge's optimistically named herbal potion 'to make women
have a quick and speedy deliverance of their children, and without pain, or at least very little'. Georgian ladies could rely on
the rather more efficacious 'liquid laudanum' – opium dissolved
in alcohol. It was completely legal, and Dr John Jones's *The
Mysteries of Opium Reveal'd* called the drug 'a sage and noble
panacea'. Queen Victoria popularised the use of chloroform
during birth, but did so in the face of enormous moral pressure not to 'succumb' to this 'weakness'. Many of her subjects
thought that 'to be insensible from whisky, gin, and brandy,
and wine, and beer and ether and chloroform, is to be what in
the world is called Dead-drunk', something shameful whatever
the circumstances. However, the rational and scientific Charles
Darwin administered chloroform to his own wife himself during
her labours.

Even after people began to understand that invisible germs
might be carried into a bedroom upon seemingly clean hands,
there was great opposition among doctors to changing their
habits. In 1865, the Female Medical Society asked that doctors
refrain from coming straight from the dissecting room to the
birthing room, but a riposte in *The Lancet* claimed that it was
entirely unnecessary: it was not infection but a woman's 'mental emotion' or overexcitement that caused puerperal fever. The
Tudor practice of remaining in bed after the birth was still followed: a book entitled *Advice to a Wife*, published in 1853,
recommended that a new mother should spend nine days on
her back before she 'may sit up for half an hour'. Only after a
fortnight might she 'change the chamber for the sitting room'.

There was, of course, a distasteful class aspect to all this resting up and seclusion. Another Victorian advice book claims
that it is 'utterly impossible for the wife of a labouring man

to give up work . . . Nor is it necessary. The back is made for its burthen.' For working women, or among the settlers in the New World, there was an unresolved tension between motherly and wifely duties. A mother-to-be was medically advised not to lift her arms above head height, yet reaching upwards was essential for the typical New England wife's task of daubing an unfinished or leaking house with clay. When Margaret Prince of Gloucester, Massachusetts, appeared in court to accuse a neighbour of casting a harmful spell upon her stillborn child, the 'daubing' accusation was thrown back at her. Yes, she had done 'wrong in carrying clay at such a time', Margaret admitted, but 'she had to, her husband would not, and her house lay open'. There was clearly a need, in rural societies, for pregnant women to carry on just as usual.

The squeamish attitudes of the nineteenth century introduced a novel reluctance to talk about pregnancy. As early as 1791, a writer in *The Gentleman's Magazine* noticed a growing trend for references to pregnancy to be seen as errors of taste. 'Our mothers and grandmothers, used in course of time to become *with child*,' he wrote, but 'no female, above the degree of chambermaid or laundress, has been with child these ten years past . . . nor is she ever *brought to bed,* or *delivered*'. The genteel lady should merely inform 'her friends that at a certain time she will be *confined*'. The downside of all this tasteful gentility was that women began to think of pregnancy as an illness, and Victorian books about childbirth began to refer to it among 'the diseases of women'. In the bedchamber, as in society at large, women began to be seen as fragile, vulnerable and incompetent at looking after themselves.

This was a great change from the more robust attitudes of the Georgian period, which saw a cruder but in some ways more assertive attitude amongst women to matters of sex and reproduction. Queen Caroline, wife of George II, would openly discuss her sexual relationships with the prime minister, Sir Robert

Walpole, and stated that she minded her husband's infidelity 'no more than his going to the close-stool'.

One cannot imagine prissy Queen Victoria ever discussing such a matter with her prime ministers. She herself was horrified by the experience of giving birth to children – 'the first two years of my married life [were] utterly spoilt by this occupation!' – and she almost certainly suffered from post-natal depression. Secrecy about childbirth only heightened the fears of the uninformed, first-time, nineteenth-century mother, and a reticence about women's bodies could be inconvenient if not downright dangerous. From the 1830s, for example, doctors knew that the mucosa of the vagina changed colour after conception, and this signal provided the earliest reliable indicator that a woman was pregnant. This would have been enormously useful for women to know. But the information was kept quiet because it implied that a doctor might actually examine a woman's private parts. The doctor who finally broke ranks and published the news was struck off the medical register as a punishment.

Alongside the idea that pregnancy was an illness, the lying-in hospital began to grow in popularity. Slowly childbirth was taken out of the bedroom, out of the home altogether, and into the public realm.

A rather sinister account of childbirth written in 1937 describes what happened, in ideal circumstances, when the expectant mother arrived at the twentieth-century hospital. She was 'immediately given the benefit of one of the modern analgesics or pain-killers. Soon she is in a dreamy, half-conscious state . . . she knows nothing about being taken to a spotlessly clean delivery room . . . she does not hear the cry of the baby when first he feels the chill of this cold world.' It didn't work out like this for Mira, the heroine of the The Women's Room (1978): 'It was not the labor that was agonizing her . . . it was the scene – the coldness and sterility of it, the contempt of the nurses and the doctor, the humiliation of being in stirrups and having people peer at her exposed genitals whenever they chose.'

Today, as a result of this sort of experience, many people would like to see childbirth return to the domestic realm. But New York midwives are, at the time of writing, not legally allowed to deliver babies in people's homes.

Another maternal duty that Queen Victoria avoided was the task of breastfeeding. In fact, it was much less common than you might assume in historic bedrooms, as a result of the once widespread practice of wet-nursing.

3 – Was Breast Always Best?

I am quite at a loss to account for the general practice
of sending infants out of doors, to be suckled ... by
another woman.

William Cadogan, 1748

For many centuries, breast was not best for upper-class women,
and newborn babies were often quickly expelled from their
mothers' bedrooms.

The early care of infants was considered vital, of course, to
their future well-being, and well-brought-up children required a
huge amount of clobber. Hannah Glasse, the eighteenth-century
Gina Ford, recommended that a baby wear a minimum of a
shirt, a petticoat, a set of buckram stays, a robe and two caps. It
seems almost cruel to squeeze a baby into tight stays, but it was
intended to ensure a straight spine. Those who grew up crooked
were thought to owe 'their misfortune to the disingenuity of
those who attended them in their infancy', who'd shamefully
failed to lace them tightly enough.

Childcare was clearly a matter requiring expert skill and
attention. And yet, for centuries, mothers did not consider that
they were the best people to care for their children.

The seventeenth and eighteenth centuries were a golden age
of wet-nursing.

Much of the evidence for this comes from one very vocal campaign group that complained vociferously about the almost universal use of wet nurses, and there was great debate on the issue (just as there is for breast- and bottle-feeding today). Only a very few ladies of 'courage and resolution' nursed their own children, it was said in the seventeenth century, and a nursing mother 'is become as unfashionable and ungenteel as a gentleman that will not drink, swear and be profane'.

But the complainers who preached so loudly on the topic were usually rather officious godly gentlemen of the Puritan persuasion. Even mothers whose milk had run dry did not escape their censure: 'sure if their breasts be dry, as they say, they should fast and pray together that this curse may be removed from them'. These views naturally held great sway in the Puritan communities of New England. In contrast to Britain, breastfeeding became the norm there at all levels in society.

While some women were incapable of providing milk, there

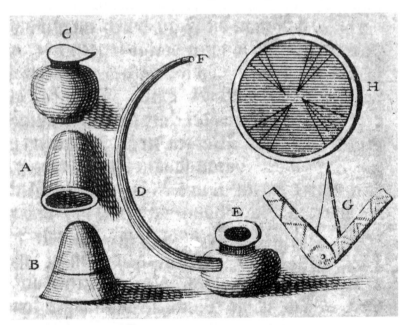

A seventeenth-century breast pump

were certainly many others who just wanted to avoid pain and inconvenience. A significant group were forbidden by their husbands to breastfeed because it inhibited the conception of the next child. Certainly a woman of property who'd given birth to a girl would be expected to return to the marital bed as soon as possible in the hope of providing a male heir to the family's estates.

Bernardino Ramazzini (c.1700) gave a list of medical risks to the breastfeeding mother: she might face problems 'when milk is too abundant, when it curdles in the breasts, when these become inflamed', or she might 'suffer from an abscess or cracks in the nipples'. Such conditions were very painful and genuinely dangerous before antibiotics came along. There were also nutritional considerations: 'atrophy or wasting may result from long-continued suckling . . . the bodies of nurses are robbed of nutritive juice . . . they gradually become thin and reedy'.

However, gentlewomen were in fact much more likely to have enjoyed good, rich and varied diets than the wet nurses they employed, and farming out the task to others came with its own risks. Half-hearted or sleepy nurses had been known to crush or 'overlie' their charges during late-night feeds. John Evelyn lost a son this way in 1664: 'It pleased God to take away my son Richard, now a month old, yet without any sickness . . . we suspected much the nurse had overlain him.'

The arguments which raged over wet-nursing are interesting for the light they throw on people's attitudes to parenthood. You might think that parents like John Evelyn who sent their children away to be brought up by strangers could not have really loved their children (this, of course, is also the reason why the question of breast- or bottle-feeding rouses such strong passions today). Historians have argued that parents in centuries past loved their babies less: high rates of infant mortality and the need to send well-born children away to arranged marriages at a young age made affection risky because of the high probability of loss and sorrow. In France, Michel de Montaigne shocks us when he fails to remember how many of his own children had died: 'two or three at nurse, not without regret, but without grief'.

So we may well ask: did people really have childhoods in the past? Or were children treated as mini-adults, fit for the world of marriage, labour and loss? A baby boy would be hard to distinguish from a girl until he was 'breeched' (put into trousers) at the age of seven, but from that point onwards he was almost a grown-up.

Certainly aristocrats had to harden their hearts in order to send their children away to early, dynastically important marriages, or to serve in the households of grander relations or the king. Daniele Barbaro, an ambassador to 1540s England from Venice, thought it shocking that the English parted from their children at such a young age, and that it showed 'want of affection'. But the noblemen he questioned countered that it was done for the child's own good. Their offspring received education and contacts in a more important household, and thus connections were forged between families that would serve everybody well.

But we also know that even when aristocratic girls were sent away to marry young, they remained attached to their birth families. Letters, visits and news carried by servants or visitors kept the links alive. Heiresses frequently chose to be buried with their fathers rather than their husbands: they were daughters before they were mothers. It's also clearly nonsensical to say that pre-modern families did not share strong affective bonds. Elizabeth Appleton, of Ipswich, New England, had a family particularly scarred by infant mortality. In 1736, she summed up her dreadful losses with heartache:

Here is an account of all my posterity. 6 sons and 3 daughters, 20 grand son and 20 grand daughters, 58 in all. 33 are gone before me. I hope I shall meet them all at Christ's right hand among his sheep and lambs. I often look over this list with sorrow.

Sarah Goodhue, also of Ipswich, movingly reminded her children in 1681 of her husband's customary behaviour on coming home from work. He was a fond and involved father, and had delighted

to take the young ones up into his wearied arms . . . you may behold as in a glass, his tender care and love to you every one as you grow up: I can safely say, that his love was so to you all, that I cannot say which is the child he doth love best.

From the late seventeenth century onwards, growing numbers of such diaries and letters record a more openly affectionate attitude towards children, and a new generation of medical practitioners began to argue that a mother should indeed breastfeed her child. The doctor William Cadogan, in his 1748 *Essay upon Nursing*, confessed that he'd simply failed to find any arguments in favour of wet-nursing. Because his book was adopted by the influential Foundling Hospital in London, it became very widely read. 'I am quite at a loss to account for the general practice of sending infants out of doors', he wrote, 'to be suckled, or dry-nursed by another woman, who has not so much understanding, nor can have so much affection for it, as the parents.' He recommended 'every father to have his child nursed under his own eye, to make use of his own reason and sense in superintending and directing the management of it'. The emphasis on 'reason and sense' is very typical of an Enlightenment physician.

A few years later, the beautiful and trendsetting Georgiana, Duchess of Devonshire, followed Cadogan's advice. Startlingly for an aristocrat, she began to breastfeed her own daughter, after having discovered that the nurse she'd employed was often drunk and 'made the bed stink of wine'.

And this was in line with the eighteenth-century ideas about childhood being promoted by Jean-Jacques Rousseau. He wrote that parents should be loving and kind to their children, letting them dress and live simply and naturally, rather than restricting them in tight clothes or closely monitoring their behaviour.

The Fashionable Mamma — or — The Convenience of Modern Dress

A fashionable mother apes the Duchess of Devonshire by eschewing a wet nurse and breastfeeding her own child

There was a resultant craze for breastfeeding, so much so that James Gillray in 1796 produced a satirical drawing showing a time-pressed fashionable mother enthusiastically squeezing out a spot of milk just before going out to dinner.

The medical establishment's continued campaign in favour of breastfeeding took a different and more serious turn in the nineteenth century. The practice of wet-nursing had by no means died out, and a new nightmare was presented in the shape of the phenomenon of baby-farming.

A woman in financial difficulty might deliberately conceive with the intention of gaining lucrative work as a wet nurse. The unwanted children of these would-be wet nurses would be sent off to 'baby farms', where they received only cursory attention, sometimes even dying from neglect. 'Why should a mother be allowed to sacrifice her child – to subject it to a slow process of disease and death – in order to make a handsome profit out of her nursing power?' asked the *British Medical Journal*.

Much campaigning eventually resulted in the Infant Life Protection Bill of 1872, whose effects are still evident today in the need the state feels to screen, register and monitor those working as childminders. Women who cared for other women's children for longer than twenty-four hours had to register their establishments, and the babies of wet nurses were less likely to 'disappear'. Also bottle-feeding had become a more practical alternative by the 1860s, with baby bottles more widely and cheaply available. Mrs Beeton thought bottle feeds 'more nutritious' and likely to prevent the child getting rickets.

Despite this new concern for the well-being of babies, the extreme separation of functions in the Victorian house saw middle-class children still kept remote from their parents. They were relegated upstairs to their own nursery or schoolroom, where they were looked after by substitute mothers in the form of nursery maids and governesses. Edward Burne-Jones, the painter, referred to his first child as 'the small stranger within our gates', summing up this lack of intimacy. In conservative families, ideal Victorian children were not seen or heard until they reached maturity and took their places in society as grown-ups. There was a great contrast between sixteen and seventeen: a sixteen-year-old might still wear the clothes and eat the food of a child, sleeping in a nursery and living a life peripheral to that of his or her parents. But a seventeen-year-old suddenly became an adult, allowed to socialise with his or her parents and their friends and given a separate bedroom.

Only in the 1950s did an interim life stage – the teenage years – begin to be recognised. This coincided with a post-war housing explosion which saw parents able to provide older children their own individual bedrooms for the first time, rather than putting them in with their younger siblings and reserving the spare room for a nursemaid. Possession of a private room encouraged teenagers to amass their own age-specific clothes, records, posters and pastimes.

But younger children were still treated as powerless, slightly inferior members of a household, with lower-priority needs and desires. Today it's quite astonishing to remember that only in the last thirty years have children been placed right at the heart of family life. Terence Conran, writing on children's bedrooms in 1974, considered that 'it's pointless spending a lot of money on decorations for young children. They won't appreciate the financial sacrifice, and will feel highly indignant when you nag about scribbles and dirty marks.' It's not an attitude shared by the Habitat shops he founded today, or by the huge industry that makes and sells furniture and gadgets for children's bedrooms. Nowadays children are treated as equally, if not more, deserving of a family's resources than parents. Despite the evidence that loving parents have existed throughout the ages, households are now more child-centred than ever before.

People often think that the practice of wet-nursing died out in Britain by the turn of the twentieth century, yet in fact it was still relatively common until the 1940s – as it remains in other cultures. And despite the danger posed by HIV, swapping babies for a feed is not unusual among laidback middle-class mothers today. Perhaps milk-less mothers who want their children to enjoy breastfeeding's benefits will once again bring back the wet nurse.

4 – Knickers

> Comfortable garments ... which all of us wear
> but none of us talk about.
> Lady Chesterfield on knickers, 1850

What do you do first thing in the morning? The Tudor physician Andrew Boorde recommends that you should 'stretch forth your arms and legs, and your body, cough, and spit, and then go to your stool to make your egestion'. Today, likely as not, you still stretch and visit the bathroom. Then, every single morning of your life, you choose an outfit, moulding your identity for the day ahead.

Bedchambers have always been places for storing clothes, unless you were grand enough to have a wardrobe. This was originally a separate room, not a piece of furniture, staffed by specialist servants. The 'wardrobe' department ('warders' of the 'robes') was a subsection of the royal household. Its members looked after the king's and queen's clothes, as well as their soft furnishings. From the time of Edward III, the wardrobe staff even had their own central depot in the City of London, handy for the cloth merchants. (Its existence is echoed in the name of the church 'St Andrew's by the Wardrobe' near St Paul's Cathedral.) By the seventeenth century, the king still had a 'Great Wardrobe', a central repository, but he also had a 'Standing Wardrobe' in each royal palace and a 'Removing Wardrobe' which travelled with him.

The wardrobe would eventually evolve into the wooden cupboard to be found in bedrooms today, but this would not happen until the nineteenth century. Textiles and hangings in medieval times were stored on a hanging-rail called a 'perch' (from the Latin '*pertica*', a rail or pole; also used as a unit of length in land surveying) or in a chest. A cupboard would not be found in a medieval bedroom. It was literally a board, or shelf, upon which cups could be placed, and it belonged in the great hall or kitchen. A chest was the more likely receptacle for linen or folded clothes, and Georgian ladies write of 'laying up' rather than 'hanging up' their dresses.

The birth of the modern, upright wardrobe followed the birth of the coat hanger. Victorian fashions for ladies involved skirts wider than ever before, and all this fabric had to be stored somewhere. Ottomans and hollow stools made their appearance in ladies' dressing rooms and bedrooms. Finally, the 'shoulder', as it was originally known, was invented. This was a narrow, wooden but still recognisable coat hanger, and it allowed clothes to be stored vertically in a cupboard. In 1904, a German visitor noted that in English women's wardrobes 'only skirts are hung on hangers and go into the hanging part of the cupboard, all the rest are laid flat, like men's clothes'. But the wire coat hanger had just been invented, and would sweep all before it: today shirts, coats, trousers and dresses alike are usually hung.

For many centuries a king or nobleman would put on his undershirt in the room where he slept. After that, a ceremony called the levee would be performed. The king would step out of his bedchamber into a more public room, where his outer clothes would be handed to him by his servants. He had to get used, then, to his courtiers seeing him in his underwear.

The nature of people's undergarments is a subject to which we can gain a surprising amount of access. Even the chivalrous, ancient and Noble Order of the Garter actually takes its name from an attempt to cover up a lady's very public wardrobe malfunction: Edward III created the order's motto when he chided some courtiers with the words '*Honi soit qui mal y pense*' ('Evil be to he who evil thinks') when they rudely laughed at the Countess of Salisbury's garter accidentally falling to the floor.

Indeed, underwear has often been put deliberately on display. This can be a sexually predatory action, common to the lacy-shirted male Cavalier courtiers in the 1630s through to the young urban males of today showing their Calvin Klein underpants above low-slung jeans. And Monica Lewinsky discovered that even the most powerful man in America could be reduced to a jelly by the sight of an intern's thong.

Generally speaking, though, to have visible underwear is regrettable. A young French housewife was addressed in the closing years of the fourteenth century in the advice book *Le Ménagier de Paris*. She was commanded to cover up carefully:

> be mindful that the collar of your shift, or your camisole, or of your robe or surcoat does not slip out one over the other, as happens with drunken, foolish, or ignorant women.

Yet to receive someone while imperfectly dressed can even mean that you respect them greatly, and the supremely self-confident Winston Churchill would famously chat to his staff while naked in his bath. On the morning of 17 June 1520, during the conference near Calais being held to celebrate their friendship, Francis I of France appeared unexpectedly in Henry VIII's bedchamber. He personally handed the English king his shirt as a sign of the close intimacy between the nations of England and France. (This tactful gesture was necessary because Francis had defeated Henry in a bout of wrestling a few days previously, and his brother king was in a royal sulk.)

In Henry VIII's case, it was usually an Esquire of the Body who would help the king into his shirt in the privacy of his bedchamber. Henry would emerge 'loosely dressed' and enter his privy chamber, a more public room, next door. Here, his Yeomen of the Wardrobe would have his outer clothes ready, and his Grooms would hand them to the more senior Gentlemen of the bedchamber. It was this latter group who would actually dress the king. The Grooms were warned to handle the king's garments with great reverence, and not to 'lay hands upon the royal person, or intermeddle with dressing', except to warm clothes before the fire.

In innumerable royal bedrooms, it was a trusted and often noble servant who had the responsibility of warming the king's shirt 'before the fire, & hold the same till we are ready to put it on', words which come from the bedchamber rules of William III. When Horace Walpole visited the French court of Louis XV in 1765, he found the king's public dressing had become so well-established and ritualised that it was almost a tourist attraction: 'You are let into the King's bedchamber just as he has put on his shirt; he dresses and talks good-humouredly to a few.' Yet even this unusually tolerant king had his limits: he would 'glare at strangers'.

The same dressing ceremonies were also found in the bedchambers of important ladies. John Evelyn, the seventeenth-century diarist, recorded how he was once invited into a bedchamber to see Charles II's mistress, the Duchess of Portsmouth, 'in her morning loose garment, her maids combing her, newly out of her bed, his majesty and the gallants standing about her'. Many other gallants and cronies of the king had also gathered to see the pleasant and titillating sight.

A little later at the British court, Queen Anne was also semi-publicly dressed by her extensive bedchamber staff. They descended in rank from the Mistress of the Robes, to the Ladies of the Bedchamber (aristocrats one and all), to the Women of the Bedchamber, to the dressers, hairdressers, and finally, the Page of the Backstairs.

The items of the queen's clothing were also ranked from high to low, and the participants were only allowed to touch garments appropriate to their status. So, the Lady of the Bedchamber put on the queen's shift, which went right next to her skin and was considered to be highly important. The Lady also handed the queen her fan at the end of the whole process, and that was the limit of her involvement. More menial work – lacing the queen into her stays, putting on her hoops and fastening her dress – was done by the Women of the Bedchamber and the dressers, and the Page's lowly role was limited to putting on her shoes. The Mistress of the Robes had the least physically demanding but most high-status job of all: she handed the queen her jewels. One pities the queen, standing cold and vulnerable in the centre of this dance of ceremony.

These records of royal dressing rituals reveal that a striking number of people were involved. The number of participants may sound excessive, and you might assume that many of them were mere flunkeys and hangers-on. But it wasn't just dressing which was subject to overstaffing: in 1512, the Earl of Northumberland had twenty servants on duty in his great chamber, or living room, in the morning, eighteen in the afternoon, and no less than thirty in the evening. Yet a vast entourage became (and remains) an indicator of a person's power and status. All this would be completely dwarfed by the absolute monarchies of the Baroque period: when Louis XIV moved his household from place to place, 30,000 horses were required to transport his people and possessions. Even people of lower status could never be satisfied with the number of servants they had. Elizabeth Spencer, who wanted her husband to stump up the wages for an additional 'gentlewoman', or female companion, wrote in 1594 that 'it is an undecent thing' for her sole existing 'gentlewoman to stand mumping alone'.

But there was another reason for all the servants: you simply couldn't get into your clothes without someone else to help. Until buttons were invented in the fourteenth century, you needed an extra pair of hands to fasten up your 'points' (the holes through which a string was threaded to attach the sleeves to the body of a gown). The batman to a medieval knight was essential to 'help to array him, truss his points, stick up his hose, and see all things be cleanly about him'. A medieval treatise recommends that a lord's 'chamberlain', or chamber servant, should act as stylist as well as dresser. 'Before he goes out', the chamberlain is advised, 'brush busily about him, and whether he wear satin, sandal, velvet, scarlet or grain, see that all be clean and nice.'

Not surprisingly, such body servants brushing their bosses in their bedchambers also became close friends. There was a moving scene after Lucius Cary, 1st Viscount Falkland, was killed in battle in 1643. Only his chamberlain could identify his master's corpse upon the field: 'they could not find his Lordship's body; it was stripped and trod-upon and mangled, so there was one that waited upon him in his chamber would undertake to know it from all other bodies, by a certain Mole his lordship had in his Neck, and by that mark did find it'.

On the other hand, the foppish 'Macaronis' of the 1780s crept into an unhealthy dependency on their personal servants, seeming to be 'absolutely incapable of motion, till they have been wound up by their valets . . . if the valet happens to be out of the way, the master must remain helpless and sprawling in bed, like a turtle on its back upon the kitchen table'.

Our medieval knight wouldn't have worn underpants as we know them today. Men wrapped the long tail of their shirts between their legs, or else wore something rather like a loose linen nappy. Early drawers begin to appear in the seventeenth century: long silk shorts with a slit in the back to facilitate a trip to the toilet. By the later 1660s, Charles II was wearing silk undershorts. William III, next king but one, had an almost garish taste in underwear. We know he favoured green socks and a red vest, items which remain in the costume collection at Kensington Palace today. Tiny in size for this minuscule king, the vest has no front fastenings. It must have been pinned, or even sewn up, each time he wore it. Neither would have been uncommon in an age before zips.

Meanwhile, sixteenth-, seventeenth- and eighteenth-century female dress quite simply precluded wearing knickers. A huge hooped skirt meant that drawers were impractical if you needed to use the toilet without completely undressing. So ladies went commando, and squatted over a chamber pot when required. This meant that toilets were everywhere and nowhere. The bed-chamber, an ante-room, even the street: all were potential places to go. (One could even use a chamber pot in bed, though it was more comfortable if it was 'warmed, and the rim covered with flannel'.)

With the slimmer, looser, less cumbersome fashions of the Jane Austen or Regency period, though, women began to adopt the male fashion for wearing protective drawers beneath their lighter, diaphanous and potentially more revealing skirts. The earliest knickers had long legs, but even so were considered terribly racy. Lady Chesterfield, writing to her daughter around 1850, described a youth spent wearing 'skirts that ended one inch above my ankles', revealing the 'frilled edges of those comfortable garments which we have borrowed from the other sex, and which all of us wear but none of us talk about'.

Despite their initially saucy reputation, drawers quickly went mainstream. Even Queen Victoria's ladies-in-waiting got swept up in the craze. Here's the Honourable Eleanor Stanley in 1859, describing how the Duchess of Manchester, climbing over a gate,

caught a hoop of her cage in it and went regularly head over heels . . . the other ladies hardly knew whether to be thankful or not that a part of her underclothing consisted in a pair of scarlet tartan knickerbockers which were revealed to the view of all the world in general.

Her use of the word 'cage' for the crinoline is particularly striking, because these stiff hooped petticoats devised from steel, string or wood literally encaged women in the sense that they restricted free movement. We all need to say thanks to the women who campaigned to end the nonsense of muffling ladies up in voluminous, unwieldy drawers and layers of petticoats. Amelia Jenks Bloomer, for one, has a worthy place in the women's movement. It was actually her friend Libby Miller who designed the 'bloomers' which Amelia championed (really voluminous Turkish pants combined with an overskirt). They were said to be especially 'fit for any sort of locomotion', including the new bicycle. 'Bicycling has done more to emancipate women than anything else in the world,' said the suffragette Susan B. Anthony in 1896. 'I stand and rejoice every time I see a woman ride on a wheel. It gives women a feeling of freedom and self-reliance.'

Despite its reputation, the voluminous bloomer was far from risqué, and so was its promoter, Mrs Bloomer herself. A dedicated campaigner for lost causes, married to a Quaker, she was also a stalwart of the Ladies' Temperance Society. She spoke against drink and in favour of bloomers at rallies all over the US (with limited success).

In Britain, the Rational Dress Society brought about similar change. It was formed in 1881 by Viscountess Harberton, and the following year a 'Hygienic Wearing Apparel' exhibition was held at Kensington Town Hall. As Lady Harberton wrote, 'no growing girl or woman of child-bearing age should wear underclothes that exceed 7 lbs in weight'. One result was the liberty bodice, a kind of sleeveless vest intended to replace the corset; another was the 1920s passion for all kinds of frivolous, light and airy knickers, often made out of the new man-made fibres. (Robert Hooke in 1664 had the idea of spinning thread from 'a glutinous substance', like a silkworm did, but 'artificial silk' or 'rayon' was not made until 1905.)

Yet ultra-respectable women wore long drawers right into the twentieth century. Rosina Harrison, maid to the first female Member of Parliament, Lady Astor, remembers how 'she was

particularly fastidious about her underwear. It was kept in sets
in silk pouches which I had to make and decorate in his lordship's racing colours, blue and pink . . . knickers fitting above
the knee.' Sobriety returned to underwear with the Second
World War and the rise of the hated 'black-outs' (also known as
'passion-killers' or 'boy-bafflers'), official-issue pants in khaki,
navy or black that came with the knee-length skirts of women's
military uniforms. Many pairs remained unworn, and were only
brought out, ironed, for kit inspections.

Once the knickers or drawers are on, the bizarre and intimate
business of body-shaping demands attention. The part of the
body most admired, or considered to be the most erogenous,
has changed enormously over time. The male calf was much
admired by the Tudors. 'Look here! I have also a good calf
to my leg,' boasted Henry VIII, slapping his muscles. Naked
female breasts made frequent appearances at the Stuart court,
just as they had at the Minoan court of Crete. Yet two centuries later, poor Caroline of Brunswick, the mail-order wife
of George IV, may have been acceptably dressed according to
her native German fashion, but offended her new compatriots
beyond measure with her décolletage. ('Such an over-dressed,
bare-bosomed, painted eye-browed figure one never saw!')

In their bedroom mirrors ladies either cursed or blessed the
biological background that gave them figures that either met
or failed the approved fashion of their times. Sometimes the
breasts were valued; sometimes not: the pendulum swung regularly from side to side. A seventeenth-century book of cosmetics
contains a prescription to 'keep the Breasts small' and 'hinder
their growth', and to 'harden soft and loose Breasts'. The stomach was in vogue in the late 1200s: perhaps it was a fondness
for fertile women that led artists to depict so many of them
with their hips thrust forward and a bulging belly. In the early
nineteenth century, William Wordsworth was dismayed by large
breasts: one pair he encountered were like two 'hay stacks,

The secrets of the perfect figure revealed, *c.*1810

protruding themselves upon the Spectator . . . you would have shrunk almost as with horror' at the sight of them. Yet a low-slung bosom was essential to the Edwardian 'pouter-pigeon' look. The bottom was also something that came and went: indeed, the late-nineteenth-century craze for the bustle sent it off into the realms of outsize fantasy.

Shaping the body is not just a feminine phenomenon. In the mid-eighteenth century, Richard Campbell mockingly described Londoners' dependence on what he called their 'Shape Merchants'. Men of fashion had no 'Existence than what the Taylor, Milliner, and Perriwig-Maker bestow upon them'. Stripped of their clothes, they appeared to be 'quite a different Species', rather like 'Punch, deprived of his moving Wires, and hung up upon a Peg'. George IV – brandy-swilling, bewigged, heavily made-up and slightly mad – was likewise a constant wearer of corsets. His baby corset, designed to encourage a straight figure, remains in the Royal Ceremonial Dress Collection at Kensington Palace. His adult corset, which doesn't survive, was designed to hold in his fat and to help him to walk. (The idea that medieval knights wore corsets, sadly, is based on the mistranslation of a Latin word. They didn't.) In the generation after George IV's, chest padding created the silhouette favoured for a gentleman seen in profile. This discreet addition to the manly chest was even adopted by Prince Albert, and can be seen inside a military outfit of his at the Museum of London.

But ladies' shapes gave away so much more about their status. A country girl, arriving fresh off the stagecoach in Georgian London, quickly found new friends suspiciously keen to 'help' her lose her bumpkin ways:

> An awkward Thing, when first She came to Town;
> Her Shape unfashion'd, and her Face unknown:
> She was my Friend, I taught her first to spread
> Upon her Sallow Cheeks th'Enliv'ning Red.

Of course, the naive country girl ended up working as a prostitute, like her friend who narrates the poem. A Georgian prostitute in prints and cartoons – and presumably in real life too – indicates her availability by lifting up one side of her skirt and showing her ankle.

The tight-laced stays necessary for eighteenth-century female costume were difficult to put on alone; in fact, one wonders how working women without maids managed. But there were short cuts. For a start, you might simply sleep in your stays rather than going to the trouble of taking them off. Also, it is actually possible to lace yourself up by running one string down from the top, and the other up from the bottom. You can tighten yourself at the mid-point by reaching over your right shoulder and under your left, grabbing the two strings and pulling them in a diagonal movement.

It was Victorian ladies who suffered the tightest lacing. A book of *Advice to a Wife* (1853) suggests that one should not lace to fewer than twenty-seven inches; to go down to the widely desirable twenty-one was to sacrifice 'comfort, health and happiness'. It was hard to persuade women to take off their stays, even under the most extreme conditions. The same writer makes the point that '*the stays should not be worn*' during labour. (Women in childbirth nevertheless expected to wear a chemise, petticoat and nightgown, with a 'broad bandage' round the abdomen.)

Stays for women can be excruciatingly painful, and Victorian ladies' manuals make recommendations for treating flesh rubbed raw and other superficial wounds. Archaeologists at the Museum of London have studied the malformation of the skeleton caused by Victorian tight lacing. They have also noticed that shoes had a crippling effect on the bones of the feet before shoes specifically designed for the left and right feet were introduced in the early nineteenth century, when shaped cobblers' lasts came into use.

The invention of the liberty bodice in the late nineteenth century saw the beginning of the end of body-shaping as an essential part of women's daily life; it had passed out of men's lives long before. In the twentieth century, the bra and girdle replaced the stays; then the girdle too eventually disappeared. But still teenagers longed for the underwear that would mark maturity: 'Are you there God?' prayed Judy Blume's fictional adolescent in 1978. 'It's me, Margaret. I just told my mother I want a bra. Please help me grow God. *You know where.*'

Before we finish with underwear, we need to make a detour

A Berlei corseted girdle
from the 1940s

into the curious history of the pocket. The variety and quality of
the items in her handbag provide a particularly intimate snap-
shot of a modern woman's daily life. The handbag's predecessor
was an even more intimate item: the tie-on pocket or pouch
worn around the waist (of the type that Lucy Locket lost, and
that Kitty Fisher found).

Some thieves specialised in stealing these particular items:
'My chief dexterity was in robbing the ladies. There is a peculiar delicacy required in whipping one's hand up a lady's petticoats and carrying off her pockets,' boasted one (fictional)
pickpocket. Putting an intrusive hand into a lady's pocket was
often used as a metaphor for seduction. In the 1760s, though,
in line with a general explosion in the number of consumer

goods of all sorts made suddenly available, handbags began to appear for carrying purses, fans, combs and shopping money. The days of the pocket as a separate item from the skirt were numbered. *The Times* of 1799 mentioned 'the total abjuration of the female pocket', and handbags quickly became known as 'Indispensables'.

The pocket became sewn into a skirt, and the handbag went from strength to strength. But both remain private places where their owners' needs, desires and aspirations are all laid bare. They have that in common with the room called the closet.

5 – Praying, Reading and Keeping Secrets

All is but vanitie.

Painted motto in a seventeenth-century
closet at Bolsover Castle, Derbyshire

Ever 'closeted' yourself away to do something private? If so, you were referring to a room whose purpose has faded away, rather like the appendix in the human body: the closet.

The bedchamber was originally a place of prayer and study as well as sleep. Then architecturally ambitious Tudors began to construct an extra little room adjoining it called the closet. Richly decorated and often incorporating cupboards for the storage of treasures, these funny little rooms became a dead end in architectural history. For a couple of centuries, though, they provided the most intimate and private space in a house. The closet was used for solitary activities – for praying, reading, meditating – or for storing precious art, musical instruments and books.

Towards the end of the Middle Ages, as literacy spread, we come across a novelty: people willingly spending time by themselves. This new trend for solitude, linked to the rise of reading, called for new, small and private rooms. The allure of seclusion is expressed in a poem written by Charles, Duc d'Orléans, while prisoner in the Tower of London. In 1440, this *duc* (the nephew

The seventeenth-century writer Margaret
Cavendish, sitting at her desk in her private
closet, her ideas swirling round her head

of the king of France) was imprisoned after the British victory at
Agincourt. He is perhaps the first recorded person to suffer from
the agonising but creative melancholy which would become so
common in the Romantic age, but which seems quite out of
place in the medieval. His homesick, miserable condition made
him want to mope about alone:

> *Tristesse*
> *M' si longuement tenu en son pouvoir*
> *Que j'ai totalement relégué ma Joie.*
> *Il vaut mieux que je m'écarte de mes semblables:*
> *Celui qui est pris d'affliction ne peut qu'embarrasser.*

> [Sadness has held me in its power so long
> that I have cast off Joy completely.
> It is better that I separate myself from my fellow man.
> He who is afflicted can only embarrass.]

Closets, these new rooms for solitude, also developed out of
a tradition of prayer. As the Bible's Book of Matthew put it,

'when thou prayest, enter into thy closet, and when thou hast
shut the door, pray to thy Father which is in secret; and thy
Father which seeth in secret shall reward thee openly'. Indeed,
the forerunner to the closet was the private oratory, like the
one just off Edward III's bedchamber at the Tower of London
(plate 4).

If your house wasn't big enough or grand enough to contain a special, dedicated closet, you could make do with other
rooms. The seventeenth-century London wood-turner, diary
fiend and depressive Nehemiah Wallington had a strong Puritan
faith which forced him to frequent prayer. His writings give an
unusual insight into the mind of an introspective and religious
man of the middling sort. One winter night, he had something
of an epiphany in his 'garret', which he'd been using as a kind
of closet:

I went up into the high garret to pray as I was used to do: and I found
a great deal of comfort in prayer and when I had done praying I went
to the garret window, and looked up unto heaven . . . seeing the stars
God's glorious creatures [I began] meditating what a glorious place
heaven is.

Occasionally, though, when Wallington was suffering from
mental-health problems, the devil tempted him to jump out of
the garret's window and end his life. He made

Much ado to resist this temptation, But God of his great love and
mercy caused me presently to go downstairs as fast as I could.

Items kept in a closet included 'Books of Hours', the pre-
Reformation prayer books which seeped out of monasteries
into people's private hands, and which were regularly used to
inspire religious thoughts. Edward IV had his Keeper of the
Great Wardrobe 'dress' his precious, valuable and well-beloved
books in what sound almost like clothes. They were to be
bound in velvet, blue and black silk, with laces and tassels of
silk, 'buttons' of blue silk and gold, and clasps of copper and

gilt adorned with roses and the royal arms. A fifteenth-century merchant's wife in York, Agnes Hull, willed to her daughter a prayer book or primer, probably much less grand but no less highly valued. She described it as the book 'which I use daily'. Such Books of Hours, made by hand, beautifully decorated and often even incorporating the owner's name, were forbidden by the Protestant king, Edward VI, in 1549. Nevertheless, many medieval books were still kept and read in secret by Catholic families, the clandestine nature of their use making them even more personal items.

Although they were originally connected with religion, closets also had secular purposes. Merchants used them for drawing up accounts and counting money. Letters to absent children were written here, and if you had any pornography, your private closet was a good place to keep it. The seventeenth-century Duchess of Lauderdale, Elizabeth Dysart, was a lady with many secrets. She is reputed to have been a lover of Oliver Cromwell's, as well as a member of the Sealed Knot, the secret society that supported Charles II in exile, before marrying the powerful Duke of Lauderdale. At her home, Ham House on the banks of the Thames, she had no fewer than two closets, an outer one for visitors to see, and an inner one for her own private use. Here she kept paintings hinting at her potentially dangerous Catholic beliefs, two sets of shelves for her private books, and a japanned box in which she kept sweetmeats and – a valuable commodity – tea.

You might also indulge in the very intimate activity of looking at miniatures in your closet. These tiny, valuable paintings of loved ones were kept wrapped and were only shown to confidants (rather as today you might show a friend photos of your children saved on your mobile phone). The Scottish ambassador was once awarded a rare privilege during a visit to Elizabeth I at Hampton Court Palace. He was taken into the queen's bedchamber, where she 'opened a little cabinet, wherein were divers little pictures wrapt within paper'. One of these proved to be a miniature of her cousin, Mary, Queen of Scots, and they looked at it together. This intimate gesture was a compliment from Elizabeth I to the ambassador, and also, by implication, to the Scottish queen.

Because closets were personal, intimate and desirable places to be, a genre of books developed which claimed to expose the goings-on in the closets of celebrities. Rather like kiss-and-tell magazine articles today, *The Queen's Closet Opened* and *The Closet of Sir Kenelm Digby* purported to be exposés by senior stewards or servants of what happened in these private places. Both are similar to recipe books, containing valued and secret methods for curing sickness and making special dishes and exotic toiletries. They were preceded in the sixteenth century by John Partridge's *The Treasurie of Commodious Conceites, and hidden Secrets, commonly called The good Huswives Closet* (1584). It contained recipes ranging from a yellow dye for gloves to a treatment for 'the loathsome disease of the French Pockes'.

As they were exclusive little rooms, closets were often richly and wonderfully decorated. In the seventeenth-century closet at Bolsover Castle made for the arch-Royalist Duke of Newcastle, there is panelling 'grained' – decorated with the imaginary grain of wood – in gold paint. In his gold-grained room, its ceiling decorated with semi-pornographic images of the gods and goddesses of Mount Olympus, the duke took off the mask of the aristocrat from time to time. Here he reminded himself of his own humanity beneath the pomp of his ducal lifestyle. As the motto reads over his window, 'All is but vanitie'.

Over time, closets developed in two contrasting directions. One use of the closet – as a storehouse for precious works of art – caused it to expand into the larger, more elaborate room known as a cabinet, and then, ultimately, into the picture or sculpture gallery. (Even today, the prime minister's 'cabinet' takes its name from this room. At one time his inner circle could

squash themselves into a closet or cabinet to hold their meetings.)
Secondly, the Pilgrim Fathers took closets over to America, and
to this day personal possessions in the US are stored in 'closets'.
The shoe-filled walk-in closet in her tiny New York apartment
represents Carrie's hopes and dreams in *Sex and the City*.

Back in the British bedroom, though, the closet died out. For
females, its purpose was to some extent replaced by the underwear drawer, the most obvious place to hide diaries and valu-
ables today. And should the Duke of Newcastle be brought back
to life as a modern man, he might well be found deep in contem-
plation in his garden shed.

6 – Sick

Take a fat cat, flay it well ... roast the cat and
gather the dripping, and anoint the sufferer with it.
Fourteenth-century recipe for a medicine
to treat a throat abscess

Medicine is another, more painful avenue to explore in the history of the bedroom.

It was in Henry VIII's reign that the profession of medicine was formalised, after the king himself set up the Royal College of Physicians in 1518. Not until the nineteenth century, though, did doctors based outside the home win a monopoly on medicine. Until that happened, people went on treating themselves in their own bedrooms.

Henry VIII was deeply interested in medicine, and would personally recommend cures to his staff. He advised Sir Bryan Tuke, his Treasurer of the Chamber, how to cure a tumour in the testicles, describing various 'remedies, as any cunning physician in England could do'.

He was not alone. Many of his subjects would likewise self-prescribe and self-medicate. In the sixteenth- and seventeenth-century bedchamber, women's and 'folk' medicine fought a long-drawn-out rearguard action against the doctors. And some of their barmy-sounding techniques worked rather well, even if their ideas about illness were totally different to ours. For centuries sickness was conceived as God's punishment. To pray was always one's first line of defence; examining the patient's actual body was sometimes thought frankly irrelevant. Consider, for example, this fourteenth-century doctor's method of diagnosis:

take the herb cinquefoil and, while collecting it, say a paternoster on behalf of the patient. Then boil it in a new jar with some of the water which the patient is destined to drink; if the water be red in colour after this boiling, then the patient will die.

Until about 1700, most physicians believed that the body was made up of the four 'humours', as described by the ancient Roman doctor Claudius Galen, and that illness occurred when one humour grew too powerful and overwhelmed the others. That's why most medical treatments involved removing liquids of one kind or another from the body. Popular remedies included vomits (medicine to make you sick), purges (laxatives), glisters (enemas) and blood-letting. The idea was to restore balance between the humours. These were absolutely basic parts of medical practice, even performed in the bedchambers of healthy people. Treatment varied from patient to patient because each individual was thought to have been born with a predominant humour which also explained their character:

Complexion	Qualities	Humour
Sanguine	Hot and moist	Blood
Phlegmatic	Cold and moist	Phlegm
Choleric	Hot and dry	Yellow or green bile
Melancholic	Cold and dry	Black bile

Today we might assume that medicine based on such a flawed concept had little chance of success. Draining much-needed blood from a sick person's veins, for example, seems likely to hinder rather than help their recovery.

But the extraordinary thing is that bleeding did actually do good. The enormous power of the placebo effect meant that a person placing him- or herself under medical treatment was given confidence, both in the healer and in the idea that they would get better. And very often people did just that.

Tudor medicine contained many wacky and gruesome-sounding recipes, but some of them were really quite efficacious. To take one example: a Tudor wife who did not desire her husband could be 'cured' of her frigidity, we are told, if her husband rubbed the 'grease of a goat' on her private parts. The intention was that something of the character of a goat – a very lusty animal – would be transferred to the woman. In practice, though, the lubrication of the grease might very well have stimulated the woman. So the medicine worked, if not for the reason that the Tudors thought.

Everyone of rank at the Tudor court enjoyed using emetics, not least because their meaty diet led to constipation. Henry VIII (once again) excelled in this area. His Groom of the Stool, or most intimate servant, had the daily duty of informing the world on the condition of the king's bowels. Enemas would be administered through a pig's bladder filled with liquid, slowly trickled into his rear end down a tube. One night his doctors reported that a very successful enema had caused the king to wake and give his close stool a 'very fair siege'. (Possibly this isn't quite the image of spectacular bombardment that our modern understanding of the word 'siege' implies. 'Sege' was also the Middle English word for a turd.)

Henry VIII set the pattern for people to make a regular habit of retreating to their bedchambers in order to be 'physicked' with enemas, baths and sweating treatments, all intended to get those humours back into balance. The Tudor and Stuart habit of retreating from the world for a few days of pampering sounds rather like a modern spa visit. But the intentions were serious, and the interventions sometimes quite extreme. Haemorrhoids, for example, could be cured – it was thought – by taking laxatives, and then 'two days after the last purge apply 6 leeches to the haemorrhoidal veins, & draw 9 or 10 ounces of blood'. (Ouch.)

There were constant new fads. For once the English were ahead of the stylish French when Liselotte, Duchess of Orléans, described in 1714 a novelty from our side of the Channel: 'a purge which was so effective that I had to retire to my close-stool no less than thirty times'. The purge was 'a new medicine, but so *à la mode* that all Paris is using it now. It is a salt from England called here *du sel d'Epsom*. You dissolve it in water.' Even the prudish Queen Victoria took a purge once a week, and the Victorians were enthusiastic users of laxatives at levels not to be seen again until the protein-based Atkins diet suddenly became popular in Britain in the early years of the twenty-first century. (Atkins enthusiasts cut down on vegetables, decreasing their fibre intake and often suffering from constipation in consequence.) The author of a book for pregnant women published in 1853 set much store by the state of a woman's bowels: 'If pregnant females, who suffer from constipation,' he wrote, 'were to take small doses of castor oil, twice or thrice a week

This doctor is about to use his enormous syringe to administer an enema. The patient in the bed looks suitably nervous

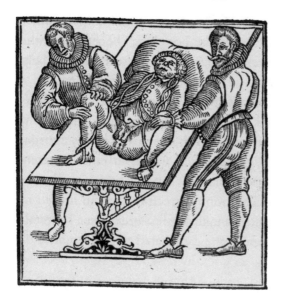

'Cutting for the stone.' Samuel Pepys underwent the operation to remove a stone from his bladder in his own home

. . . difficult cases of labour would very rarely occur.' For their enemas, the Victorians dropped the rectally damaging syringe, which had held sway since the seventeenth century, in favour of the pipe and squeeze-bag.

Even while the medical profession was becoming established, the bedroom at home remained the scene of many a crisis. When Samuel Pepys, for example, had a stone in his bladder removed, his surgeon came to his house to perform the operation. The preparations took place in his own bedchamber. He was tied down on a table so that he could not thrash about, and two strong men were also present to 'hold him by the knees' and 'by the arm-holes'.

With the Enlightenment, though, the bedchamber began to lose its role as an operating theatre. Those in need began to turn to the professionals. There were physicians who would still visit you at home for a fee, but also surgeons who could perform operations in their own shops, and apothecaries and chemists who could sell you herbal remedies and drugs from commercial premises. Early hospitals (places for the provision of hospitality) were mainly places for the relief of the poor and indigent, rather than for curing the middle and upper classes. So on into the nineteenth century a professional nurse might still arrive to help a wealthy family with a sick member turn a bedroom into a sickroom. Eventually, though, by the twentieth century, illness became firmly associated with the surgery and hospital. Today, the very idea of a doctor making a 'home visit' sounds unusual and retrograde: it seems like a practice from a more leisurely past.

Medical drama in the bedroom is much rarer than it used to be. Now that 58 per cent of us take our last breath in a hospital, we've forgotten that once everyone expected to die at home.

7 – Sex

Would you rather sin with Elinor Glyn on a tiger skin?
Or would you prefer to err with her on some other kind of fur?
Verses on Lord Curzon's lover, romantic
novelist Elinor Glyn, 1864–1943

We tend to assume, along with Philip Larkin, that 'Sexual inter-course began/ In nineteen sixty-three . . . Between the end of the *Chatterley* ban/ and the Beatles' first LP.' There was a curious reluctance to talk about sex for well over a century, between 1800 and 1960. Yet before that copulation was openly dis-cussed, with much less stigma and shame.

Nor was sex restricted to the bedroom. Edmund Harrold, a priapic wig-maker living in late-Stuart Manchester, kept a detailed diary of his sex life, including comments such as 'did wife 2 tymes couch & bed in an hour an[d] ½ time'. In 1763, James Boswell exceeded him with a clever actress/prostitute named Louisa: 'a more voluptuous night I never enjoyed. Five times was I fairly lost in rapture . . . I was somewhat proud of my performance.' On this occasion they were in a bed, but it's only fair to point out that the lanes and fields were far more attractive to medieval and Tudor young people who lived in otherwise communal spaces. The fact that early bedrooms were shared could certainly inhibit romance. The seventeenth-century

Abigail Willey of Oyster River, New England, would stop her husband 'coming to her' when she didn't feel like it by making her two children sleep in the middle of the bed rather than taking their usual position at the sides.

We don't hear Harrold's wife's or Louisa's side of the story, and there's a widely held notion that the church has always encouraged the missionary position as it kept a woman in her rightly subordinate place. But Harrold would have sex with his wife both in the 'old fashion' (missionary position) and the 'new fashion' (her on top), the latter especially when she was pregnant. And in fact, pre-modern female sexuality was considered to be powerful, formidable and valuable.

Medieval women who considered their husbands to be unsatisfactory could always pray at the shrine of St Uncumber in Westminster Abbey to be rid of them. ('If the man's member is always found useless and as if dead, the couple are well able to be separated.') Alison, Geoffrey Chaucer's 'Wife of Bath' in *The Canterbury Tales*, devoured no less than five husbands in her attempt to satiate her sexual appetite, and male impotence is no modern bedroom problem. Sir Tristram in Sir Thomas Malory's *King Arthur and his Knights* could not perform with his wife because of intrusive memories of his former lover, Isolde. As soon as Isolde popped into his mind, he became all 'dismayed, and other cheer made he none'. And having spoken of Henry VIII's impotence was one of the accusations made of Anne Boleyn at her trial in 1536.

Medieval women were considered to have a right to an orgasm. As the author of the thirteenth-century *Romance of the Rose* put it, 'one should not abandon the other, nor should either cease his voyage until they reach port together'. One fourteenth-century Oxford doctor recommended that frustrated sisters should simply do it for themselves: a woman should get her midwife to lubricate her fingers with oil, insert them into the vagina and 'move them vigorously about'.

Yet society also condoned a long-standing division of labour between a mistress (provider of pleasure) and a wife (mother of children), and only a minority made a successful transition from the former to the financial security of the latter. Anne Boleyn was a notable exception, and did so by making Henry VIII wait six years before consummating their relationship. She allowed him addictive tasters along the way. As he wrote to Anne when they were apart, Henry was often lost in daydreams about her: 'wishing myself . . . in my sweetheart's arms, whose pretty duckies I trust shortly to kiss'. Once Anne was married, though, she had to put up with the occasional infidelity, especially during her pregnancies, when she was curtly told by her husband to 'shut her eyes and endure as her betters had done'.

To modern eyes, a striking emphasis was placed upon a woman's sexual pleasure in medieval times. This was because in medical terms the medieval female body was thought of as simply a weaker version of the male, a kind of mirror image of it, with the sexual organs placed inside rather than outside. The female orgasm, therefore, was thought essential to conception, just as the male orgasm was. (At the same time, Tudor medicine books contained remedies for complaints affecting a man's 'womb'.) The idea that a female orgasm led to conception was put like this in the seventeenth century: if a man feels during intercourse 'a kind of sucking or drawing at the end of his yard . . . a woman may have conceived'. This was why Samuel Pepys was careful not to allow his many and varied mistresses to enjoy themselves, even while he insisted on taking his own pleasure. For women, another dreadful drawback to this belief was what happened in cases of rape. If a raped woman became pregnant, she must have experienced an orgasm, therefore she was not raped.

However, during the eighteenth and nineteenth centuries, the female orgasm entered into decline, and people began to question its very existence. Physicians discovered, during the course of the Enlightenment, that orgasm is not in fact necessary for conception. As a result, the importance society attached to sexual pleasure for women plummeted. Thus we get the stereotype of the frigid Victorian age, with females frightened of sex. Victorian women were not expected to experience orgasms; the official line was that their doctors and husbands thought them incapable of it.

This change in biological understanding had enormous implications for society. Women gradually shed their medieval stereotype as insatiable temptresses in order to become the Victorian ideal of pure, chaste, virginal angels. A society where sexual order was maintained by physical chastisement gradually began to give way to internal moral codes, where behaviour was policed by social forces such as shame and expulsion from the community for sexual transgression. Even before the end of the seventeenth century, the historian Laurel Thatcher Ulrich notes, the New England county courts which had dished out whippings and convictions in the early settler period began to lose their grip, and fines began to replace beatings. The result: less violence, but more psychological repression. So the modern mentality was born. Only when, in the later twentieth century, sex began to be considered as something pleasurable for women in its own right – not merely as wives or mistresses – did the female orgasm return to prominence in scientific and public discourse.

Despite the earlier emphasis on female pleasure, a respectable married woman was monogamous. In the medieval and Tudor ages, the sexual urges of young men were cleverly sublimated through the cult of chivalric love: they were supposed to devote themselves to the service of ladies of superior social status, and to expect nothing physical in return. (Favours, patronage and promotion at court were all acceptable alternatives.)

The chivalric cult had a strange parallel in the sleeping arrangement known as 'bundling', which was common both to rural areas of seventeenth-century Wales and to eighteenth-century

New England. This was likewise a non-sexual relationship, where a young man and woman passed the night alone in a bedroom together, but remained fully clothed. Sometimes they were even tied down or a board was placed down the middle of their bed. The idea was to make it through to morning without having sex, in order to find out whether they got on well enough together to marry. Until 1800, when it began to arouse a new moralistic disapproval, to 'bundle' was considered both chaste and sensible as it led to more successful marriages:

> Cate Nance and Sue proved just and true
> Tho' bundling did practise;
> But Ruth beguil'd and proved with child,
> Who bundling did despise.

The other explanation for this curious custom can be found in the architectural design of pre-modern rural cottages. Obviously, in an age when houses contained far fewer rooms than there were family members, the young people were short of private places in which to become acquainted. It was a kindness on the part of a girl's parents to leave a young couple alone together in the upstairs bedchamber, the rest of the family gathering in the kitchen or parlour below instead. The ropes and the board assuaged the parents' conscience, as they were responsible for finding their daughter a suitable husband, yet also for preserving her virginity. On the other hand, pre-marital sex was not seen as disastrous for people of the middling or lower sort, and a pre-marital pregnancy could be welcome proof of fertility. 'You would not buy a horse without trying it first,' explained one Norfolk farmer to his vicar.

The process of creating royal or aristocratic children, though, was the business of the whole nation, and its importance was so great that it took place in a semi-public context. The proxy bedding of Henry VIII's sister, Mary, sounds rather undignified, yet the process saw her legally wed. Mary lay on a bed in what was described as a 'magnificent *déshabille*' with bare legs. The

French king's ambassador took off his own red stockings and lay beside her. As their naked legs touched, 'the King of England made great rejoicing'. (When Mary finally reached France, its elderly king was delighted with his new bride and boasted 'that he had performed marvels' on his wedding night.)

A century later, another English princess named Mary, aged only ten, had to endure a public bedding with her brand-new husband, the fourteen-year-old Prince of Orange. The bride's father, King Charles I, 'had some difficulty in conducting' his new son-in-law through the thick throng of spectators gathered around the bed where the young princess lay waiting. Once in bed, the boy prince 'kissed the Princess three times, and lay chastely beside her about three-quarters of an hour, in presence of all the great lords and ladies of England'. After this, his duty was considered done.

We also know a good amount about what actually happened when a king and queen were left to it to attempt to produce an heir. Details of such matters survive because they were of vital political importance: the stability of the kingdom and alliances between nations hung in the balance.

In 1501, the ritual for the bedding of Katherine of Aragon with Henry VIII's older but short-lived brother, Arthur, was similarly well recorded. The princess was led from the wedding feast by her ladies, undressed and 'reverently' placed in bed. Prince Arthur entered the bedchamber in only his shirt, accompanied by a crowd of courtiers and musicians. The shawms, viols and tabors died away for a change of mood: the solemn blessing of the marriage bed by bishops. The young lovers were then left alone.

But the business of what happened next was mightily raked over in later times because it became central to the issue of whether or not Henry could divorce Katherine of Aragon. Henry argued that his marriage to Katherine had been fatally flawed because the Bible decreed that he shouldn't have married his brother's widow. Meanwhile, Katherine herself argued that this was irrelevant because she hadn't been truly married to Arthur: he had never penetrated her. Yet Henry's supporters claimed to 'remember' the young Arthur coming out of the bedroom the morning after his first night with Katherine and calling for wine to refresh him after his 'long journey into Spain' and back.

The success or failure of Henry VIII's own sex life could literally result in life or death for his intimate servants. In June 1540, Thomas Cromwell, Henry's latest chief minister, was arrested. He had been the prime mover behind Henry's fourth marriage, to Anne of Cleves. Henry had been persuaded into marrying Anne only because Cromwell thought an alliance with the German state of Cleves was a good idea. When he actually met his promised bride, however, Henry was gravely disappointed by her appearance. He was desperate to find a way out of his marriage, and required Cromwell to put it about the court that it had been unconsummated because of Anne's lack of physical charms. Cromwell obediently spread reports recounting the king's words to him: 'I have felt her belly and her breasts, and thereby, as I can judge, she should be no maid. Which struck me so to the heart . . . that I had neither will nor courage to proceed any further.'

But once Cromwell had contributed his 'evidence' that the marriage was invalid, and once the divorce from Anne was under way, Henry had no reason to keep his former favourite minister alive. He was executed on 28 July 1540.

The undressing of a bride remained a semi-social bedroom ritual right into the early nineteenth century, and it involved throwing things around just as bouquets and confetti are still thrown today. The bride's men would 'pull off the bride's garters' and fasten them to their hats, while the bride's maids would carry the bride into the bedchamber, 'undress her, and lay her in bed . . . the bridemen take the bride's stockings, and the bride maids the bridegroom's; both sit down at the bed's feet and fling the stockings over their heads'.

In the seventeenth century, Lady Castlemaine, Charles II's mistress, once had herself married to her friend Mrs Stuart as a saucy joke which mirrored the contemporary ceremony of getting the bride ready for bedding. Their 'wedding' was solemnised with the aid of a 'church service, and ribbons and a sack posset in bed, and flinging the stocking'. At the end of all the titillation, though, it was said that 'Lady Castlemaine, who was the bridegroom, rose, and the King came and took her place'.

This idea that a newly married couple needed the encouragement of spectators persisted into the early nineteenth century, but by then it was starting to look old-fashioned. When Percy Bysshe Shelley eloped with and married Harriet Westbrook in 1811, he found himself blissfully alone at last with his bride in a bedroom in an Edinburgh lodging house. Suddenly there was a knock at the door. It was the landlord, with the unwelcome news that 'it is customary here at weddings for the guests to come, in the middle of the night, and wash the bride in whisky'. The sight of Shelley brandishing his pistols convinced the disappointed landlord that no whisky-washing would be taking place that particular night.

Only in the Victorian period does the bedroom door swing closed upon the newly married couple, though in her own journal Queen Victoria records her pleasure at having Albert, her new husband, help her on with her stockings. Once sexual matters had become a matter of private business for the couple involved, rather than a concern for their wider community and subject to open discussion, information grows harder to come by.

This changed once more with the 1950s revolution in Britain's bedrooms. In this decade, British marriage rates were at their highest ever. It was partly a result of the post-war housing shortage: young people forced to live with their parents saw marriage as a step on the way to finding a home of their own. The return of the men from the war to the workplace meant that many women lost their jobs, or found their earning power reduced. So they devoted themselves instead to home improvement and enthusiastic baking.

The 1950s are often seen as a conservative, stable period, optimistic but with an undertone of prudery and repression. Despite this urge for conformity, though, a new model for marriage now emerged in which husband and wife were considered to be equals in a 'companionate' relationship. A mutually satisfying sex life began to be prized, and numerous authors went into print to help the nation achieve it.

Helena Wright was a pioneer with books such as *The Sex Factor in Marriage* (1930) and *More About the Sex Factor in Marriage* (1947), and this kind of writing ended up in the Marriage Guidance Council's famous series of 1950s pamphlets. They now seem quaint, gingerly administering rather limited advice, but they did give much-needed information about sex in a straightforward fashion. ('Husbands and wives should get rid of the feeling that there is anything indecent, immodest, or wrong about their sex relationship.')

Additionally, books which actually spelt out that a man should not have intercourse with a woman against her will were still very necessary. 'The first point to remember is that sexual intercourse must not be attempted *till the wife is ready for it*; and it is the husband's business to make her ready,' reads one of the Marriage Guidance Council's guides. Meanwhile, the Family Planning Association, which promoted birth control, finally became respectable. Until 1956, when the Minister for Health, Iain Macleod, visited the association to celebrate its silver jubilee, the media had been forbidden to mention its existence and work.

Despite these steps forward, the respectable married couples of the 1950s who might have read and profited from the Marriage Guidance Council's leaflets still remained largely ignorant and dismissive of homosexuality and pre-marital sex – both were still thought immoral and dangerous. But they would become much more acceptable after 1960 and the lifting of the ban on the publication of D. H. Lawrence's *Lady Chatterley's Lover*. During the trial, the judge was widely derided for asking the jurors to imagine whether they would like their 'wife or servants' to read it. His idea of social relationships seemed deeply anachronistic. Now the Swinging Sixties would see more and more people having more than one partner.

So the image of twin beds flanking a Teasmade may represent repression to us today, but the seeds of the Swinging Sixties were planted in the bedrooms of the 1950s. Many think these seeds have sprouted and grown too vigorously, with porn available via the computer in the corner of many bedrooms, and children exposed to sexual imagery at a younger and younger age.

The fact that sex has become a matter for public conversation is a dramatic reversal of the silence of a hundred years ago. But it's often pointed out that we've only exchanged one sort of silence for another. The Victorians were reticent about sex, yet they were far better than we are at talking openly and with acceptance about ageing, death, grief and mourning.

8 – Conception

Your breeches and your very balls be blessed!
Fourteenth-century compliment

Nowhere did biology determine female destiny more than in the area of fertility. For a princess, quite bluntly, your health and happiness depended upon your abilities in the bedroom, where your task was to provide your husband with an heir.

The queens who suffered accordingly included Katherine of Aragon and Anne Boleyn (neither were strictly infertile, as both frequently conceived, but they produced only one healthy baby apiece). The Stuart Queen Anne became pregnant no less than seventeen times in a desperate but ultimately futile attempt to produce an heir. Royal doctors were always adamant that the failure lay with the woman, while the properties of royal sperm were never questioned. When Anne of Cleves, Henry VIII's fourth wife, failed to produce a child, the king made sure that his physician Dr Butts spread word round the court that Henry – in truth by now quite possibly impotent – was very 'able to do the Act with other than with her' and still had wet dreams in the night.

At the other extreme end of the scale, we hear of distressingly fertile young women, like poor Elizabeth Chappin of Kent, a servant without a husband who was unfortunate enough to give birth in 1602. (This was despite the fact that recipe books often contained instructions for potions to 'bring on the courses', code for abortion. The herb rue was especially valued for its ability to cause uterine contractions.) Elizabeth's parish elders wanted to know the name of the father, because unless he took responsibility she and her baby would become a charge upon the parish. Only in her very worst childbirth pains – while she was 'wishing that all the devils in hell might tear her in pieces' – did Elizabeth finally admit that 'the right father of her child' was her master and employer. He refused to help, she and her baby had to claim poor relief, and her life was ruined.

A single woman whose baby was stillborn stood in grave danger of being suspected of infanticide, hence the many heartbreaking court records which reveal women being sharply interrogated about bad birth experiences. Elizabeth Armitage, another spinster, gave birth in 1682 and told the magistrate that her labour pains had woken her in the night. Nobody came to help her, the baby was certainly born dead, and 'she had had a night would have killed a horse'. In 1668, a court instructed a team of expert midwives to conduct a forensic examination of the clothes of a single woman accused of having done away with an illegitimate baby. They reported that her petticoat had indeed been 'the first receptacle of a child born into the world very lately', and that a murder charge should certainly be considered.

Men were never criminalised in the same way for becoming parents outside marriage – how could they be? The master who made his maid pregnant had huge power over her. Society saw him as the deputy of the king, indeed of God, in the little kingdom of his own household. To criticise him would be to suggest that there was something wrong with the social order, and this was impossible. In 1593, the House of Commons considered plans to punish men as well as women for having illegitimate children, but, as one member baldly put it, it wouldn't work. The requirement to undergo a whipping 'might chance upon gentlemen or men of quality, whom it were not fit to put to such a shame'.

For female servants in a large household, the predatory habits of their employers were a constant curse. The eighteenth-century Jane Peareth had the misfortune to work for the 'low, lewd and wicked' Mr Hall, who told her he had 'lain with all his maids, and that he would lie with her'. Mr Hall's wife, a straight-talking woman, told him 'that if he must have a whore he should go abroad for one and not meddle with her maids'. But it cannot have led to domestic harmony.

Mary Mercer, Samuel Pepys's maidservant, was high in her master's favour, but had to endure his indulging himself daily by the 'handling of her breasts in a morning when she dresses me, they being the finest that ever I saw in my life'. Eliza Haywood, author of *A Present for a Servant-Maid* (1743), had some stout advice for maids like Mary who had to negotiate life in the house of an amorous master. On such occasions, a maid should 'remonstrate to him the Sin and Shame he would involve you in', Haywood warned. 'Let no wanton Smile, or light coquet air give him room to suspect you are not much displeased with the Inclination he has for you.' Jonathan Swift had more mercenary (if satirical) advice for the serving maid: 'never allow him the smallest Liberty, not the squeezing of your Hand, unless he puts a Guinea into it . . . Five Guineas for handling your Breast is a cheap Pennyworth . . . never allow him the last Favour under a hundred Guineas, or a Settlement of twenty Pounds a Year for Life.'

These were wise words, for 'servants and the poorer sort of woman have seldom an opportunity of concealing a Big Belly', according to another commentator named Bernard Mandeville. But one particularly sad form of Georgian impregnation was performed by the 'child getters' whose services were known to be available for hire in prisons such as Newgate. They would enable convicted women to 'plead their bellies' and escape from the gallows for a few more months until their babies were born.

Illegitimate babies were no strangers even in high society, but there their birth could be much more easily hushed up. In the chapel of Georgian St James's Palace, some babies mysteriously 'dropped in the court' were baptised; no one knew who their mothers were, but various Maids of Honour seemed suspiciously willing to stand as godmothers. By the early nineteenth century, poor Princess Sophia, daughter of George III, could not be found an appropriate Protestant prince as a husband because of a shortage in supply, and marriage to a commoner was out of the question. So, in desperation, she embarked upon an affair with one of the very few men she knew: an equerry of her father's called Colonel Garth, thirty-two years older than herself and described by his colleagues as 'a hideous old devil'. She gave up her child.

It's very noticeable just how much bigger Victorian families were than Georgian ones: an average of six children as opposed to 2.5. Part of the reason was a decline in the age of marriage. In the seventeenth and eighteenth centuries, most non-aristocratic women got married in their mid-twenties (having saved up a nest egg through work). They were therefore well advanced into their fertile years even before they began to procreate. (Once they'd started, though, they did not readily stop, but frequent infant deaths brought the average number of children down.) In an industrial economy, though, so much more wealth was generated that a man could go out to work and win the wages to support a wife at home. Victorian marriages therefore took place at a younger age, and more babies survived.

For those who didn't want babies, condoms were available from the late seventeenth century onwards, and there was always the method of coitus interruptus (rather quaintly described as 'to make a coffee-house of a woman's privities, to go in and out and spend nothing'.) Reliable contraception in the twentieth century, as we know, has had an enormous effect on society, and to read certain newspapers infertility or 'leaving it too late' seems almost as big and regrettable a social issue as unwanted pregnancy.

9 – Deviant Sex and Masturbation

I used to masturbate whenever I thought about Lady Jane Grey,
so of course I thought about her continually.

Nancy Mitford, 1948

A piece of pornographic graffiti pencilled onto a staircase wall by a bored page at Hampton Court Palace in 1700 shows a lady with legs akimbo, naked except for a pair of very beautifully drawn shoes. Given the sketchy nature of the rest of the depiction, and the care lavished on the footwear, it seems safe to conclude that he must have been a foot fetishist.

The main point to make in a history of sexual deviancy is that sexual preferences and orientations formed very little of a person's social identity until the late twentieth century. So there were no labels of 'homosexual' or 'lesbian' (or even 'child molester' or 'voyeur'), just people who, from time to time, performed such aberrant actions. The Earl of Castlereagh, executed at the Tower of London in the early seventeenth century for sodomising his footman, was tried and condemned by his peers. What really upset them was not the sodomy but the fact that he'd slept with one of his servants.

The beginnings of a homosexual subculture do appear in the early eighteenth century in the 'molly-houses' caricatured by the London writer Ned Ward. From these origins grew a whole group of people who would eventually publicly describe themselves by their sexuality.

Strikingly, lesbian actions are described in medical textbooks long before any hint is given that males might have sex with each other. Perhaps it was a matter of salacious interest for their male authors. Certainly the seedy seventeenth-century uncle of one Nicholas LeStrange would say 'whensover he saw two women kiss, (otherwise then in the way of salutation) Oh how my breech waters at that'. Queen Anne suffered from negative rumours that she had 'no inclination for any but of one's own sex'. But behind the accusations lay fears that women were too powerful at her court, and that they were disrupting the flow of political advice that should stream to the queen from her male courtiers. The practice of sharing beds meant that homosexual actions were surely an accepted part of life for many of both sexes, and they only caused problems when they emerged from behind the bedroom door.

The most interesting period in the history of masturbation was the nineteenth century, when the anti-masturbatory propaganda and scare-mongering information issued to young people had much in common with the anti-drug campaigning material of today. Why did this great wave of fear grip society and cause so much guilt in the bedroom?

Excessive lust seems to have been a problem as old as humanity. Hildegard of Bingen in the twelfth century recommended wild lettuce as a medicine which 'extinguishes lust in a human. A man who has an overabundance in his loins should cook wild lettuce in water and pour that water over himself in a sauna bath. He should also place the warm, cooked lettuce round his loins.' But the first book devoted to the dangers of masturbation – *Onania, or the heinous sin of self-pollution, and all its frightful consequences in both sexes considered* – appeared in Georgian London in 1715, where urban life was booming. One explanation for the anti-masturbation movement may lie in the fact that cities distanced people from nature. They created a growing concern with appearances and correct behaviour, and people moved from being producers to consumers. Then there was the influence of the new 'rational' trend in thought and habits. If you prided yourself upon your enlightened rationality, you might well have considered that sexual pleasure without reproduction was pointless and therefore wasteful and wrong. The writer of *The Ladies Dispensatory* (1739) thought female masturbation simply dreadful: women who'd learned to become 'capable of pleasuring themselves', he said, were foolishly and wrongly turning down good offers of marriage.

By the nineteenth century, young men were routinely warned of the 'dangers' of masturbating, and there were even devices available to make sure it didn't happen. While it's quite upsetting to imagine generations of youngsters genuinely believing that they might go blind through pleasuring themselves, the nineteenth-century solutions for preventing them from doing so were often amusingly and crazily Heath Robinson-like in character. The 'Leather Jacket Corset' (invented in 1831) included a metal penis tube and 'prevented access to the testicles', while 'The Timely Warning' was a penis-cooling device that employed cold water to cool 'the organ of generation, so that the erection subsides and no discharge occurs'.

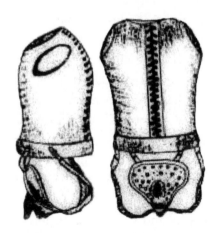

'Dr Fleck's leather corset', one of many inventive Victorian anti-masturbation devices

Now, most people think that as long as the bedroom door is closed, anything goes, and masturbation is a topic for humour not shame.

10 – Venereal Disease

Oh! Now I have a pressing need to make water ... Oh!
It scalds me to Pieces ... 'tis like Fire ... – I have heard
and read of pissing Pins and Needles, But never felt
what it was till now.

So wrote a sufferer from venereal disease in a striking blow-by-blow account of his symptoms on 9 September 1710. He was experiencing its classic symptoms: pain in urinating and purulent matter dripping from the urethra. 'These damned twinges, that scalding heat, and that deep-tinged loathsome matter are the strongest proofs of an infection,' ranted fellow victim James Boswell in 1763. He believed himself to be afflicted by 'Signor Gonorrhoea', but at this point people still couldn't distinguish between gonorrhoea and syphilis. The latter was the more serious: years after the first infection, the symptoms could reappear and culminate in flesh decay, paralysis, madness and a horrible death. Whichever of the two he had, Boswell was understandably gloomy at being confined to his bedroom for several weeks of treatment.

In common with their predecessors and successors in practically all other periods, commentators writing during the First World War thought that the morals of young people were in rapid and dangerous decline. 'Social customs and traditions are altering rapidly in a most undesirable direction,' thundered the

An old procuress, with patches covering up her pox, takes an innocent country girl under her wing

author of *The Changing Moral Standard*, as 'girls, unmarried women and young married women of all classes' had started behaving like prostitutes. In the early twentieth century, the arguments of campaigners against gonorrhoea shaded into eugenics. One pamphlet issued by the National Council for Combating Venereal Diseases claimed that couples who wanted to marry should obtain approval from a priest and a lawyer, but also from a doctor: 'surely there can be no sanctity in any marriage unless blood-cleanness and freedom from infectivity are regarded as essentials?' A printed warning issued to soldiers proposed a more practical solution to the problem of venereal disease: a visit to 'special treatment centres . . . where examination is SECRET, FREE OF CHARGE, and CARRIED OUT BY EXPERT DOCTORS'. (People could find the location of their nearest centre by asking a policeman.)

Syphilis first reached Europe from the New World late in the fifteenth century, and then spread rampantly through sexual contact. It could not be transmitted through the air, even though the over-powerful Cardinal Wolsey was accused of having 'breathed' syphilis over Henry VIII. While the humour-based concept of medicine still reigned, the recommended treatment was with mercury. ('Five minutes with Venus may mean a lifetime with Mercury.') The intention was to make the body sweat excessively, which would restore equilibrium. Syringes for injecting mercury into the urethra sank with the *Mary Rose* in 1545, to be rescued by modern divers. Otherwise a mercury ointment could be rubbed onto the skin, and there were even bizarre anti-venereal underpants coated with the chemical. The mercury did indeed cause a patient to sweat, but the resultant black saliva thought to indicate that the treatment was working was in fact a symptom of advanced mercury poisoning.

It's often been suggested that Henry VIII's various health troubles were caused by syphilis, and he did indeed make potions and salves of his own devising 'to dry excoriations and comfort the member'. But at no point did he disappear from public life for the standard six-week mercury treatment, as did his French contemporary, Francis I. So the case seems unproven. (Syphilis, known in England as 'the French disease', was called 'the English disease' in France. The other conditions thought abroad to be peculiarly English were flagellation, suicide and bronchitis.)

Anyone using a prostitute in seventeenth- or eighteenth-century London would have run a high risk of getting venereal disease. 'A Whore', asserted one moraliser, making a good point but in a particularly unpleasant way, 'is but a Close-Stool . . . that receives all manner of filth, she's like a Barber's Chair, no sooner one's out, but t'others in.' No wonder James Boswell, after his visit from 'Signor Gonorrhoea', reluctantly decided to try the reusable animal-gut condoms that were increasingly available.

Some of the saddest syphilis cases were the wives and children infected by straying husbands. But most heart-rending of all were the victims of the strange and horrible Georgian idea that a man could get rid of his syphilis by having intercourse with a small child, even a baby. His young partner would remove his disease, it was thought, leaving him clean and cured.

Since the 1950s, it's been easier to control syphilis, and if detected early, the patient will make a full recovery. But be warned: the numbers of new cases being reported today are on the rise!

11 – What to Wear in Bed

What do I wear in bed? Why, Chanel No. 5, of course.
Marilyn Monroe

As bedrooms were communal places throughout so much of their history, people were used to being seen in their night-clothes. Instructions written for a medieval pageboy describe how he should undress his master and get him ready for bed. (They have the amusing effect of making the master/king/lord in question sound rather like a doll.) When your sovereign lord wants to go to bed, the page is told, you must spread out a foot sheet for him to stand upon, and take off his robe. Then you put a cloak on his back, before pulling off his shoes, socks and hose. ('Hose', or leg coverings, consist of 'upper hose', or breeches, and 'nether hose', or stockings.) You should throw the hose over your shoulder before combing his head and putting his kerchief upon it, then putting on his nightgown.

This kerchief, wrapped around the head, would develop into the nightcap. The thought of sleeping with an unprotected head was abhorrent in an age when sickness was thought to travel through the air in a cloud of evil 'miasma'. People really believed that they might die from sitting or sleeping in a draught. They were paranoid about keeping their heads warm (but without overheating: some nightcaps had a hole in the crown, so that

84

'the vapour may go out'). My own mother wasn't allowed by my grandmother to leave the house with wet hair even in the 1950s.

Cardinal Wolsey, Henry VIII's minister, was the son of a humble Ipswich innkeeper and butcher, yet rose through the ranks of the church, one of the few careers open to young men of modest means. He revelled in his rich cardinal's robes of red, but during his frequent work binges he stayed in his nightclothes all day. His talent at statecraft and his industry under pressure were both enormous: during negotiations with the French in 1527, Wolsey worked for twelve hours continuously from four in the morning, yet 'never rose once to piss, nor yet to any meat, but continually wrote his letters with his own hands, having all that time his nightcap and kerchief on his head'.

Most people slept in a shirt (men) or shift (women) just like the one they wore as underwear in the daytime; sometimes even the very same one. A family forced from their beds by a fire in their house on the old London Bridge in 1633 took to the street with 'nothing on their bodies but their shirt and smock'. Those with the money bought special nightshirts with slightly fuller sleeves and a deeper neck opening than those worn during the day.

A surprising number of daytime fashions started out as bedroom wear. Anne Boleyn was bought nightgowns by Henry VIII, notably one of black satin bound with black taffeta and edged with black velvet. Something like a modern dressing gown, 'nightgowns' such as Anne's were warm, loose and often hooded garments. They were worn over other clothes, and taken off at the point of getting into bed.

Being snug and practical, nightgowns made their way out of the bedchamber and into public areas (rather like 'housecoats' in the twentieth century). Count Egmont wore a 'red damask' nightgown to his own execution in 1568, while in 1617, Lady Anne Clifford even went to church in her 'rich night gown'. In time, the nightgown evolved into the smartest and most formal dress ever invented: the eighteenth-century court mantua, a dress with an enormously wide hooped skirt. The mantua began as bedroom wear, but developed into a stylised and strangely fossilised uniform for formal occasions. In the slow-moving world of the court it was still worn in the 1760s, but looked like an extreme parody of the off-duty outfits of nearly a century earlier.

The nineteenth century saw the development of specialist nightgowns, and voluminous white cotton was the textile of choice in the age when Britain's mills dominated the world. No woman would have worn pyjamas until after the First World War. In the 1920s, the influence of Hollywood films brought about a revolution in bedroom wear. When the stars appeared in scenes set in bedrooms, they were put into satin so that they'd shimmer in the studio lighting. Around the same time, Madame Vionnet's invention of the 'bias' cut allowed clothes to cling more closely to the body, so a generation of shiny, slinky, peachy or flesh-coloured nightgowns appeared. They could also be made out of the new synthetic rayon for those who couldn't afford silk. However glamorous your very own Hollywood-inspired, peach-coloured 1930s boudoir might have been, though, in Britain it probably still lacked central heating, and those bias-cut silk nightgowns would have disappeared under thick, quilted, satin dressing gowns.

Pyjamas also became standard wear for female Hollywood stars, inspired by decadent, exotic, Chinese garments rather than the striped cotton pyjamas of conventional male nightwear. Shanghai and Hong Kong were glamorous travel destinations, reached by cruise ships on which pyjamas were considered appropriate leisure wear for the fashionable.

Since the 1920s, pyjamas and nightdresses have evolved in line with contemporary cut and choice of fabric, but there has been no real revolution in nightwear for the last few decades.

The first generation of pyjamas for ladies, from a 1920s ladies' magazine

Perhaps the surprising thing is that, with central heating and duvets, anyone needs pyjamas at all. Certainly the dressing gown has an archaic air, and belongs more to the communal world of the hotel or house share than to most people's private bedrooms.

12 – Sleeping with the King

The crowd is ushered through the King's chambers to view a . . .
magnificent bedchamber hung with fine canopies.

César de Saussure, visitor to London, 1725

We've heard about royal dressing ceremonies, and there was a similar kerfuffle in the evening when the king or queen wanted to go to bed.

The origins of the royal putting-to-bed ceremony can be seen in the preparations performed for a medieval knight or squire. These were identical wherever he happened to lay his head as he travelled from castle to castle upon a journey or progress:

See his sheets be clean, then fold down his bed, and warm his night kerchief and see his house of office be clean, help off his clothes, and draw the curtains, make sure the fire and candles, avoid [chuck out] the dogs, and shut the doors.

The middle-class fifteen-year-old French housewife to whom the advice book *Le Ménagier de Paris* is addressed must similarly serve her husband's needs at night, with extras thrown in too. Her duties include:

Removing his shoes in front of a good fire, washing his feet, offering clean shoes and socks, serving plenteous food and drink, respectfully honouring him. After this, she puts him to sleep in white sheets and his nightcap, covered with good furs, and satisfies him with other joys

A royal levee. The king is ceremonially dressed before his courtiers

and amusements, intimacies, loves and secrets about which I remain silent.

Royal ceremonies were along exactly the same lines, but multiplied vastly in terms of complication and the number of people involved.

Henry I's household accounts mention many of the numerous people who prepared the king's bedchamber, including the 'porter of the king's bed', who received an extra three halfpence for his 'man and a packhorse' (remember the bed was still being carried about from castle to castle). The king's 'ewerer' got a penny for drying the king's clothes, and 'when the king has a bath 3 pence'. (But the accountant didn't know everybody's wages: 'Touching the laundress there is a doubt.') All these people who worked in the bedchamber together made up the innermost department of the royal household.

The household rules for Henry VIII describe exactly how his bedchamber staff went about making his bed. He slept upon eight mattresses, and his servants had to roll upon them to make sure that enemies had hidden no dangerous daggers inside. When the bed was made with fresh sheets, his servants had to make the sign of the cross over the bed, kiss the places where they'd touched it, and sprinkle it with holy water.

For the very highest in status, bedroom politics were not merely sexual. Until the late seventeenth century, the royal bedchamber was used for receiving guests and audiences and for ceremony. This proved so onerous that monarchs would sneak out of their state bedchambers into more private, secondary bedrooms when they actually wanted to sleep. William III's private bedroom, tucked away downstairs beneath the state apartments at Hampton Court Palace, has its locks on the *inside* of each of its three doors. Finally the king could be alone there.

This desire to control access to the royal presence helps to explain why keys were such a big deal in a palace. The Groom of the Stool was the king's most important servant and attended him on the 'Stool', which is the close stool or toilet. As his badge of office, the Groom of the Stool wore the bedchamber's single 'gold Key in a blue Ribbon', and there were strict instructions that 'no other Keys for the Bed-Chamber &c. be made or allowed'.

Until modern times, kings rarely slept alone. But Henry VIII would not sleep with his wife unless he wanted to have intercourse with her – for this purpose he would visit her in her own chamber. Generally, in his bedroom, a small wheeled bed was pulled out each night from beneath the king's big bed for one of his gentleman attendants. Favoured servants such as Thomas Culpepper 'ordinarily shared [the King's] bed'.

Over time, though, Henry VIII grew annoyed that so many people considered themselves entitled to barge into his bedroom any time they wanted. So he built himself a new bedchamber in his so-called 'secret lodgings' at Hampton Court, and here he tried to start afresh with a much stricter access policy. He issued new orders to his bedchamber staff, insisting that his six Gentlemen of the Bedchamber could no longer enter the royal bedchamber without permission. Only his favourite, Henry

Norris, had that right, and 'the King's express commandment is, that none other of the said six gentlemen, presume to enter or follow his Grace into the said bed chamber, or any other secret place, unless he shall be called'.

Queens likewise had an extensive bedchamber staff, and also ended up with many more people than they wanted in their bedrooms. But it was very difficult to eject anyone who thought they had permission, established by precedent, to be there. On one occasion the eighteenth-century Queen Caroline had to spend a whole hour hearing the rival arguments of her Ladies of the Bedchamber and her Lord and Vice Chamberlains. Their dispute was whether the two men were allowed into the queen's bedchamber, 'a right always pretended to by them & always contested by the Ladies'.

People would brag about their privilege of entry, if they had it, because it was such an important sign of status. Once, when Caroline was recovering from a miscarriage, the Countess of Manchester insisted that her husband's high position gave her the right to visit Caroline's bedside. She marched right into the bedchamber of a desperately ill woman, just to prove to her peers that she could.

This all seems rather trivial to modern eyes, but it really was of the greatest importance. The people who spent time with the king or queen, from day to day, could affect the very government of the country. It's easy for powerful people, through inattention or laziness, to fall under the thumb of their closest servants and advisers, and to make poor decisions as a result. So the history of the royal bedchamber department, from the Tudors to the Stuarts, also tells the story of royal power.

Henry VIII successfully retained control over his bedchamber staff, as the resetting of his relationships with them upon the construction of the 'secret lodgings' demonstrates. The structure of power at court changed under Elizabeth I because, as a woman, she spent more time in her bedchamber and privy

lodgings. Yet her Ladies of the Bedchamber were not as powerful as their male predecessors had been. There was less access to
the queen by her male courtiers, but Elizabeth was a powerful
enough personality to use this to her advantage, rigidly insisting
on making her own decisions and imposing them on her court.

Her successor James I, however, was a weaker character.
When he came down to London from Scotland, he staffed his
bedchamber with old Scottish friends. A little clique developed,
and James fell rather under the spell of the manipulative Duke
of Buckingham, his favourite, who was well able to get the king
to agree to what he wanted without bothering with the Privy
Council. It was this sort of high-handed rule by an arrogant
inner group that led James I and then Charles I into trouble.
Eventually their subjects became so weary of their imperious-
ness that they rebelled. So some of the seeds of the cataclysmic
English Civil War – in which a greater proportion of the population was killed than in the First World War – were sown amid
the politics of the royal bedchamber.

Great aristocrats also found their bedchambers distressingly
public places, where the conflicts of the various factions in their
households were played out. From the seventeenth century
onwards, though, bedrooms were less important places for politics. With the decline of personal power and the rise of a more
democratic form of government in the shape of the Parliament,
the bedrooms of the great became period pieces, interesting for
what had gone on there in times gone by. They became tourist
attractions, rather than places of power.

The indefatigable tourist and house-snooper named Celia
Fiennes infiltrated the Duke of Exeter's own apartments and
saw his blue velvet bed at Burghley House near Stamford in
1698. She found the rooms 'very large and lofty and most deli-
cately painted', but the Duke's pictures rather upsetting: their
subjects 'all without Garments or very little, that was the only
fault, the immodesty of the Pictures especially in my Lord's

apartment'. One feels disappointed in the duke, obviously, for his objectification of women, but he also deserves a little sympathy for being obliged through courtesy to let the super-nosy Celia Fiennes poke about in his bedroom.

But even while royal power was gradually dwindling, aristocrats in their great country houses often maintained a special bedroom – and indeed a special bed – for visiting sovereigns. These 'state beds', rarely slept in, are like colossal temples to luxury, and they've often survived astonishingly well because of their lack of use. In fact, whether or not the beds were really intended to be slept in is a matter of hot scholarly debate. Some might merely have been commissioned out of a sense of self-importance and tradition (plate 1).

People visiting country houses were simply staggered by the sight of some of these state beds. A poet was moved to verse by the sight of the one at Harewood House in Yorkshire:

> Hail, glorious structure! Noblest of our isle,
> Finished by artists bred on every soil,
> What gold can finish or what taste can shew
> Beyond conception strike the astonish'd view.
> Such costly furniture, such beds of state!

Thomas Chippendale in 1761 recommended that a state bed should measure 7 ft across and 8 ft long, with a canopy 15 ft high (by comparison, a standard modern double bed measures 4 ft 6 ins by 6 ft 3 ins). The Duke of Bedford's state bed at Woburn Abbey was commissioned from Samuel Norman of Soho Square. It cost £378, but if its current worth is calculated according to average earnings today, the sum would be nearer half a million pounds.

While a state bed may seem sumptuous, kings and queens often wished they could sleep somewhere lower-key. Sickness in a state bed, for example, was a miserable experience. Pitiful, aged Elizabeth I passed the last few nights of her life upon a pile of cushions 'laid for her in the privy chamber hard by the closet door', rather than in her 11-ft, ostrich-feather-topped and decidedly inconvenient bed.

During the last week in the life of Mary II, which she spent in her grand bed at Kensington Palace, her husband William III passed his nights with much more humble sleeping arrangements. One morning in December 1694, Mary had woken up to discover on her arm the rash heralding smallpox. She put her affairs in order, paid her bills and resigned herself to death, which came a week later. During these final few days, her distraught husband slept on a lowly servant's pallet bed in the corner of her bedchamber, so as to miss none of the few remaining hours he had in the company of his beloved wife. 'You can believe what a condition I am in, loving her as I do,' he wrote. 'If I should lose her, I shall have done with the world.' One might suggest that, as a constitutional king whose power was limited by the Bill of Rights, William III could willingly sleep in a bed at which Henry VIII would have turned up his nose whatever the circumstances.

So the decline of the power of the monarchy was accompanied by the decline of the stateliness and scale of its beds. It's remarkable to think that Queen Elizabeth II and Prince Philip spent their honeymoon on the royal yacht *Britannia* each sleeping in their own narrow single bed. There was not one double on board.

13 – A History of Sleep

Sleep may be reckon'd one of the Blessings of Life.

Sarah Cowper, 1712

There are two ways of telling the time: by the hands of a clock, or by the shadow on a sundial. That's why we still give the hour 'o'clock', of the clock, and by implication not 'of the sun' or 'of the dial'. Until the eighteenth century, when ordinary people began to get access to clocks, the sun told most people when to get up and when to go to bed.

The cost of candles and firewood meant that only the richest and most powerful Tudors could turn night into day. Yet it did sometimes happen: once, eager for a building project to be completed, Henry VIII made his workmen labour all night by candlelight, and rewarded them with beer and cheese.

But consider the difficulty of coping with a long winter night if you couldn't afford the lighting to ease its passing. There's a fascinating theory, promoted by the historian Roger Ekirch, that people living in pre-industrial times dealt with the darkness by sleeping in two spells, the 'first sleep' and the 'second sleep', with a couple of hours or so of wakefulness in between.

The British night lasts fourteen hours in winter, and human beings simply don't need to sleep for that long. Modern experiments have shown that the body clocks of humans kept regularly in darkness for fourteen hours at a stretch gradually gravitate towards two periods of slumber, with a middle stretch spent awake. Could this sleep pattern have been widespread in the days when nights were still long and dark?

There are indeed occasional documentary references which support this theory. A pattern of two sleeps a night would explain why, for example, in the sixteenth-century story *Beware the Cat*, its hero, 'newly come to bed', has a quarrel with his two room-mates, who had 'already slept' their 'first sleep'. Also, in *A Treatise of Ghosts* (1588), the author can refer in a matter-of-fact manner to the time 'about midnight when a man wakes from his first sleep'. Perhaps these forgotten wakeful hours in the middle of the night were an important part of life for medieval and Tudor people.

How might they have passed the time? Maybe they chatted to a husband or wife. The French doctor Laurent Joubert recommended in the sixteenth century that this was the best time to conceive children: 'after the first sleep' couples should have 'more enjoyment' and 'do it better'. He recommended that afterwards they 'get back to sleep again, if possible, or if not, at least to remain in bed and relax while talking together joyfully'. Perhaps people even felt their way around their houses in the dark. Certainly they must have had a drink or relieved themselves: the Tudor Andrew Boorde recommends that 'when you do wake of your first sleep you shall make water if you feel your bladder charged'.

Some people even left their beds to go about their business. Poor men went out to rob houses, and women got up to 'brew a Load of Malt in the Back Kitchen' or to put a load of washing to soak. 'Often at Midnight, from our Bed we rise,' explains Mary Collier in *The Woman's Labour* (1739).

If there really was such a broken pattern of sleep at night, it's not surprising to discover that people made up for it with naps in the middle of the day. 'At noon he must have his sleeping time,'

complained Bishop James Pilkington about the ordinary working man, and Thomas Rowlandson's *Haymakers at Rest* (1798)
shows labourers literally asleep in the fields. A workman's right
to sleep during the daytime was officially recognised in 1563 by
The Statute of Artificers: half an hour was to be allowed daily
to each workman 'for his Sleep when he is allowed to sleep . . .
which is from the middest of May to the middest of August'.

Samuel Pepys recorded taking real pleasure in a broken night.
He delighted in falling asleep and waking up again and again:

there being now and then a noise of people stirring that waked me;
and then it was a very rainy night; and then I was a little sleepy, that
what between waking and then sleeping again, one after another, I
never had so much content.

It's striking that he thought this was a good night, as it is so far
from the modern ideal of a solid eight hours' sleep.

By the mid-eighteenth century in London, the middle hours of
the night were often disturbed by noise and movement: highway-
men, drunkards, pickpockets and nightwatchmen 'had not yet
gone to bed, while pigeon fanciers, cow keepers, water workers,
and the women who attended the fish markets had already got
up'. Maidservants collected water from the pumps to avoid the
daytime queues; 'Drunken Husbands' wandered 'home to their
half-starved disconsolate Families'.

And it seems that when city life developed, and when artificial
light became more readily available, the pattern of first and second sleep was disrupted. If you had the money – and candles –
to stay up later in the evening darkness, then you tended to sleep
for the six or eight continuous hours usually recorded in the diaries of upper-class seventeenth- and eighteenth-century individuals. Richard Steele in 1710 condemned the new habit of staying
up late. He found it a 'perverted relish' to prefer 'sea-coals and
candles to the sun, and exchange so many cheerful morning
hours for the pleasures of midnight revels and debauches'.

But Steele underestimates the sheer pleasure of conquering

night with light to those unused to it. Louis XIV's fabulous Hall of Mirrors at the Palace of Versailles was glitteringly marvellous by day, yet really came into its own in darkness, when the astonishing mirrors reflected and magnified the light of the candles. This was perhaps the first room in modern history with artificial light levels approximating what we would today consider necessary for a social gathering, and the French court made great use of it for evening parties on a scale never before seen.

It would be the factory whistle and the steam train that created the modern toe-tapping attitude to time, in which hours and minutes are carefully demarcated and utilised. Until these developments, events had rarely been timed to the minute. Stagecoaches went when all the passengers were aboard, early-modern workplaces (often in people's houses) kept quite flexible hours, and meals were served when all the family were present. But the departure of a train or the start of a shift in the mills waited for no man (or woman or child).

The heads of Georgian households tried to instil a similar sense of urgency into their domestic staff. Time became money in the Georgian age, and promptness and efficiency were increasingly demanded in servants' manuals. 'Do everything at the proper time. Keep everything in its proper place. Use everything for its proper purpose,' ran *The Cook's Oracle* of 1817, while Thomas Broughton in his *Serious Advice and Warning to Servants* (1768) sternly warned his readers: 'when you hired yourselves, you sold all your time to your masters, except what God and Nature more immediately require to be reserved'.

A new housemaid, for example, might be presented with a daunting card listing her weekly duties in fifteen-minute blocks. 'On first sight I could not see how one could possibly perform all those duties in one day,' wrote housemaid Lavinia Swainbank, who was born in 1906 and started work as a teenager, yet 'to this day I have not lost the clockwork precision instilled into me by a succession of head housemaids and timetables forty years ago'. The time to sleep and the time to wake were now subject to a level of control which seems far from the dreamy awakening and sleeping again of medieval times.

And yet, as today's market in self-help books promulgating time management reveals, the idea that time should be divided into neat chunks has always been more successful in theory than reality. At home today, the dividing line between work and leisure remains blurred: there is housework, there is computer work and there is down time, but no set hours for any of them.

And the same goes for sleep. While the healthy ideal since the Industrial Revolution has been for a solid eight hours, most people get nothing like that. Next time you're suffering from insomnia, just tell yourself that you're experiencing a medieval sleep pattern and maybe you'll relax enough to drop off.

14 – Murdered in Our Beds

I lay in some disquiet all night, telling of the clock
till it was daylight.

Samuel Pepys

There's a good reason why we talk about people being murdered 'in their beds' rather than in their living rooms or bathrooms. The bedroom is an excellent dark and private place to do away with somebody. One of the earliest and most compelling images of child murder is that of the pillow held over the mouths of the sleeping fifteenth-century boy Princes of the Tower in Shakespeare's *Richard III*, a crime that has been pulled inside out without the evil-seeming Richard III's guilt having ever been finally proved (plate 5).

In bed we feel at our safest, which means a foul deed performed there seems all the more shocking. In 1381, the boy king Richard II took refuge from the Peasants' Revolt in the Tower of London once again, while a mob burned his palace in the Strand and his Archbishop of Canterbury was murdered on Tower Hill. When Richard rode out of the Tower to meet his citizens, the protestors burst in, 'pulling the beards of the Guard'. The rebels 'arrogantly lay and sat and joked on the king's bed, whilst several asked the king's mother [. . .] to kiss them'. This was the king's mother Joan. The rebels abused her in this particularly intimate manner because she had the reputation of being a sexual libertine.

Thomas Deloney's Elizabethan novels kicked off the literary genre of the whodunit, in which beds would play a prominent part. In one of his books, a traveller named Thomas Cole arrives at the Crane Inn (a kind of sixteenth-century Bates Motel). He falls into a strange melancholy state, depressed by the screech owls and ravens which 'cried piteously . . . hard by his window'. 'What an ill favoured cry do yonder carrion birds make!' he said, as 'he laid him down on his bed, from whence he never rose again'.

He was killed in his sleep by the inn's evil keeper, who'd fashioned a trapdoor beneath the bed. When the pins holding the trap were removed in the middle of the night, unfortunate guests would whistle straight down into an enormous cauldron in the kitchen below, there to be 'scalded and drowned'. In this particular case, the murderer was discovered, for the innkeeper had overlooked one detail: he told everybody that his guest had never arrived, but Cole's horse wandered off from the inn, was recognised, and gave the game away.

The privacy of the bedroom also makes it a favoured place for suicide. John Evelyn recounts how the 'extraordinary [*sic*] melancholy' Lord Clifford, formerly Lord Treasurer, had been found strangled 'with his cravat upon the bed-tester'. Clifford's servant, however, had looked in 'through the key-hole, and seeing his master hanging, brake in before he was quite dead, and taking him down, vomiting a good deal of blood'. He was just in time to hear Lord Clifford's last words, which were 'there is a God, a just God above'.

It's therefore not surprising that bedchambers are also the most haunted rooms of a house. James Boswell, that bundle of bravado and insecurity, was not immune to frights in the night. Sharing a room with his friend Lord Mountstuart, they lay one night talking about superstitions: 'I was afraid that ghosts might be able to return to earth, and for a time wished to get into bed with my Lord. But I lay quiet.'

In the previous century, though, the philosopher Thomas Hobbes treated the question with his usual rationality. His brilliant work aroused jealousy, and his enemies spread false reports:

One was that he was afraid to lie alone at night in his Chamber; I have often heard him say that he was not afraid of Sprights, but afraid of being knockt on the head for five or ten pounds, which rogues might think he had in his chamber.

Most people, though, were with Boswell rather than Hobbes. Going to bed in an age when witches, ghosts and robbers were all equally real in the mind required a good deal of resolution. Preparing to survive the trials of the night was a much more arduous task than it is today, when you merely set the alarm and switch off the light. The precautions one could take ranged from a pragmatic attention to household security, to prayers and rituals designed to scare off even the most awful evil spirits. First you had to get into the right frame of mind: 'Discompose yourselves as little as may be before Bed-time,' was the sensible advice of Humphrey Brooke in 1665, 'the Master of the Family prudently animating and encouraging his Wife, Children and Servants against Fear and Disorder.' It was wise to pray for protection each night against 'sudden Death, Fears and Affrightments, Casualties by Fire, Water or Tempestous Weather', and obviously, 'Disturbance by Thieves'. There was also symbolic protection to be gained by placing a pig's heart over the hearth, or putting a shoe among rafters in the roof, or carving the protective letter 'M' (for Virgin Mary) by the window or chimney through which a witch could conceivably enter. You might also put rosemary leaves under your bed in order to 'be delivered of all evil dreams'.

One could also take the practical step of locking all the doors; a Georgian house at night was described as 'barricaded', 'bolted' and 'barred', both 'backside and foreside, top and bottom'. 'I always go round every night to see that all is fast,' explained the London laundress Anne Towers, concerned that thieves would try to steal her customers' linen overnight. Rural robbers might try to steal a family's pig, and its male members would blunder outside with their sticks or cudgels in a literal attempt to 'save their bacon'. Burglar alarms are an older invention than you might think. In *The Footman's Directory* (1827), the retiring footman is encouraged to lock up carefully, and 'if the shutters and doors be secured by an *alarm-bell*, be sure to put the wire of the alarm-bell to them, so that they cannot be opened without its going off'.

Today, night fears are more about intruders and serial killers than ghosts, but they still persist. Many people think that the 3 a.m. existential angst is a modern phenomenon. Like most human problems, though, people have suffered from it for centuries.

PART TWO

An Intimate History of the Bathroom

Separate rooms for washing were not standard in people's homes until at least the middle of the twentieth century. In this section we nevertheless cover the activities of washing, defecating and grooming, which today take place in that most private of places, the bathroom. Bathrooms are now usually the only rooms in a house with a lock on their doors, yet the activities that take place within did not always require privacy.

Nor did people's bodies inevitably grow cleaner as the years marched on. It's surprising to discover that the many enthusiastic users of medieval communal baths probably smelled better than their Tudor descendants, who thought that bathing was dangerous. The Georgian period saw an enthusiasm for baths and washing return after an absence of more than two 'dirty' centuries. But many people had to make do with a bowl of water in the bedroom well into the twentieth century.

It seems horrible today to imagine life without hot water, but our notion of what it really means to be clean has changed dramatically. Developing ideas about cleanliness and social habits have dominated the history of the bathroom. Technological improvements in the art of plumbing have merely followed, rather than led, change.

15 – The Fall of Bathing . . .

GLOUCESTER: O, let me kiss that hand!
LEAR: Let me wipe it first; it smells of mortality.
William Shakespeare, *King Lear* (1608)

Notice that King Lear doesn't wash his hand; he merely 'wipes' it. This is deeply significant in the history of personal hygiene. The actor playing the first King Lear probably washed himself far less frequently and thoroughly than his medieval predecessors.

The word 'medieval' is often – and wrongly – used to mean something primitive, dirty and uncomfortable. This is really unfair to the people of the Middle Ages, where art, beauty, comfort and cleanliness were widely available (at least for those at the top of society). Washing their bodies was an important part of life for prosperous people, and from medieval towns there are numerous records of communal bathing after the Roman model.

More commonly than taking a bath, though, medieval people washed their hands and faces in a basin (the very same word for the much more sophisticated, plumbed-in bowl that you'll find in your bathroom today). In art, you often see the baby Jesus being sponged down in such a dish. The head of the household usually had his own personal basin, and one of his servants would have had the job of pouring water into it from a special jug: we know about this because people often left valued basins and jugs to each other in their wills.

It was particularly important to wash your hands just before mealtimes, and the attention you paid to this was a marker of status. Once Cardinal Wolsey dared to dip his fingers in water that had just been used by the king; his presumption in doing so was considered to be outrageously arrogant.

A medieval bathhouse. Its patrons enjoy baths, saunas, drinking and social interaction

This was the kind of minor, intimate but telling detail that led to his downfall.

But medieval people also immersed their whole bodies in bathwater relatively frequently. A bath was not just for getting clean; it could also be a hugely significant element of ritual purification as well. The ceremony of baptism involved water, priests would wash carefully before taking Mass, and bathing was an important part of the ritual of conferring knighthood. In Britain, this was especially important to the Order of the Garter's younger sibling, the Order of the Bath. Just before Henry VIII's coronation in 1509, twenty-six would-be companions of the order had a ritual bath at the Tower of London – denoting 'future purity of the mind' – before keeping an all-night vigil in the castle's medieval chapel.

A knightly bath sounds rather pleasant. The knight's servant was supposed to hang sheets, flowers and herbs around the wooden tub, and to place in it sponges upon which the knight would sit. The servant then took a basin full of hot, fresh herbal potion in one hand, and used the other to scrub his master's body with a soft sponge. The lucky knight was then to be rinsed with rose water, taken out and stood upon his 'foot sheet', wiped dry with a clean cloth, dressed in his socks and slippers and nightgown, and sent to bed.

If the knight required a 'medicinable' bath (perhaps after jousting), it might have contained hollyhock, mallow, fennel, camomile and 'small-ache' (wild water parsley). In his royal palaces, the king had even better baths: as early as 1351 he had 'two large bronze taps . . . to bring hot and cold water in'. Henry VIII's bath at Hampton Court could be found in a room in the Bayne Tower (from *bain*, French for 'bath'). It was filled from a tap fed by a lead pipe bringing water from a spring more than three miles away. Henry's engineers performed the amazing feat of passing this pipe beneath the very bed of the River Thames, all this effort being necessary to create, through gravity, the pressure of water to spurt up the height of the two floors to the royal bathroom. The bath itself was made of wood, round like a barrel cut in half and lined with a linen sheet to stop the king from getting splinters in his bottom.

The king may have had his own private bathtub and bathing room, but a great many of his subjects made regular visits to public bathhouses, or 'stews'. The Crusaders had returned home from the East with reports of the enjoyable Turkish 'hammams' they'd visited, and in 1162 there were eighteen bathhouses recorded in the London district of Southwark alone. They were perhaps called by their colloquial name of 'stews' from the 'stoves' which heated the water, but alternatively it's worth noting that fish were bred and kept in ponds likewise called 'stews'. Medieval Londoners loved water as much as fish.

London's numerous communal bathhouses were concentrated in Southwark, on the south bank of the river, a district devoted to pleasure and packed with playhouses, bear-baiting pits and gardens. When the water was hot and the steam ready at any particular establishment, boys would run through the streets shouting out the news and drumming up custom. (They were ordered to refrain from doing so before dawn because it woke everybody up.)

The bathhouses were used by large numbers of men and women *all together*. Bathing was a social experience, just like the sauna is in Nordic culture today. People in the Middle Ages – professional hermits excepted – were used to being in a group, and rarely spent time on their own.

While many bathhouses were respectable institutions offering a useful service to the public, some of them shaded over into houses of ill repute, just as many twenty-four-hour massage parlours do today. A prudish monk who visited a communal bathhouse in the 1390s was less than impressed: he found that 'in the baths they sit naked, with other naked people, and I shall keep quiet about what happens in the dark'. In medieval songs and stories, taking a bath was often an erotic affair. The dynamic and heroic Sir Lancelot is often offered baths or massages by the various damsels he rescues from distress. Just like his twentieth-century equivalent, James Bond, a beautiful and flirtatious girl inevitably appears whenever he's swimming or bathing.

In literature, it's sometimes not clear whether a medieval bath is being offered in hospitality or out of feminine designs upon the hero's body. But in the thirteenth-century story of *The Romance of the Rose* it's pretty explicit. The 'Old Lady' character warns its juvenile hero that

sooner or later you will pass through the flame that burns everyone, and you will bathe in the tub where Venus steams the ladies . . . I advise you to prepare yourself before you go to bathe, and that you take me for your teacher, for the young man who has no one to instruct him takes a perilous bath.

By the sixteenth century the bathhouses' reputation had become well and truly tarnished, and they had become synonymous with brothels. In fact, Georgian brothels were often called *bagnios*, even though no actual bathing was happening there any more. Visits to bathhouses were sometimes cited in later medieval divorce cases: like a weekend in Brighton, a person's spending time at the stews could be taken as evidence that he or she'd been unfaithful.

What was it like, exactly, in a medieval bathhouse? Well, numerous illustrations show rows of individual baths, or even shared communal tubs, in a large room. The heat for the water might conveniently be provided from a baker's oven next door. Baths themselves were often draped with sheets, partly to make them more comfortable and partly so the sheets could be raised to form a tent-like steam bath. Hot stones might be provided to give extra heat, and spices – cinnamon, liquorice, cumin, mint – to scent the water. The twelfth-century Hildegard of Bingen suggests various combinations of herbs suitable for water to be poured over the head, to be splashed upon rocks in the sauna, to be rubbed directly onto the body, or for a soak. In the bath-houses of thirteenth-century Paris, a steam bath cost two deniers and a slosh in the bathtub itself twice as much. It all sounds delightful: medieval illustrations even show bathers, seated in their tubs, eating meals served on boards laid across the bath.

Perhaps the most sophisticated water systems were to be found in monasteries. Monks were immensely keen on bathing too; it was just they liked to make it single-sex and do it in ascetic cold water rather than hot steam. (A monk named Aldred, chronicler of Fountains Abbey, found it helpful to sit in cold water up to his neck whenever he was plagued by 'worldly thoughts'.) The monks of Canterbury were mysteriously exempted from the Black Death in 1348–50. What was chalked up at the time to superior praying power may well have been their hyper-efficient plumbing. The monks had five settling tanks to clear the water feeding their frater, scullery and kitchen, bakehouse, brewhouse and guest hall, as well as lavers or fountains trickling into basins for hand-washing.

But many medieval people couldn't afford the bathhouse. And even if they could, their unwashable fur, leather or woollen clothes were seldom as clean as their skin.

The best way to keep clothes clean was to brush them. A book of advice for young men training as body servants gives these recommendations for robes: 'brush them cleanly, with the end of a soft brush', and never let 'woollen cloth nor fur pass a sennight [a seven-night, a week] unbrushed & shaken'.

The medieval household manual *Le Ménagier de Paris* (1392) gives various recipes for getting rid of fleas, such as scattering a room with alder leaves or attempting to trap the insects on slices of bread smeared with glue. Fleas were particularly hard to remove from furs, but infested garments could be 'closed up and shut away, as inside a chest tightly strapped, or in a bag tied up securely and squeezed'. Then the fleas should 'quickly perish'. There was an important social distinction between being afflicted by lice as opposed to fleas. Fleas were almost unavoidable; everyone had them. But to 'be lowsie' was an indicator of poor personal hygiene. According to the Georgian entomologist Thomas Muffet, lice were an embarrassing disgrace. (Mr Muffet was the father of the Little Miss Muffet who finds the spider beside her in the nursery rhyme.)

Around 1500, though, something fundamental in society shifted, and the practice of bathing entered into two hundred years of decline and neglect. The bathhouses of London were finally closed down for good in 1546 by Henry VIII. This was done with a flourish and sense of occasion: the stews 'were by Proclamation and Sound of Trumpet, supress'd, and the Houses let to People of Reputation and Honest calling'.

So began the two 'dirty' centuries, from about 1550 to around 1750, during which washing oneself all over was considered for the greater part to be weird, sexually arousing or dangerous. For the few people who could afford to have them at home, baths became medicinal, rather than cleansing, in purpose.

The superlative state bed at Kedleston Hall, intended for a visiting king.
Disappointingly for Nathaniel Curzon, who commissioned it, his sovereign never
actually came to stay.

A recreation of Edward I's bed at the Tower of London (top). Demountable, it would have been carried with the king as he travelled. Most medieval furniture was similarly portable, hence the French word 'mobiliers' or 'removables'.

A depiction of the conception of the wizard Merlin (centre). This manuscript illustration showing Merlin's mother's bed was one of the sources for reconstructing Edward I's.

Edward I's oratory at the Tower of London. The forerunner of the closet, his oratory was per-haps the only room in which the king could expect to be alone.

This is the bed associated with the story of the 'warming pan'. It was put about that James II's son was born dead, and an imposter smuggled in using a warming pan. It's probably untrue, as there were at least 51 people present at the birth in 1688.

Thanks to Shakespeare, the 'Princes of the Tower' are perhaps the best known victims of being 'murdered in their beds'. They're shown here in Delaroche's historical painting of 1831.

A medieval Caesarian takes place in a woman's bedchamber (top left).

Pregnant Jacobean ladies often had their portraits painted just before giving birth. If they died, their husbands and children would at least have a souvenir of a lost wife or mother.

The 'Man-Mid-Wife', a caricature of 1793. To the left is the new, masculine face of the birthing profession; to the right, his female predecessor. Before its medicalisation, childbirth was one of the few areas of domestic life where women were totally in charge.

Queen Victoria's split drawers. Ladies first began to wear knickers in the nineteenth century. Early drawers were often split like this to facilitate the use of a chamber pot.

A bedroom in a working family's 'back-to-back' house in Birmingham. Perhaps eight or nine family members would have been packed top-to-toe into two beds.

'Slumberdowns' or 'continental quilts' revolutionised bedding, ending centuries of sheets and blankets. This 1970s Habitat catalogue shows another novelty: children placed at the heart of family life.

A public bath-house. These places of pleasure were immensely popular in medieval cities. Used by both sexes simultaneously, they developed rather a dubious reputation. By the eighteenth century, a 'bagnio' was basically a brothel.

Queen Caroline, interested in medical innovations, pioneered the habit of bathing when it returned to fashion in the 1700s after centuries of being considered dangerous. This is her bathroom at Hampton Court Palace.

An earth closet, an enduring form of toilet. Without the need for water or plumbing, they were always the poor person's choice, and are returning to favour once again in the form of today's sustainable composting toilets.

The fishing pavilion at Kedleston Hall, Derbyshire (top left). Its lower storey houses a plunge pool for a cold dip, intended to cure 'weakness of Erection, and a general disorder of the whole Codpiece Economy'.

A lady's maid from the 1730s soaping her mistress's linen (top right). The laundry-maids were the servants least supervised in any household, and the most fun.

18, Folgate Street, Spitalfields, London. Built in the 1720s, townhouses like this would dominate the next two centuries. Their bedrooms were starting to become private places.

In most workers' homes, the kitchen was the bathroom, and the whole family took turns to use the same tub. It was easier 'to throw the baby out with the bathwater' than you might think. Families bathed eldest to youngest, and the water grew dirty and dark towards the end.

Pregnant women were advised to avoid the shower bath, as it 'gives too great a shock, and may induce miscarriage'. Charles Dickens possessed a model aptly named 'The Demon'.

Why did this happen? For a start, many holy wells and baths were closed down in the Reformation because worshipping the saints to whom they were dedicated had become idolatrous and illegal; their secondary purpose of keeping clean was a casualty of this. Bathing also declined because of fears that water spread illness, especially the new and frightening disease of syphilis. As cities grew, it became harder and harder to maintain a supply of clean water. People became increasingly concerned that polluted bathwater might penetrate their skin or gain access to their bodies through their orifices. Sir Francis Bacon's instructions illustrate how the Tudors and Stuarts believed that they needed to defend their bodies against water:

First, before bathing, rub and anoint the Body with Oil, and Salves that the Bath's moistening heat and virtue may penetrate into the Body, and not the liquor's watery part.

A description of the nasty things that lurked in a common bathing pool makes such precautions understandable:

> Mad and poison'd from the Bath I fling
> With all the Scales and Dirt that around me cling:
> Then looking back, I curse that Jakes obscene;
> Whence I come sullied out who enter'd clean.

Hot water might even open up the pores in your skin so that the evil 'miasma' of the air could enter, bringing sickness with it.

To say that bathing fell out of fashion, though, is not to say that people positively enjoyed being dirty or that they had no concept of cleanliness. It was simply different in scope. Another Tudor health writer recommended that people should dress of a morning but then wash their faces with extreme care, even opening their eyes under water to remove 'the gum and foulness of the eye-lids that do there stick'. An unpleasant personal odour was still worthy of mention and disparagement. The 'evil smells' and 'displeasant airs' of Anne of Cleves caused Henry VIII to be unable to consummate his fourth marriage.

In the Tudor or Stuart concept of hygiene, clean underwear played an important part. The wearing of clean linen next to the skin was considered essential in the 'dirty' centuries. People thought it was dangerous to immerse their bodies in water but perfectly safe to use linen to absorb the body's juices, and then to wash the linen regularly.

In fact, a show of brilliant white linen at the collar and cuffs was important to publicise the cleanliness of your body – and, by implication, the purity of your mind. To the Elizabethan George Whetstone, in his *Heptameron of Civil Discourses* (1582), a woman with dirty linen 'shall neither be praised of strangers, nor delight her husband'. Spotlessness of the visible outer clothes was extremely important, as proved by the list of linen possessed by the seventeenth-century headmaster of Westminster School. He had only two shirts but fifteen pairs of cuffs. Natural linen is a grey colour, and a great deal of effort is involved in bleaching it to a sparkling white. So, as well as attesting to virtue, to wear white also signified status and wealth.

How did the Tudors wash their underclothes? The first job was to make 'lye', or caustic soda, the main detergent. This was done by dribbling water through ash from a fire that had been collected in a wooden tub with a hole in the bottom. The water was passed through the ash again and again, absorbing its chemicals and growing stronger each time. Dirty linen was then soaked in the lye to loosen the dirt, a stage analogous to the pre-wash in a modern washing machine. The receptacle used for soaking, a big wooden tub, was called the 'buck'. (Hence the name for the laundry tub's smaller sibling, the 'bucket'.)

A more concentrated stain-remover was to be found in the form of urine. Hannah Woolley in 1677 gave these instructions 'to get Spots of Ink out of Linen Cloth':

Lay it all night in urine, the next day rub all the spots in the urine as if you were washing in water; then lay it in more urine another night and then rub it again, and so do till you find they be quite out.

Urine remained a prized stain-remover right into the twentieth century. In country houses where a heavy and muddy programme of fox-hunting caused the gentlemen's scarlet coats to need urgent and nightly attention from the valets, a butler named Ernest King remembered that when coats were truly filthy,

> . . . we would ask the housemaid to save us the contents of the chamber pots, at least a bucketful. It was truly miraculous in getting the dirt out.

One suspects that the gentlemen were not told how their coats had been cleaned.

Next on Tudor laundry day came a vigorous stage of scrubbing the linen with soap and beating the dirt out of it with a wooden bat called a 'beetle' (i.e. a tool for 'beating'). As I discovered when I attempted this, it's very tempting to thwack the balls of soap about with the bats, and there's a theory that it was the children of laundresses who invented the sport of cricket. This stage of scrubbing and beating was like the main washing cycle in your own machine at home today.

Henry VIII paid his laundress Anne Harris £10 a year to wash his tablecloths and towels, but out of that sum she had to provide her own soap. The soap used in the laundry involved even more lye, or caustic soda. To make it, lye is boiled with animal fat, a process which makes a truly ghastly smell. In seventeenth-century London, the noxious fumes created by soap-makers formed 'an impure and thick mist, accompanied with a fuliginous and filthy vapour' over the city. Soap would often come like jelly in a barrel, though it was also formed into hard balls or blocks.

The soaped linen needed a good rinse and then to be squeezed out (today's spin cycle). Here a cross-shaped post in the ground was a useful anchor for twisting a rope of linen round and round to wring out the drips. Finally, instead of the tumble drier, clothes and sheets were then laid out on bushes to dry in the sun. Rosemary is ideal, for its sweet smell, and hawthorn is also extremely effective as its prickles act like little clothes pegs to hold the fabric in place.

All this effort was worth it, not just to wear clean clothes, but to have a clean body, and underclothes performed part of the function of the still non-existent bathroom. A clean shirt 'today serves to keep the body clean', wrote a French architect in 1626, 'more conveniently than could the steam-baths and baths of the ancients, who were denied the use and convenience of linen'.

But he was writing just a few decades before bathing began, in advanced circles, to return to favour once more.

16 – ... and Its Resurrection

Slovenliness is no part of religion ... cleanliness
is indeed next to godliness.
John Wesley, in a sermon on dress, 1786

Why did bathing inch its way back into fashion in the eight-eenth century?

There had been people bold enough to brave the dangers of bathing throughout the sixteenth and seventeenth centuries, but they'd usually been undergoing some kind of medicinal treatment bath under the orders of their doctors. Henry VIII, for example, was prescribed herbal baths for the treatment of his suppurating leg ulcer. A seventeenth-century aristocrat was sometimes pre-scribed a mineral bath, although his doctor's instructions give a good idea of the precautions thought necessary:

let the liquor be as warm as you can suffer it when you first go into the bath & have hot ready to pour in as it first cools ... drink a draught of warm broth or caudle, keeping yourself from cold for some times after.

And it was also under doctors' orders that bathing began to make a return to everyday experience. The seventeenth century saw the beginning of a huge upheaval in contemporary medi-cal understanding. With the Enlightenment, the Galenic concept that the human body was made up of the four humours would

A Tudor tap from Hampton Court Palace. Did it once fill Henry VIII's bath?

gradually become discredited. The perceived risks which went with bathing were much reduced once people stopped believing that water could throw their bodies out of equilibrium.

Additionally, there was a new understanding about the nature of sweat. That a large but largely invisible volume of perspiration comes out of our skins every day was proved by the measurements of the physician Sanctorius, whose works became increasingly widely disseminated. By 1724, an English physician could write that it was 'now known by everybody' that washing the body freed the pores of 'that glutinous foulness that is continually falling upon them'. But hot water was still seen as rather risky. It was cold water which returned to favour first.

So a chilly dip began to be considered beneficial for health. It provided a useful jolt to a sluggish system. A cold bath 'excites the drowsy spirits', as Sir John Floyer, author of *The History of Cold Bathing*, put it, and 'the stupid mind is powerfully excited'. But Floyer had an ulterior motive behind his promotion of cold bathing on medical grounds: he thought that the ceremony of baptism ought to involve complete immersion of the body, as in ancient times, and wished the church would restore the practice.

Immersion in cold water, suggested Joseph Browne's *Account of the Wonderful Cures Perform'd by the Cold Baths* (1707), could cure a multitude of ills: scrofula, rickets, 'weakness of Erection, and a general disorder of the whole Codpiece Economy'. Browne was not alone in thinking that a cold bath would have a welcome effect on a limp libido:

> Cold bathing has this Good alone
> It makes Old John to hug Old Joan
> And gives a sort of Resurrection
> To buried Joys, through lost Erection.

Dr Richard Russell, author of a *Dissertation on the Use of Seawater*, thought seawater should be drunk for its properties as an excellent laxative – 'a pint is commonly sufficient in grown persons, to give three or four sharp stools' – while his colleague Dr Awsiter revealed that 'in cases of barrenness I look upon seawater to stand before all other remedies'. Bathing in the sea became a popular Georgian holiday activity, and contributed to the growth of the seaside resorts springing up along England's south coast.

Given the amazing health benefits supposedly to be found in cold water, the next step for enthusiasts was to bathe in their very own homes. At Kedleston Hall in Derbyshire, the Curzon family created a private plunge pool down by their lake (plate 15). It formed the lower storey of a fishing pavilion (you stuck your rod out of an open upper window). The less plutocratic took a mini-cold-water plunge in a simple bucket. Horace Walpole, afflicted by gout in his face, relied upon the remedy of dipping his head 'into a pail of cold water, which always cures it'.

Bathing for everyone did genuinely become less dangerous as water supplies grew cleaner. In the Georgian city, houses of the middling sort began for the first time to receive supplies of uncontaminated piped water. Back in 1582, the Dutchman Peter Morritz had noted the existence of a waterwheel at London Bridge. When the tide was right, it would lift river water to supply people's houses. But the river was also Elizabethan London's sewer, and its citizens' own faeces were being recycled back to them.

Wooden pipelines bringing water to Georgian London ran along roads like strings of sausages

One of the most impressive engineering achievements in the history of London was the seventeenth-century New River. This artificial waterway, a wiggly forty miles in length, brought fresh water from a Hertfordshire spring into the heart of Islington. A statue of its builder, Sir Hugh Myddleton, still stands proudly in the middle of Upper Street in Islington today. As an engineering achievement, the New River ranks with the Channel Tunnel and the Great Western Railway. The feat of seventeenth-century surveying involved in getting the waterway to follow the correct contours is quite staggering.

From the New River's head, great rafts of elm pipes were buried beneath the Georgian city's roads. Sometimes they even ran along the surface, looking like strings of enormous sausages. This was because the pointed end of each hollow trunk slotted into a larger hole at the end of its neighbour. In winter, these surface pipes would be heaped with manure to protect them from frost. Elm was the preferred wood because of its durability in wet conditions, and only in the nineteenth century was it replaced by iron. These great pipelines marching down London's roads were tapped at intervals with lead 'quills', smaller pipes that ran into the basement kitchens of individual houses.

The whole system worked through gravity, so water pressure was low and often even failed. During the Great Fire of London in 1666, panicking people dug up and punctured the pipes in the streets, ruining the pressure so that the supply quickly fizzled away. In Georgian London, the water supply might be turned on once a week – the 'water day' for a particular street – and would run only for a couple of hours. Householders would diligently fill up their cisterns, pots and pans for just as long as the flow lasted. They'd have to purchase extra water from a water-seller roving the streets if they ran out during the week.

The slightly unpredictable nature of the system meant that basements sometimes received no water at all, or else were unexpectedly flooded. Charles Dickens found his arrangements annoyingly inadequate: while living in Tavistock Square in 1853, he complained that his 'supply of water is often absurdly inefficient'. Even though he paid an extra charge for 'a Bath Cistern', he wrote that 'I am usually left on a Monday morning as dry as if there was no New River Company in existence – which I sometimes devoutly wish were the case'.

The New River Company was London's best-known concern, but it faced competition from the Hampstead Waterworks Company (providing its supplies from the ponds on Hampstead Heath), the Chelsea Waterworks Company and others. In the early days, there was a period of joyful guerrilla warfare between the rival companies, reminiscent of today's war between rival mobile-phone suppliers. Each company would cheerfully steal another's customers, or cut the pipes of competitors. Other dramas included the unexpected appearance of wildlife: the lack of filtering meant that sometimes fish got into the pipes, and once a dozen eels nearly two feet long were found in the vicinity of Pall Mall.

IF WALLS COULD TALK

Once houses had piped water, even if only to a single tap in their basement, washing the body obviously began to require much less labour. Even during the 'dirty' centuries people had continued to wash their faces, hands and other body parts in basins, using linen towels as washcloths. The French word for a linen cloth, a *toile*, would give its name to the process called the *toilette*, or basin wash. In due course, it would morph into the modern word for a water closet, a 'toilet'.

In Georgian times, the very beginnings of the bathroom – which would eventually become a separate room – appeared in the corners of bedrooms. Georgian *toilette*, or dressing, tables held brushes, mirrors, perfume bottles, jewels and make-up, and next to them stood a three-legged stand for the washbasin. Furniture catalogues containing such stands, or cabinets with basins set into their tops, are recording the beginnings of what would eventually become the washbasin and vanity unit in modern bathrooms.

It's worth noting that even if a few top doctors were now recommending full bathing in addition to this bedroom-based lick and splash, society at large was exceedingly slow to catch up. A Georgian high-society ball in Bath still smelled awful, if one of Tobias Smollett's characters is to be believed: 'of mingled odours, arising from putrid gums, imposthumated lungs, sour flatulencies, rank armpits, sweating feet, running sores and issues'. In 1750, John Wilkes observed that 'the nobler parts are never in this island washed by women', and John Hervey even described the courtiers in the royal palace, crammed into a hot room, as 'sweating and stinking in abundance as usual'.

It would be the involvement of religion that would help tip the scale towards Britons becoming bathers once again. The Methodist John Wesley promulgated the idea that cleanliness is next to godliness. He thought that 'slovenliness is no part of religion', and he would not even preach in a place where no toilet was provided for his use. The 'little house' was essential, he said. 'Wherever it is not, let none expect to see me.'

Others agreed. The leaders of various radical Protestant religious movements discovered that creating the urge to keep clean among their followers also encouraged them to become self-disciplined, self-motivated and increasingly devout. The poor little chimney sweep in Charles Kingsley's Victorian children's story *The Water Babies* learned that he could only go to heaven if he kept himself clean; he needed to 'work very hard and wash very hard' before he could be considered worthy. This nexus of religion, cleanliness and a Protestant work ethic lay behind the great nineteenth-century movement in favour of sewers, public toilets and drains. As the historian Keith Thomas puts it, public health became 'a religious duty, a form of moral crusade'.

But even with divine endorsement, bathing was still not an accepted part of daily life by the turn of the nineteenth century. A *Family Cyclopaedia* published in 1821 had separate entries on 'personal cleanliness' and 'bathing' because they remained slightly different things. As late as 1857, hot baths still had a racy, somewhat dangerous reputation: by no means 'to be trifled with, and in medical cases where there is time to obtain it, advice should be had recourse to before using them'.

The next stage in the general acceptance of bathing came about when taking a bath became a classy thing to do, one of the marks of a gentleman. Beau Brummell, a leader in Regency high society, and a hugely influential figure in men's dress and grooming, advocated that men should no longer wear effeminate perfumes. A daily bath was therefore necessary if they were not to smell of sweat. In due course, the lower and middle classes would aspire to copy his upper-class lifestyle.

Now, at last, bathing was becoming not just a healthy or religious duty, it was a social one too. Victorian etiquette books began to spell it out: a clean body was the beginning of good manners. By 1869, *Cassell's Household Guide* had finally dropped the idea that baths had a medical aspect, and insisted instead on the importance of the 'Saturday night wash' for simple hygiene reasons.

Society was ready for the next step: the birth of the bathroom.

17 – The Bathroom Is Born

Although the bathroom has long been of exceptional
importance in eastern cultures, it is the most recent
addition to the accommodation of our northern houses.

Hermann Muthesius, *The English House*, 1904

In 1871, a French visitor to England described a stay in a particularly luxurious Victorian country-house bedroom. It had a
dressing table holding three jugs of different sizes, one of which
was for hot water. There were two porcelain basins, a dish for
toothbrushes, two soap dishes and a water bottle with a glass.
On the floor near by stood a 'large shallow zinc bath for morning bathing'. Each morning, a servant came in, drew his curtains
and delivered 'a large can of hot water with a fluffy towel on
which to place the feet'.

Until the arrival of the plumbed-in bath in the 1860s,
Victorians put their servants through incredible feats of water-
heating and water-lugging – with possible spillages – in rooms
not really intended for the purpose. The relatively low cost of
domestic labour put people off installing upstairs plumbing.

A full-length bath, filled only 15 cm deep, requires 45 litres
of water weighing 45 kg. In a townhouse this would typically
have to be carried up from the basement by hand. Then the
used bathwater had to be carried down afterwards. 'Men will

A bedroom suite with a washstand (left), forerunner of
the modern bathroom's washbasin and vanity unit

do much for glory and vainglory,' wrote Florence Caddy in
1877, 'but then I never heard of a man who took the trouble
to empty his bath after using it.' Clearly, when it came to taking their own baths, the servants themselves cut corners. The
six laundresses employed at Chatsworth House in Derbyshire
in the 1920s bathed in half a wooden beer barrel on Saturday
nights: 'The head was first to get in, followed by her five helpers
in order of seniority.' Pity the most junior!

Emptying the contents of a washstand and chamber pot was
called 'slopping', and it took place within individual bedrooms;
chamber pots and basins were not carried down the stairs. It
worked like this: the housemaid would bring two buckets into
the room, one empty, the other full of clean water. The contents of the basin, chamber pot, used water glass and any other
waste went into the empty one, and the vessels were rinsed out.
Then the rest of the clean water was poured into a jug and left
for the return of the bedroom's occupant. Chamber pots were

only taken out of the bedroom twice a week to be scalded clean (though the slop bucket was scalded every day).

In larger establishments, the housemaids might have been aided by special 'watermen'. At Belvoir Castle in Leicestershire, recollected Diana Cooper, these were troll-like figures:

the biggest people I have ever seen . . . On their shoulders they carried a wooden yoke from which hung two gigantic cans of water. They moved on a perpetual round . . . they seemed of another element and never spoke but one word, 'Water-man'.

From the 1860s, piped water to the first-floor bathroom began to make all this effort obsolete. The new bathrooms were at first pretty simple. The cartoonist Linley Sambourne had only a cold supply to his tub in his pioneering bathroom at Stafford Terrace in London (he introduced a clever folding shelf so he could develop pornographic photographs in his bath as well as washing himself). But what was originally a plain and functional room grew more decorative over time. Early fitted bathrooms of the 1880s were often described as 'Roman' or 'Pompeiian' in style, in deference to the Romans' reputation for good plumbing.

From around 1800, the kitchen range had begun to creep into British kitchens, and with it houses gained a permanent supply of hot water. But the range was often left unlit in summer. Another innovation from around the middle of the nineteenth century was the self-heating bath. The 'gas bath' made use of Robert Wilhelm Bunsen's breakthrough eponymous burner, which consumed gas enriched by oxygen. Models such as the 'Prince Albert', the 'General Gordon' and the 'Prince of Wales' were proudly installed in upper-middle-class homes.

But gas baths required a thirty-minute wait for the water to heat, and were not particularly reliable. 'A call on the hot water supply . . . did not meet with an effusive or even a warm response,' recollected Lord Ernest Hamilton of the baths of the 1860s.

A succession of sepulchral rumblings was succeeded by the appearance of a small geyser of rust-coloured water, heavily charged with dead earwigs and bluebottles . . . these huge enamelled iron tanks were not popular as instruments of cleanliness.

In due course, a quicker result could be achieved by Mr Maughan's patent 'Geyser' boiler, which appeared in the trade journal *The Ironmonger* in 1874. The Geyser, a marvellous invention, would ultimately provide wonderful hot water for thousands of homes, but would always retain a reputation for fearsome and unpredictable behaviour. 'At the head of the bath', wrote a resident of Bath in the 1940s, 'towered a dragon-like copper geyser with a gas meter below for shillings. When lit, the geyser burst into life with a deafening roar and spluttered out much steam and a little water.'

The plumbed-in bath and the hot-water Geyser represented an investment beyond the reach of working-class householders, and remained a novel sight to many. The Edwardian Duchess of Portland would invite local miners' wives to sewing classes at her magnificent mansion, Welbeck Abbey in Nottinghamshire. These women would 'form a queue to use the lavatory, and none of them missed the opportunity to see the lavish bathrooms, try the hot and cold running water, and use the luxurious soap'.

And cleanliness still remained a vital indicator of class. 'The lower classes', complained John Stuart Mill in 1874, 'seem to be actually fond of dirt.' George Orwell went ever further. 'The real secret of class distinctions', he said, 'is summed up in four frightful words . . . bandied about quite freely in my childhood. These words were: *The lower classes smell*.'

No wonder. As Diana Athill wrote of her Edwardian grand-mother, she expected her servants 'to be ninnies, and to be dirty, and how they managed not to be the latter is hard to see, con-sidering that it was years before anyone thought of putting in a bathroom on the attic floor where they lived'. Old habits pre-vailed, and into the 1900s bathrooms were still seen as optional rather than necessary. Edward Lutyens, for example, built at least two mansions (Munstead Wood and Crooksbury) in the early twentieth century without bathrooms. New working-class homes were not expected to have baths with hot and cold water until legislation was passed in 1918, and of course many older houses remained without for decades after that date.

Even in aristocratic circles something of a lingering suspicion of plumbing and hot water persisted into the twentieth century. To keep *too* clean seemed somehow degenerate. 'There is in the taste for sitting down in a bathtub a certain indolence and softness that ill suits a woman,' wrote Countess Drohojowska in 1860, and the *Manual of Hygiene* of 1844 recommended that the private parts be washed no more than once a day. 'We will content ourselves with observing that everything which goes beyond the boundaries of a healthy and necessary hygiene leads imperceptibly to unfortunate results,' was all its authors had to add. James Lees-Milne stayed in a house without plumbing in 1947. Each day, an 'old retainer brought into the room a red blanket which he spread before the empty hearth-grate. Then he brought a brass can of tepid water, enough to cover the bottom of the bath. The room must have been several degrees below zero. He might have been a ghost performing the customary function of a hundred years ago.'

This conservatism caused a culture clash when visitors from across the Atlantic arrived in Britain with much higher expectations of bathroom technology. The 'dollar princesses', American heiresses sent over to find themselves English noblemen for husbands in the 1890s, were horrified by the primitive bathing conditions they encountered in English country houses. But they were even more horrified by the prospect of failing to snag a duke. Afraid to return to America empty-handed, one of Edith Wharton's characters said she'd 'rather starve and freeze here than go back to all the warm houses and the hot baths' at home.

The en-suite bathroom was first seen in the New World, and

from the 1920s onwards hotels in America often had a bathroom for each bedroom. The ascetic British were slow to follow and en suites were at first only to be found in the luxury hotels where an international clientele required them. The art deco bathrooms added to Claridge's hotel in Mayfair in the 1920s, with their marble surfaces, eau de Nil colour schemes, mirrors, separate showers at head and at shoulder height (so as not to get your hair wet) and bells for maid or valet, are perfect examples. One can imagine a Hollywood star frolicking in a bubble bath in such a room, perhaps to the disapproval of the English dowagers next door.

The other innovation from America was the stand-up shower to be taken separately from, and in preference to, the bath (plate 20). Even within the US, the shower was a West Coast idea that worked its way east over time. Over-bath showerheads had appeared in Britain in Victorian plumbing catalogues (Charles Dickens favoured a model called 'The Demon'), but in Europe such devices were seen as rather treacherous: certainly a pregnant woman should avoid their use, as 'a shower bath gives too great a shock, and may induce miscarriage'. The European modernist houses of the 1930s, designed as rational 'machines for living', still had bathtubs in preference to showers, and even today few British flats are built without baths, despite their heavy claim upon ever-dwindling supplies of water.

So long was the en suite considered a little bit racy that bathrooms entered through the bedroom only became common in British homes in the 1980s. Terence Conran was a little ahead of the game as usual when he wrote in 1974 that 'along with central heating and a good fitted kitchen, there is nothing like a bedroom/bathroom suite to bump up the value of your property'. But even then he still felt it necessary to justify spending money on a room used merely for washing oneself:

attitudes to bathrooms have been changing. These rooms are no longer limited by Puritan traditions according to which you used them only for ablutions, if not cold baths, or groped your way through clouds of rolling steam and yards of pipes.

It was in this continued Puritan spirit that my mother took me, only a few years after Conran was writing, on a day out to marvel – but also to scoff a little – at the luxurious bathrooms for sale in Harrods.

So this vital room has a much shorter history than you might assume: a matter of decades, not centuries. The bathroom's decorative journey from Victorian Pompeiian pomp via art-deco glitter reached an endpoint in the stripped-down, minimalist, designer bathrooms of the 1990s, where function and aesthetics were as one. 'The best contemporary bathrooms are those that cloak fitness for purpose in a Spartan simplicity,' proclaimed a guide to the most desirable trends of the 1990s. The bathrooms designed by John Pawson look like temples to serenity, while Philippe Starck transformed familiar bathroom fittings into sleek and eye-catching alien shapes. Their simplicity of form, though, did not preclude endless supplies of hot water and piped music, and an atmosphere of luxury.

By the end of the twentieth century, the bathroom had become only secondarily a place for washing. 'Thinking in the bath', a form of meditation, is now one of the bathroom's intimate activities. As the only room in the modern home in which the user can turn a key against his or her family, the bathroom has quite a lot in common with the Stuart closet.

18 – Don't Forget to Brush Your Teeth

A few grains of gunpowder ... will remove every blemish
and give your teeth an inconceivable whiteness.
The Gentleman's Magazine, 1764

Until the eighteenth century, there was no such thing as a dentist. The barber-surgeons of Tudor times did all the jobs about the body requiring blades, removing rotten teeth along with amputating limbs and cutting hair.

Tudor and Stuart people did indeed clean their teeth: with water, with powdered cuttlefish, with salt or rosemary rubbed on with cloths, twigs or sponges. But they also had sugar, and therefore cavities. (The aged Elizabeth I was a fearsome figure with 'nose a little hooked, her lips narrow and her teeth black'.) Popular sweet treats included fiendish dental challenges such as 'subtleties', fabulous gilded edible sculptures of fortresses, beasts or even (as once served by Cardinal Wolsey) a model of St Paul's Cathedral. Crafted in sugar and almond paste, they provided a severe 'assault for valiant teeth'. Once decay set in and teeth were yanked out, rudimentary false teeth of ivory or bone were worn.

The late seventeenth century saw the development of a new branch of medicine: dentistry. Charles Allen's book *The Operator for the Teeth* (1685) is the earliest dental treatise in

English. He emphasises the need to have healthy teeth for chewing, and regrets the pain caused by toothache. His eighteenth-century successors agreed that strong teeth were useful for eating, but they also exhibited a new and more refined set of values. Additionally, the Georgians wanted a fine set of teeth in order to be able to talk genteelly, and they wanted their snappers to *look* good: 'the ornament of the mouth'. This is the century in which toothy smiles begin to appear in portraits for the first time.

There was still no sure way, though, of protecting your teeth from decay. One hardly believes in the powers of a 'pleasant ODORIFEROUS TINCTURE' advertised in the *Weekly Journal* in 1725, which promises to make even the 'blackest and most foul teeth extremely white, clean and beautiful at one using'. A vinegar gargle against bad breath sounds rather more efficacious, less so a potion containing powdered cumin and white wine, said 'to help a Stinking breath, which comes from the Stomach'.

Salt remained an enduringly popular toothpowder, as did bicarbonate of soda. The twigs of earlier times were gradually replaced by pig or horsehair bristle brushes. In 1721, Sir John Philipps begged his wife not to use the new toothbrushes: 'using a brush to your teeth and gums (as you constantly do) will certainly prove in time extremely injurious to them both . . . I beg of ye for the future to use a sponge in its room.'

George Washington (1732–99), first president of the US, is celebrated for his false teeth made of hippopotamus ivory and cow tooth. During the Revolutionary Wars, the capture in 1781 of his letter requesting cleaning tools for his teeth alerted the British forces to his whereabouts – the tiniest details may determine the course of empires. And indeed most people requiring false teeth preferred not to advertise their need. Customers in search of the services of Mme Silvie, a Georgian dentist, were assured of her discretion: 'Those who don't choose to make their

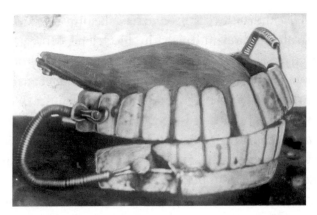

George Washington's false teeth. The lower denture was
carved from hippopotamus ivory

grievances known by asking for the Artificial Teeth-maker may
ask for the Gold Snuff-box and Tweezer-case Maker' instead.
The Dental Journal of 1880 describes the sad case of a lady who
complained of a pain in her throat. She was too embarrassed to
tell her doctor what he soon discovered for himself: that she had
swallowed her top set of false teeth.

The new Georgian art of fixing up the mouth was part of
the boom in unnecessary but charming additions to daily life
designed to display your status, wealth and the fact that you had
leisure time to squander – just like shopping trips, enormous
feathered hats, ceramics and the other luxuries produced by the
Industrial Revolution. Unfortunately the wealthy eighteenth-
century ladies who longed for a 'fine mouth' may well have
rotted their own teeth through drinking the newly fashionable
sugared tea. A country character in a book published in 1703
despises extravagant London 'dames': what 'with drinking hot
Liquors, and eating Sugar-Plums at Church, not one in ten has
a Tooth left'. Another reason for the poor state of people's teeth
was the use of 'vomits' or emetics, an important component of
medicine based on the concept of the four humours. A person
making him- or herself sick on a regular basis will damage the

teeth by introducing strong stomach acids into the mouth.

One strange byway through the history of dentistry was a short-lived craze for live tooth transplantation, which took place in the comfort of your own home. The surgeon John Hunter (1728–93) was a pioneer of the new art of transplanting live organs from one body to another, and this included the teeth. A rich patient requiring teeth would buy from a pauper, and the transplantation from mouth to mouth would be carried out as quickly as possible with pliers and alcohol.

The practice came to an end in the nineteenth century for three reasons. Firstly, there were moral concerns about poor people selling their healthy teeth (just like the concerns over the sale of livers and kidneys today). Second was the very reasonable fear that diseases could be transmitted along with the teeth. And finally, the new porcelain false teeth, once they had become available, were so lovely and white and durable. Gradually porcelain replaced all the earlier materials, which had included ivory, mother-of-pearl, silver, agate and the teeth of walruses. But even porcelain falsies must have been extremely uncomfortable: an 1846 dental textbook admits that they were usually 'too insecure in the mouth to admit of any attempt at complete mastication of the food without displacement'. Only the discovery, importation and growing use of Indian rubber would make them comfortable to wear.

Once false teeth that fitted reasonably snugly were available, they became an object of great desire. You could avoid pain and expensive dental treatments by having all your natural teeth whipped out at a young age. In 1918, T. S. Eliot overheard women in a pub discussing their teeth in connection with the return of their husbands from the First World War:

> Now Albert's coming back, make yourself a bit smart.
> He'll want to know what you done with that money he gave you
> To get yourself some teeth. He did, I was there.
> You have them all out, Lil, and get a nice set.

Still, the practice of live tooth transplantation took a long time to die out completely. In 1919, the Royal College of Surgeons' examiner in dentistry was still able to write a text describing how exactly how to perform this arcane art. But by then dentistry had moved out of the home and into the specialised surgery, and beyond the boundary of our intimate history of the home.

19 – An Apology for Beards

Long hair is one of the sinful customs and fashions
of the wicked men of the world.
                                        Thomas Hall, 1630s

'There's more to life than hair, but it's a good place to start,'
say the Aussie shampoo adverts, and it's true that hair is a terrific indicator of status, wealth and aspirations to fashion. In
fact, your hair provides you with a vast canvas for personal and
political self-expression.

Hair speaks especially stridently in the area of religious beliefs.
The twelfth-century monk who wrote *An Apology for Beards*
argues that the 'marvellous mystery' of matted, greasy facial
hair indicates 'interior cleanness' and 'divine virtue'. But five
hundred years later, the strictly Puritan writer William Prynne
found long hair on men to be 'graceless', 'whorish', 'ungodly'
and 'horrid'.

Norman commentators seem to have alternated regularly
between criticising dashing young knights who'd grown their
hair too long and complaining that they'd cut it too short. A
convincing explanation is the fear medieval people felt if other
people looked like they were trying to escape from their allotted
stations in life. Men whose job was fighting looked shamefully
like women if they wore their hair long, while the same men

with short hair were trespassing on a look reserved for the tonsured clergy.

Throughout the medieval period, at least in Western Europe, there was a preference for blond hair which endures to this day. It can be seen in the names of the heroines of the French romances of the chivalric age: we have 'Clarissant' (clear), 'Soredamor' (golden) and 'Lienor' (bright). The thirteenth-century Anglo-Norman text *Ornatus Mulierum* has a positively modern ring in its promises to reveal an infallible method of turning white hair blond again. (Apply overnight a paste of ashes boiled for half a day in vinegar. Clearly it was a bleaching agent like 'Sun-In'.) An Elizabethan recipe 'to make hair as yellow as gold' includes rhubarb and white wine among its ingredients.

Depilation was another modern-sounding beauty treatment sought by medieval women. All-over removal of body hair ('in order that a woman might become very soft and smooth and without hairs from the head down') might be achieved from a recipe made up of cucumber, almond milk and (worryingly) quicklime. Users were warned 'that it is not to stay too long on the skin, because it causes intense heat'. Identical warnings are still found on hair removal creams today.

In the Tudor period, Henry VIII had particularly 'political' hair, and his frequent changes from the pageboy look to the crop and back again were slavishly copied by his courtiers. In 1520, he heard that Francis I had shaved his head after an injury, so he had his own hair cut very short in sympathy. On another occasion, anxious for a meeting with his ally, he promised not to shave until he and Francis were once again in each other's company. But Katherine of Aragon, disliking her husband's tickly chin, made him break his vow. A diplomatic incident nearly ensued, neatly averted by Francis's mother, Louise of Savoy, who declared that the love the two kings bore one other was 'not in the beards but in the hearts'.

Henry went through a daily routine of being shaved by his

barber, Penny, probably using a basin with a notch for the neck rather like those discovered in the wreck of the *Mary Rose*, which you can see in the museum at the Royal Naval Dockyard in Portsmouth today. The basin contained clove-scented water, and Penny also used knives, ivory combs and scissors to carry out his job. Because he was so close to the king, Penny had to keep himself scrupulously clean and healthy, and avoid 'misguided women'.

Later on in life, though, with Katherine of Aragon well out of the way, Henry became a regular beard wearer, and he died wearing whiskers. When his coffin was opened in 1813 and his corpse examined, 'some beard remained upon the chin'.

Like Henry VIII, his daughters Elizabeth and Mary and their stepmother Katherine Parr were uniformly ginger and proud (though Elizabeth in later life wore dyed wigs: her hair was described as 'a light colour never made by nature'). Katherine Parr's hair survives in exceptionally large quantities. Her body, buried at her third husband's home of Sudeley Castle, was dug up numerous times in the eighteenth century by nosy antiquarians, who cut off various locks of hair and even pulled out a tooth as a souvenir.

Every Tudor person possessed their own comb because it would have been simply intolerable not to disentangle the inevitable parasites from their hair. In 1602, William Vaughan ascribed awesome powers to the humble comb, recommending that you should 'comb your head softly and easily with an ivory comb, for nothing recreateth [provides recreation for] the memory more'. Samuel Pepys once got into trouble when he asked his maidservant for a little hairdressing help. He described going 'after supper to have my head combed by Deb, which occasioned the greatest sorrow to me that ever I knew in this world; for my wife, coming up suddenly, did find me embracing the girl'. Later, the vengeful Mrs Pepys literally seized the iron while it was hot: 'she came to my side of the bed and drew the curtain open, and with the tongs red hot at the end made as if she did design to pinch me with them'.

The person who cut your hair, your barber, might also have performed more extreme services. The Company of Barber-Surgeons combined two professions concerned with knives. Both would offer home visits, whether it was a haircut or a major piece of surgery that was required. (Doctors were supposed to restrict themselves to the classier business of prescribing medicine, rather than getting splattered with blood as surgeons did.) Barbers and surgeons therefore had overlapping skills, even after their two professions began to diverge. The wig-maker Edmund Harrold of Manchester, who'd trained as a barber, was typical. Some days he would help women struggling to breastfeed by 'cupping' their breasts, placing a hot glass over the nipple. Other days he would go out in search of flaxen hair to buy for his wig-making business. A head of long and beautiful hair was a valuable resource for a woman. Even a well-born (but down-on-her-luck) Georgian courtier named Henrietta Howard investigated what she might get for selling hers to a wig-maker, and received an offer of eighteen guineas.

Just like bathing the body, washing the hair also went through a couple of centuries of extreme disfavour from 1550 onwards. Contemporary doctors greatly 'misliked' the 'bathing of your head in cold water especially in winter'. This chimes in with Randle Holme's description of the duties of a seventeenth-century barber. He was not to *wash* anyone's head, but only to 'rub the hair with a napkin to dry it from its sweatiness and filth'.

The age of the Whigs was also an age of wigs. The gentleman's wig first made its appearance in London in the 1660s: Charles II had grown used to wearing one during his years of exile in fashionable France, and brought the look back with him on his Restoration to the English throne. Samuel Pepys was at first suspicious of the new trend, then tempted, and finally, four years later, he splashed out on a wig of his own. He did so, as he wrote, because 'the pains of keeping my hair clean is so great'. Wigs worn over a shaven head became the staple headgear of gentlemen: when James Boswell lost his, in 1789, he was devastated and rushed twenty-five miles to buy a replacement ('I could not long remain an object of laughter').

At first wigs were worn mainly by men, but women adopted them too. By 1751, 'The Black, the Brown, the Fair and Carroty, appear now all in one livery; and you can no more judge of your Mistress's natural complexion by the Colour of her Hair, than by her Ribbons.' Even after the wig fell from favour, towards the end of the century, the natural hair was combed, curled, piled and powdered to artificial perfection. 'Those who had to preserve a genteel appearance spent an hour each day under the hands of the hair-dresser,' wrote Charles Knight about the 1800s, at the tail end of the age of big hair, and the Earl of Scarborough kept an astonishing 'six French *fizeurs*, who have nothing else to do than dress his hair'. A duchess visiting London complained vociferously that the city was nothing but 'knock, knock, knock, all day; and friz, friz, friz all night'. Time spent like this showed, however, that one was in the privileged position of having no business more pressing than preening.

Why did the wig finally lose favour in the early nineteenth century? A bold theoretician might link the decline of the wig to the decline of absolutism. Along with shoes in which it is impossible to walk and dresses in which it is impossible to sit, hair requiring hours of preparation is reserved for the aristocrat of limitless wealth. After many such people lost their lives at the guillotine in the French Revolution, those surviving lost their nerve.

Shorn hair has always gone with radical politics, as demonstrated by the eighteenth-century French revolutionaries, the English Roundheads of the previous century and 1970s skinheads. Those governing France after 1789 left off 'their curls, *toupees*, and *queues*; some of them go about with cropped locks like English farmers without any powder'. After the revolution, many unemployed French hairdressers and barbers came over to seek work in a jumpy Britain. Here, their whispering and their caressing of the heads of their clients in many a bedroom caused conservatives to wince. Were these Frenchies spreading dissent along with their powder and pomatum?

In these perilous times, when you submit your chin to a barber never talk about politics till you ascertain his principles on these matters. It is dangerous to put one's throat in the mercy of a man armed with a razor, especially if he be a red-hot politician; which all shavers are, without exception.

As a result, the very profession of hairdressing came in for some striking criticism after 1789. 'The art and mystery of barbery' has sunk 'exceedingly from that high estimation in which it was anciently held', it was written in 1824. The virtuous, the high-minded and the patriotic simplified their own hairdressing routines, so much so that by 1830 a Bristol newspaper described the hairdresser as no 'longer the important personage he used to be'. Smooth, simply dressed hair became the mark of gentility in the Victorian age.

But the menservants who worked in large and lavish households were still made to wear powder, and grand footmen looked like extras from *Cinderella* right up to the Second World War. They hated powder and its application:

They ducked their heads in water, rubbed soap in their hair to make a lather, and combed it stiffly through. Powder puffs came into action as they took turns to dust each other's hair with either violet powder or ordinary flour. This dried to a firm paste.

That was Eric Horne, a former footman, writing in 1923. 'I constantly had a cold in the head', he went on, 'through having to re-powder after going out with the carriage, one's head is seldom dry.' As well as giving them head colds, footmen thought that powdering discoloured their hair and made them prematurely bald.

Once the plumbed-in bath made its appearance in the purpose-built bathrooms of the late nineteenth century, new and better shampoos began to be invented, replacing the curious mixtures of cow fat and perfume, or eggs and lemons, which had been used previously. Like dentistry, the art of dressing the hair became the focus of scientific innovation as the Victorian age drew towards its close, and gradually moved out of the home and into the specialist studio.

It was Monsieur Marcel of France who invented the Marcel wave, or, as it was originally known, his '*ondulation*' in his Paris salon. He used a pair of ordinary crimping tongs, and it was a German, Karl Nessler, who had the idea of making the *ondulation* permanent by electrically heating the tongs. So the 'perm' was born, and grew to maturity during the craze for short hair amongst the flappers of the 1920s. This step towards liberation was supported by Lady Astor, the first female Member of

The Marcel wave, popular in the 1920s, created a kind of corrugated-iron effect

Parliament. She once had this conversation with her butler:

One of the housemaids asked if she could have her hair bobbed. . .
  'Why should she want her hair bobbed', her ladyship demanded.
  'I understand it's the fashion, my lady'.
  'Tell her she must keep it as it is, I don't want fashionable maids'.
  'Very well,' said Mr Lee, 'but I think I should inform you that if you adopt this intransigent attitude you will shortly be lucky to get house-maids with any hair at all'.
  Lady Astor dissolved into laughter, and told him that the maids could do anything they wanted with their hair.

Grooming was made easier for men, too, when the cut-throat razor became obsolete. The American King C. Gillette patented the first safety razor with a disposable blade in 1901, and the invention of the electric razor in the 1920s made the then popular pencil-thin moustache and clean cheeks and chin much easier and cheaper to achieve.

Despite the rise of the hair salon, home hairdressing has not entirely disappeared. In my 1970s childhood we were visited by a hairdresser who came to our house and cut our hair as we sat in state upon the kitchen stepladder. That seems like a time long gone, but a fascinating barometer of the recent recession was provided by the increasing sales of hair dye as people cancelled their expensive salon appointments.

Hard times send people back to the bathroom to do their own hair.

20 – War Paint

> I now observed how the women began to paint themselves, formerly a most ignominious thing and only used by prostitutes.
>
> John Evelyn, 1654

John Evelyn was charting a change from sobriety to revelry as the serious years of the English Civil War gradually gave way to a more hedonistic and courtly Restoration age. But make-up, long associated with prostitutes, had also been used by royalty and courtiers, actresses and actors. It has always been employed by anyone who needs to play a part before the eyes of the world.

The Tudors literally didn't know what they looked like. They had no glass mirrors, only the cloudy view provided by polished steel or water. (The royal peacock, Henry VIII, had several of these metal 'glasses to look in'.) In such an age, it's not surprising that an exact likeness was low on the list of the requirements of portraiture. Instead, a portrait presented the patron's abstract idea of what the sitter should look like: usually richly dressed, stately, well-born; but often strangely inhuman, like a cipher not a person.

Grand ladies had their skins daily painted lead-white by their maids to make them look more like the stiff, splendid, stately symbols of lineage and power seen in contemporary portraits.

Jacobean fashions required lengthy doings 'with their looking glasses, pinning, unpinning, setting, unsetting, forming and conforming, painting blew veins and cheeks'. Paleness was sought because only the labourer was burned by the sun.

The seventeenth century saw the rise of rouge, the rosy cheek and reddened lip. But now the arguments began. The Puritans insisted that sexy and more naturalistic make-up was nothing short of sinful. Paint and perfume represented vanity and self-absorption, and covered up an impure soul. One particularly strident Puritan complained that cosmetics were 'putrifaction', and that a painted woman was nothing more than 'a dunghill covered with white & red'. On 7 June 1650, Parliament even proposed 'an Act against the Vice of Painting and wearing black Patches and immodest Dresses of Women' (it never actually reached the statute book).

When Charles II returned from French exile in 1660, he brought with him a daring French fondness for rouge. (His unfortunate queen, Catherine of Braganza, was observed with make-up running down her sweating face during a stifling banquet in 1662.) But red cheeks were still not widely accepted as respectable or even desirable, and ladies' man Samuel Pepys preferred his prey pale: he found one female acquaintance 'very pretty, but paints red on her face, which makes me hate her'.

Beauty spots, or black stick-on patches, were originally used to cover pimples or smallpox scars. But the rules for their shaping and positioning soon developed into quite a sophisticated system of meaning. In the reign of Queen Anne, Whig ladies wore them on one cheek and Tories on the other. According to *The Spectator* in 1711, one '*Rozalinda*, a famous Whig Partizan', had the misfortune to possess a natural and 'beautiful Mole on the Tory Part of her Forehead; which being very conspicuous, has occasioned many mistakes' about her political allegiance. In the twentieth century, Thomas Harris's fictional serial killer Hannibal Lecter, delighting in esoteric knowledge,

The positioning of this lady's face patches proclaims her
Whiggish political tendencies

could still read the language of beauty spots: he was delighted
when his beloved FBI agent Clarice Starling acquired a gunpowder scar on her cheek just in the position symbolising 'courage'.

It's easy to forget just how pustular and pock-marked
seventeenth-century skin must have been, with sores and pus-
filled spots seen on nearly every face, not just upon the faces
of adolescents as today. There were no antibiotics to prevent
an infected pustule from possibly becoming a long-lasting and

dangerous wound. James Woodforde, an Oxford undergraduate, writing in 1751, described how he was given great pain by a boil on his bottom. It was bad enough to give him a fever, until luckily it 'discharged itself in the night excessively'.

Lepers and syphilitics, whose conditions showed upon their skins, were thought to be suffering from moral as well as physical decay, so no wonder there was a strong urge to cover up evidence of imperfection. Skin preparations were largely made and applied at home, from asses' milk to make 'a woman look gay and fresh, as if she were but fifteen years old', to bean-flower water, 'which taketh away the spots of the face'. Not all of them were benign: the ingredients for Eliza Smith's Georgian recipe for pimple cream included brimstone, while Johann Jacob Wecker suggested a fingernail preparation containing arsenic and 'Dogs-turd'.

As well as covering up imperfection, though, make-up heightens femininity, and therefore complements masculinity, so it did become accepted by the men who would otherwise regret their wives looking like prostitutes. 'Alas! The crimsoning blush of modesty will be always more attractive, than the sparkle of confident intelligence,' regretted one particularly enlightened male in 1798. 'Too much' make-up, though, has in all periods always signalled sexual availability. In 1953, Barbara Pym describes a female character in her novel *Jane and Prudence* with eyelids 'startlingly and embarrassingly green, glistening with some greasy preparation'. 'Was this what one had to do nowadays when one was unmarried?' the narrator wonders. 'What hard work it must be.'

Make-up for men too grew more important in the eighteenth century. Indeed, the new social stereotype of 'the fop' was 'more dejected at a pimple, than if it were a cancer'. He and his over-groomed friends might use a conical mask to protect their lungs from the powder blown over their wigs and coats 'abundantly', while their gloves were 'essenc'd' and their handkerchiefs 'perfum'd'. Then it was 'time to launch, and down he comes, scented like a perfumers shop, and looks like a vessel with all her rigging under sail without ballast'.

Effeminacy was an accusation frequently flung about in the eighteenth century. While sodomy remained a crime punishable by death, though, men wearing make-up were much more in the mainstream of society than the puritanical, moralistic Victorians would allow them to be. It was the influential Beau Brummell in late eighteenth-century Bath who advocated the scrupulously clean but absolutely unpainted and unperfumed body for men, and this more 'manly' ideal persisted throughout the next two centuries.

Female make-up began finally to lose some of its association with prostitution in the twentieth century. Red lips were (and remain) desirable but dangerous, associated with independence and subversion. The suffragettes, revelling in their newfound sense of feminine freedom, adored shop-bought, very red lip-stick, so much more enjoyably risqué than beauty products made at home. *The Daily Mirror Beauty Book* of 1910 gives a recipe for lip rouge to be made by the timid or thrifty in their own kitchens: boric acid, carmine, paraffin and 'Otto of Rose, sufficient to perfume' are all required. As the suffragette movement gained force and credibility, even the staid and respectable ladies' magazines began to contain discreet adverts for ready-made make-up.

The next generation, coming of age in 1920, found nothing at all disreputable about lipstick, and it finally became universal and classless. Cinema and television had a great effect on make-up styles; what showed up well on screen was also copied on the street. Greta Garbo was responsible for the pencil-thin eyebrows of the 1930s, and set every cinema-going girl a-plucking. 'Never take out lip-salve, mirror and powder-puff at the dinner table' an etiquette guide of the 1920s had to counsel the over-enthusiastic face-painter.

Nurses in hospitals between the wars complained vociferously when they weren't allowed to wear lipstick, and the princesses Elizabeth (b.1926) and Margaret Rose (b.1930) were brought up to wear make-up as a matter of course. It was now perfectly respectable. It is surprising and a little touching to learn that in 1953 the new queen, quite adept enough, did her own make-up for her televised coronation.

21 – The Whole World Is a Toilet

The sideboard is furnished with a number of chamber pots
and it is a common practice to relieve oneself while the rest
are drinking; one has no kind of concealment and the practice
strikes me as most indecent.

François de La Rochefoucauld on
English table habits, 1784

Having once had occasion to visit the ladies' at the Goldman
Sachs investment bank, I was not entirely surprised to see free
tampons provided. What did impress me was the provision of
three different brands. And it's always been true that the conditions in which you relieve yourself reveal a huge amount about
your social and economic status.

Many people in the Middle Ages simply used nature itself.
After all, as the Bible said, every man could use a spade, and
'it shall be, when thou wilt ease thyself abroad, thou shalt dig
therewith, and shalt turn back and cover that which cometh
from thee'.

Settlements, however, required more formal arrangements.
The Anglo-Saxons under King Alfred began to organise their
towns into 'burghs', fortified rectangles with a grid system of
streets that can still be seen today in places like Winchester
and Wallingford. Now communal cesspits were created for

the disposal of waste. I have had the privilege of handling the human excrement from one such pit, excavated in Winchester and kept in the freezer in the town's museum. Occasionally it is defrosted and lucky visitors are allowed to handle it, and even to pick out the cherry pips which have been proven by archaeologists to have passed right through a Saxon stomach.

But it was the Normans who introduced the first fixed-position indoor toilets to be seen in Britain since Roman times. The Norman White Tower at the Tower of London, built just after the Conquest, has garderobe shafts in the thickness of its walls, all positioned on the north or east elevations of the building. These sides faced away from the city of London, so its newly subjugated residents wouldn't be able see the stains left by their conquerors' faeces.

The little closets called garderobes were also literally places to 'guard robes' (keep clothes), because hanging your robe in an ammonia-rich environment like over the loo would kill the fleas. In fact, a well-brought-up person might still ask the way to the 'cloakroom' instead of the toilet when visiting a strange house today. The well-appointed garderobe could be quite a pleasant place: the ninth-century author of *The Life of St Gregory* recommends it for uninterrupted reading.

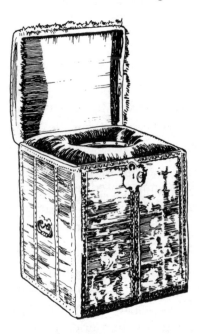

A velvet-covered seatless 'close stool' like William III's model at Hampton Court Palace

At the Tudor court there were three main ranks of toilet. Royal and noble people used the close stool, a padded, seat-less chair placed over a pewter or ceramic chamber pot, often placed in a dedicated 'stool room'. Henry VIII possessed several close stools, stuffed with swansdown, covered with velvet and decorated with gilt nails and fringes. The stool room had two doors, one leading to the owner's bedroom and one to the outdoors for servants to remove the waste. (This easy access made the stool room a favoured place for trysts between Henry VIII's fifth wife, Katherine Howard, and her alleged lover Thomas Culpepper. Charles I also planned to sneak his lady friend Jane Whorwood into 'the stool room which is within my bedchamber' during his imprisonment on the Isle of Wight, in order to 'smother' her with embraces.)

The next rank down, courtiers senior enough to have their own rooms, also possessed their own personal chamber pots. The physician Andrew Boorde decried the smell of these 'piss pots' and thought them unhygienic. The Tudor 'piss pot' excavated in the Privy Garden which remains on display at Hampton Court has been scientifically proved still to contain traces of genuine Tudor urine.

But the lowest servants at Hampton Court used the great communal toilet capable of seating fourteen people at once named the 'Common Jakes' or the 'Great House of Easement'. This giant facility discharged into a tank which was washed clean by the waters of the moat. Even so, the tank emitted a dreadful smell and frequently had to be scrubbed clean. The unfortunate servants who performed this role were known as the 'gong scourers' ('gong' was another euphemism for toilet).

Rather than walk to the Great House of Easement, though, people at court still insisted upon relieving themselves in the fireplaces and passages. There were hundreds of male servants, and not enough official toilets. In occasional vain attempts to improve hygiene, the palace management would have crosses chalked onto the walls in the hope that people would be reluctant to desecrate a religious symbol. Urinating into the kitchen fireplaces was also made the subject of a special prohibition, implying that it had previously been a common practice.

Bizarre as the Great House of Easement sounds, the vast communal toilet had been a feature well known in the ancient and medieval worlds. In Britain, twenty Roman soldiers at once could have used the latrine at Housesteads Fort on Hadrian's Wall. And medieval London contained no less than thirteen shared public toilets, the best known among them being the gigantic, fifteenth-century, eighty-four-seater in Greenwich Street named 'Whittington's Longhouse' after Dick Whittington, mayor of London. It was situated on the street now called Walbrook (then still literally a brook) and was flushed out by the Thames at high tide.

Obviously Londoners used chamber pots in their own homes, and the emptying of the pot out of a house's upper window gives one of the rival explanations of the word 'loo', meaning toilet. 'Gardez l'eau!' was the call to warn passers-by. Alternatively, and to my mind more convincingly, the 'loo' may be the 'lieu', the French name for the 'place' of easement. Some houses had garderobe closets suspended over streams at the back. It was a constant struggle to keep the city clean, and by 1300, Sherbourne Lane, once adjacent to 'a long bourne of sweet water', had been renamed by the locals as 'Shiteburn Lane'.

And many town dwellers simply used the open street to excrete. This wasn't just a medieval problem. In the seventeenth century, Samuel Pepys's wife suffered from some kind of bowel complaint, and once he 'was forced to go out of the house with her to Lincoln's Inn walks, and there in a corner she did her business'. A century later, when Casanova visited London, he was surprised to see the 'hinder parts of persons relieving nature in the bushes' even in St James's Park.

We know most about toilet habits at the highest levels, because until 1700 the king himself was constantly accompanied, even when relieving himself. At Henry VIII's court, one courtier

'*Gardez l'eau!*' The call warning pedestrians that a chamber pot was about to be emptied may provide the explanation for our word 'loo'

apologises for not attending a meeting because he simply couldn't get away from toilet duty, there being 'none here but Master Norris & I to give attendance upon the king's highness when he goes to make water in his bed chamber'. It was understood that his most intimate servants would ask Henry VIII for favours 'in the evening, when he was comfortably filled with wine, or when he had gone to the stool, for then he used to be very pleasant'.

So royals and indeed many other important aristocrats were accustomed to relieving themselves before others. Instructions for the late-seventeenth-century household of William III reveal that enormous efforts were made to ensure that the king never had to go to the loo alone. During visits to the 'Secret or Privy Room, when we go to ease ourself', he ordered that he should be accompanied by the 'Groom of the Stool (if present) and in his absence the Gentleman of our Bedchamber in waiting, & in his absence the Groom of our Bedchamber in waiting'. At the Palace of Versailles in eighteenth-century France, the homo-sexual Duc de Vendôme gave audiences while sitting upon his close stool, and fawning guests would call out that he had the 'culo d'angelo' as he wiped his bottom. Even Samuel Pepys, much lower down the social scale, did not seem to consider that his own bowel movements were restricted to private moments: he kept his own 'very fine close-stool' in his drawing room. (Probably he was proud of it.)

The declining power of the monarchy might be traced through the decreasing levels of respect paid to royal toilets when the eighteenth century is compared to the sixteenth. One cannot imagine that anyone at court was bold enough to make free with Henry VIII's close stools, or with Elizabeth I's (her special 'stool carriage' transported them in her wake from palace to palace). Yet during the coronation of George III in 1761, the Duke of Newcastle was spotted using the queen's own appointed toilet behind the altar: he was caught 'perk'd up & in the very act upon the anointed velvet closestool'.

There's a quotation from the witty Lady Mary Wortley Montagu that's often used to suggest that grand court ladies too didn't mind urinating in the presence of other people. The French ambassador's wife, for example, was notorious for the 'frequency and quantity of her pissing which she does not fail to do at least ten times a day amongst a cloud of witnesses'. But do note that the lady is from France. It was almost a given, in eighteenth-century England, that most French habits were immoral, dirty or both.

However, the voluminous skirts of eighteenth-century ladies did allow them to make use of the gravy-boat-like jugs known as 'bourdaloues', or 'carriage pots'. They take their name, we're told, from a fêted French preacher. He was so popular that hordes of ladies would arrive hours before his sermons began, and therefore needed discreet relief while waiting.

The great advantage of the chamber pot or close stool was that you could use it in the privacy of your bedchamber, in a closet or ante-room, or anywhere else you pleased. It remained in use for so long because it was exceedingly convenient. Its only disadvantage was that someone had to empty it. This person, often female, was known as a 'necessary woman' (she emptied the 'necessary'). A seventeenth-century servant-maid was required to see 'that your close stools and chamber pots be duly emptied, and kept clean and sweet'. In the royal palaces, there were whole teams of 'necessary women' who emptied the chamber pots and cleaned the bedchambers, and were paid additionally for their mops, brooms and brushes on top of their wages.

Remarkably, they went on performing their labours for at least two hundred years after you might think they could reasonably have stopped: at the invention of the flushing toilet.

22 – The Wonders of Sewers

The Civilization of a People can be measured by
their Domestic and Sanitary appliances.
George Jennings, installer of flushing public
toilets at the Great Exhibition, 1851

Britain's first flushing toilet was built in late Elizabethan times,
but the idea didn't catch on until the nineteenth century.

Sir John Harrington was its pioneer, installing the first
flusher at his home near Bath, and then another at the Palace of
Richmond for Elizabeth I. (There's a theory that Americans call
the toilet 'the john' in honour of Sir John.) Harrington wrote a
book about his achievements called *A New Discourse on a Stale
Subject: Called the Metamorphosis of Ajax*, published in 1596.

The title was a joke. 'Ajax' in this case was not the hero of
classical mythology, but 'a jakes', the common euphemism for
a toilet. Harrington's version had a cistern, seat and stool pot
below. Opening a cock in the cistern caused water to rush down
and flush the system out, and he claimed that this needed doing
only once a day, even 'though twenty persons should use it'.
I've helped to make a reconstruction according to Harrington's
instructions, and the flush was impressively powerful – it successfully carried away a handful of cherry tomatoes.

I'm less convinced you would only need to flush it once every twenty uses, and Harrington did admit that 'the oftener it is used and opened the sweeter'. He suggested that pitch and wax, applied to the pot, would also help keep it fresh. But Harrington's invention was a blip in the history of sanitation, and few people adopted his idea.

Flushing water closets could be found here and there, usually in great houses or palaces, throughout the seventeenth and eighteenth centuries. Queen Anne's husband George, for example, had 'a little place with a seat of easement of marble with sluices of water to wash all down', and at Chatsworth House in Derbyshire no fewer than ten water closets were installed during a remodelling in the 1690s, with fittings of brass and bowls of local marble. Yet these were oddities, frequently commented upon with wonder by those who saw them, and they remained remarkable.

In the later eighteenth century, the design of the flushing toilet underwent several improvements which helped to make it more popular. Alexander Cumming in 1775 made the vital step of inventing the S-bend, the kinked waste pipe which stopped smells from coming back into the room. Previously water closets had featured the D-bend drain, but this design trapped stinking water in the system.

In 1778, Joseph Bramah patented his own particular model of water closet which featured a fifteen-second flush timed by a brass air cylinder. (Bramah also invented the hydraulic press and a famously complicated lock: some northerners still refer to a particularly knotty problem as 'a Bramah'.) He was born on a farm in Yorkshire in 1748, but an early accident put an end to his labouring life and he became apprenticed to a cabinet-maker instead. He was installing a water closet for a client when he realised that he could create a better one himself. His excellent design would lead the field for the next century.

Bramah's showmanship and his eagerness to promote and install his water closets made his a well-known name. He claimed to have fitted 6,000 closets across the country by 1797. Queen Victoria would order one of his models for Osborne House on the Isle of Wight, where it still remains in working order. But even Bramah's water closets were not perfect. They had a hinged valve at the bottom of the pan, and inevitably this leaked a little.

Indeed, there were problems with all the various Georgian water-closet systems. They needed priming with water daily, and did not always flush successfully. The valves could malfunction, wood could splinter, and their iron pots retained smells and 'ancient ordure'. Another difficulty with water closets was their position off corridors. As the eighteenth century wore on, sensibilities grew more refined. There was no more public pissing; people, especially ladies, did not want to be seen or heard leaving their bedrooms at night to use the facilities. So chamber pots continued to be used. Simple, tried-and-tested earth closets (just a wooden seat positioned over a midden) in the backyard also remained popular in rural areas.

Another problem which delayed the widespread adoption of the flushing toilet was its requirement for a proper sewerage system. For most of the seventeenth and eighteenth centuries, people's faeces were collected in cesspits behind or beneath their houses. They were periodically emptied by 'night-soil men', who in London took excrement to use as manure on market gardens to the north of the city. By 1800, the city's million residents had 200,000 cesspits between them. But from each of them polluted water would leak through the soil into London's rivers.

Cesspits completely failed to cope with the arrival of the flushing toilet, which produced waste now mixed with a large amount of water. In 1815, it was made permissible for individual houses to link their drains into the London sewers intended to carry rainwater from the streets down to the river. By 1848, this became mandatory. There was no longer any need for cesspits and night-soil men, but the result was that raw sewage was being piped straight into the Thames. In 1827, a pamphleteer

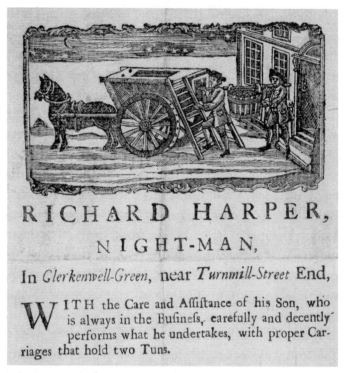

RICHARD HARPER,

NIGHT-MAN,

In *Clerkenwell-Green*, near *Turnmill-Street* End,

WITH the Care and Affiftance of his Son, who is always in the Bufinefs, carefully and decently performs what he undertakes, with proper Carriages that hold two Tuns.

The trade card of Richard Harper, one of the 'nightmen' who carted away London's nightsoil

described the river as 'saturated with the impurities of fifty thousand homes . . . offensive to the sight, disgusting to the imagination, and destructive to the health'. This was the very river that still supplied many people with their drinking water.

Obviously, such a primitive means of sewage disposal presented a major public health hazard. London suffered from four major outbreaks of cholera during the nineteenth century, in 1831–2, 1848–9, 1853–4 and 1866. But the link between cholera and an infected supply of drinking water was not made for a considerable length of time. The scale of the problem was underestimated because of contemporary misunderstandings about the nature of disease.

Rather than realising that cholera was water-borne, people

still persisted in believing that a 'miasma' of disease moving unstoppably through the air made you ill. The idea that houses should be better ventilated took priority over drainage. Even Florence Nightingale, in her *Notes on Nursing* (1869), condemned the idea of connecting houses to drains, because she thought odours rising from the drains would bring with them scarlet fever and measles. She was not alone in her suspicions: when Linley Sambourne installed a plumbed-in wash basin in his wife's bedroom at Stafford Terrace, Kensington, she kept the plug in the basin at all times as a guard against evil vapours.

It took a long battle by the heroic Dr John Snow to get anyone to appreciate what he had understood from 1854 onwards: that cholera was spread through water, and that better drains and sewers would help, not hinder, health. Snow's surgery was in Broadwick Street, Soho, and he noticed that many local cholera victims had been using a pump fed by a well in his street. This well was in close proximity to a sewer. Certain that water from the well was causing deaths, Dr Snow persuaded the parish council to remove the handle from the pump so that people couldn't use it. Deaths consequently fell. But he had great difficulty in persuading his colleagues of his findings, because the water that actually contained the cholera bacilli looked perfectly clean and wholesome.

Yet everybody became persuaded of the need to invest in a proper sewerage system by the Great Stink of July 1858. A particularly hot spell of weather caused the Thames to give off a terrifically dreadful smell. It even penetrated the Palace of Westminster, giving the country's legislators a graphic and timely reminder that London lacked proper sewers. They had to hang sheets soaked in lime across their windows as a barrier to the stench.

In fact, improvements were already in hand. London's Metropolitan Board of Works had been established in 1856, with Joseph Bazalgette as its chief engineer. Bazalgette was in the process of creating a network of sewers beneath London which would not take waste directly to the Thames but eastwards instead, so that sewage would enter the river downstream of the city and its water supplies. It was noticeable, in the fourth cholera bout of 1866, that only the East End was affected – the sole area yet to be connected to the not-quite-yet-complete sewerage system.

Bazalgette's work was one of the true marvels of the Victorian age. He would eventually use 318 million bricks to construct over a thousand miles of sewer, and his works to drains, embankments and bridges cost more than twice as much as Brunel's Great Western Railway. Most remain in use today, underground cathedrals of brick and water.

Bazalgette's sewer revolution would allow the water closet to become standard in most homes. The Great Exhibition of 1851 had also helped to popularise the flush, through the public toilets provided for its visitors. (Those for ladies were a late addition to the project: initially only men's needs were considered.) Some 14 per cent of the six million visitors to the exhibition used the facilities, many of them experiencing the flush for the first time. This was despite the fact that they cost a penny to use – hence the expression 'spending a penny'.

So flushing toilets entered many homes, and now Thomas Crapper became a household name. The famous motto for his toilets, produced from 1861, was 'a certain flush with every pull'. His is the best-known name in the history of sanitary innovation, but this was really because he became a figurehead for the new industry of sanitaryware rather than because of any particular technological breakthrough he made. His genius was in sales and promotion. He was a self-made man who walked from his native Doncaster to London, at the age of eleven, to find employment with a plumber in Chelsea. Perhaps the apogee of his career was his royal warrant, won after installing toilets at Sandringham House for the Prince of Wales, and his company survived until 1966.

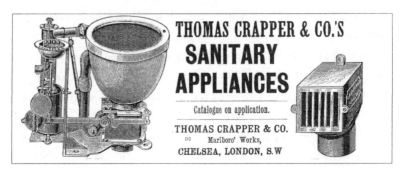

An advertisement for Thomas Crapper's products . . . but, contrary to popular opinion, he did not invent the flushing toilet

Despite the suggestions made in his company's advertising, none of his nine plumbing patents were actually for the marvellous flushing siphon cistern. The credit for inventing this new and thunderous flush, produced by a pivoted arm balanced by a counterweight, must go to Joseph Adamson of Leeds, who took out his patent in 1853. Crapper did not even manufacture his own toilets: the products which bore his name were made by various other firms, mainly in Staffordshire, and he merely sold them on. (It was not unusual for one firm to stamp another's name on its bathroom wares.) Stoke-on-Trent, with its good local supplies of coal for firing the kilns, was becoming the toilet capital of the world.

Contrary to popular opinion, the *Oxford English Dictionary* notes that the verb 'to crap' was in use long before Crapper's company became widely known. 'Crap' was an old English word for rubbish, taken by the Pilgrim Fathers to America and used over there as a slang expression for 'faeces'. When American soldiers came over to Britain in 1917 to help fight the First World War, they were highly amused to encounter toilets with cisterns marked 'CRAPPER'. But this was just a coincidence.

Unfortunately not every toilet was a Crapper cracker. The obsolete D-bend remained in use in many places, despite the condemnation of professionals. At the Sanitary Exhibition in

Croydon in 1879, an engineer called William Eassie still felt it necessary to insist that he 'should above all like to see abolished the filthy D trap with its furrings of faecal matter'.

The best form of toilet pan would eventually turn out to be nothing like the complicated valve-based system installed in the houses of rich early adopters. An alternative, robust and cheap model had begun to emerge in the 1840s, consisting of a crude ceramic bowl placed over an S-bend pipe. All across the country, the 'Bristol Closet', the 'Liverpool Cottage Basin' and the 'Reading Pan' were developed by local manufacturers. These simple devices were the direct forerunners of the modern toilet bowl sold today.

What about the terminology? The word 'lavatory' really means a place for washing, i.e. a washbasin, and its use to signify a water closet is a polite euphemism. There's an argument that the word 'toilet', another euphemism, owes its existence to the railways. One's *toilette* was originally nothing to do with defecation; it meant washing and dressing. Early train carriages had two separate rooms involving water: the 'toilet', for washing, and the 'WC' or water closet. When, in the early twentieth century, the washbasin and lavatory joined together into just one little room, the more discreet 'toilet' was the only word that remained on the single door.

Here's George Jennings, the Victorian toilet impresario, using yet another, rather charming euphemism for the loo:

although my proposition may be startling I am convinced the day will come when Halting Stations replete with every convenience will be constructed in all localities.

He was writing with considerable prescience. Once the social and technical glitches had been ironed out, nothing could stop the triumphant progress of the flushing toilet. Two hundred and fifty years after its invention, it became an integral part of the British home.

23 – A History of Toilet Paper

See the privy-house for easement be fair, soot and clean;
And that the boards thereupon be covered with cloth fair and green ...
Look there be blanket, cotton, or linen to wipe the nether end,
And ever he clepith [calls], wait ready and entend [prompt].

John Russell, *Book of Nurture*, c.1452

A research study in 1994 revealed that the average person flushes their toilet 3.48 times a day and uses 11.5 sheets of toilet paper. Quite a variety of materials have done duty over the centuries before paper became the material of choice.

The superior Roman option was a sponge on a twig, possibly providing the origin of the phrase 'to get hold of the wrong end of the stick'. Once the Romans had left Britain, standards declined, and 'arsewisp', a handful of straw, was quite acceptable in the Middle Ages. However, there were much fancier options available for the medieval super-rich. A fifteenth-century instruction manual addressed to a medieval squire or body servant explains that the servant must make sure that his master's garderobe was fresh, clean and neat, and well provided with toilet paper. The 'paper', though, was actually a cloth: 'Look there be blanket, cotton, or linen to wipe the nether end.'

And so linen was the chosen material for wiping the bottoms of royalty and the aristocracy. It sounds rather repellent, but these linen cloths would be boiled and reused. William III had his own personal laundress who washed his shirts and also his 'stool ducketts', items which appear alongside sheets and napkins on the royal laundry list. Probably looking rather like napkins, the stool ducketts would have been laid out ready for use on the table in the stool room. Royal stool rooms were actually quite spacious: Mary II's at Kensington Palace, for example, contained a painted portrait of herself and her husband.

This practice of laying out the napkins on a table handy for the close stool had a lingering echo in a very conservative household of the late twentieth century. Only twenty years ago, the housekeepers of Grimesthorpe Castle in Lincolnshire, home of the De Eresby family, maintained a tradition of arranging sheets of toilet paper in a fan upon a table in the toilet. This must have been an echo of how the linen ducketts were presented before they were replaced with pieces of paper.

Paper was initially too valuable a commodity to be sacrificed to the once-only use of bottom-wiping. By 1751, though, one William Wyndham had clearly moved onto the more modern material. In making plans for a new privy at his house, Felbrigg, in Norfolk, he mentioned the need to have it 'as light as possible. There must be a good broad place to set a candle on, and a place to keep paper.'

But no one wasted valuable *new* paper in going to the toilet. The term 'bumf' for junk mail actually comes from 'bumfodder': one's read newspaper or unwanted post would be torn into squares, skewered in the corner, tied up with string and hung in the privy. I've had a go at performing this task, which must have once been a regular chore for housewives, if not delegated to their children. It's gentle and pleasantly therapeutic, but all too easy to get distracted into reading the stories.

Purpose-made toilet paper first appeared in America from 1857, when Gayety's Medicated Paper company was formed. The novelty spread to England, where the British Patent

Perforated Paper Company, makers of market-leader Bronco, appeared in 1880. Hard and shiny Bronco was first sold from a barrow in London, but it would become dominant in the toilet-paper market until the 1950s; Izal was its main rival. At their offices, civil servants were provided with a special HMSO variety stamped with the baleful words: 'GOVERNMENT PROPERTY NOW WASH YOUR HANDS'.

Soft tissues were invented in 1936, but were at first marketed as being only for gentlemen's noses and sold solely at Harrods. However, people soon realised that soft tissue was much more pleasant to use than Bronco, and rolls of it began to appear in bathrooms. Its colour was restricted to white until 1957. For a long time toilet-paper manufacturers made their paper thicker for the North American market, on the understanding that Europeans 'folded' (a legacy from linen-using days?) but Americans 'scrunched' the paper.

Pastel colours, patterns, quilting and extra-strong paper all followed. Other cultures, especially in the East, manage without toilet paper and use a hose instead, and this certainly saves trees and waste. A hideous innovation of the 1990s was 'moist' toilet paper, fragranced, dermatologically tested and super-cleansing. It really does sound like something from the last decadent days of the Roman Empire.

24 – Menstruation

So many troubles are brought on by constipation,
painful menstruation being no exception.

Leona W. Chalmers, *The Intimate
Side of a Woman's Life*, 1937

Leona W. Chalmers, writing in 1937, may have had some funny
ideas about what causes painful periods, but she had a com-
mendable urge to teach women about their reproductive organs.
'Women should be given the opportunity of learning how these
organs are constructed,' she wrote, and 'what their functions
are'. And yet how could females be expected to acquire reliable facts, Chalmers asked, 'when such knowledge has not been
made available'?

The Book of Leviticus shows that even in ancient times men-
strual blood was already firmly taboo, something to be hidden
away and not discussed:

If a woman have an issue, and her issue in her flesh be blood, she shall
be put apart . . . and everything that she lieth upon in her separation
shall be unclean . . . And whosoever toucheth her bed shall wash his
clothes, and bathe himself in water.

The Book of Isaiah describes a 'menstruous cloth' as a horrible thing, to be discarded as quickly as possible. Scraps of old
cloth were the enduring means of dealing with the flow for many

centuries, and the words for the shameful fact of menstruation remained vague and elliptical: it was the 'French lady's visit', the 'Redcoats' were coming, or the 'moon' was full. Richard Mead wrote in 1704 that 'everyone knows how great a share the moon has in forwarding those evacuations of the weaker sex', and he thought that women living nearer the equator must have stronger periods.

It's hard to find out very much about how Victorian women viewed menstruation because they would rather have died than talk about it. 'The first sign that leads a female to suspect that she is pregnant, is her *ceasing to be unwell*,' is how the author of *Advice to a Wife* somewhat opaquely described a missed period in 1853.

The Victoria.

From a circular advertising the New Victoria Protector. 'Astonishing Success! Enormous Sales!' reads the accompanying text. 'When on the person there is absolutely no chaffing sensation . . . as with the more common napkin or cloth'

In 1896, the company of Johnson and Johnson began to manufacture 'Lister's Towels', history's first recorded disposable pads. But because they were unable to market their products – it was unacceptable to mention menstruation in public – the line failed and was withdrawn. It was during the First World War that nurses noticed that the cellulose bandages used for wounded soldiers on the battlefield soaked up blood far better than the cotton or linen cloths they had been using for themselves for so long. So, in 1921, the oldest surviving brand of sanitary product, Kotex, began to make its disposable pads. They were originally buttoned into or hooked onto a special pair of pants or a belt, until in the 1970s the adhesive strip was invented. The convenience and liberation that sanitary pads brought to women was not entirely welcome to men. The literary giant William Faulkner, jealous of the enormous commercial success of Margaret Mitchell's ultra-romantic *Gone with the Wind* (1936), peevishly dismissed it as a trivial product of an over-feminised 'Kotex Age'.

Tampons were invented in 1933, and caught on despite concerns from the Catholic Church that they were a bit too much like a contraceptive device. There's an interesting theory that applicator tampons are more popular in countries with a Protestant heritage – keener on aestheticism and purity, more afraid of getting bloody fingers – and that women in less squeamish Catholic countries prefer the type without the tube.

Only in the 1970s, with the rise of outspoken feminism, did menstruation become something to be publicly talked about. In the novel *Are You There God? It's Me, Margaret* (1978) by Judy Blume, the narrator is shown a disappointing educational film at school: 'The film told us about the ovaries . . . it didn't really show a girl getting it. It just said how wonderful nature was and how we would soon become women and all that.' Afterwards, one girl asked if she should use Tampax, a question then still bold enough to cause consternation. 'We don't advise *internal protection* until you are considerably older,' was the pusillanimous answer. The dangers of toxic-shock syndrome from tampons were at first underestimated by their manufacturers: when its existence emerged in the early 1980s, some feminists came to believe that the products would have been better tested if intended for use by men.

The disposal of sanitary towels has long been a vexing issue. For much of the twentieth century they were burnt, either at home or in the boiler of a college or office building, which created a foul smell. Since then, the legislation concerning the disposal of sanitary products has been heavy-handed: the bins provided in public toilets have to meet standards set by the Environment Act, and must be emptied by specialist clinical-waste contractors. In order to reduce the frequency of empty-ing, and therefore of cost, the bins are bigger than convenient, take up a large amount of a cubicle's space, brush against users and transfer germs. Alternative, women-led designs for toilet cubicles tend to incorporate chutes in their walls to receive used sanitary products.

In 1976, when the first cultural history of menstruation, *The Curse*, was published, one of its authors spoke to a meeting of psychiatrists:

During her talk Mary Jane deliberately mentioned that she was men-struating . . . afterwards, many of the participants expressed shock that she had so revealed herself. 'Why, my own wife doesn't tell me when she is menstruating,' said one.

The psychiatrist's wife was well in line with an attitude which had persisted for millennia. In more recent years, it's been interesting to compare the rhetoric about nappies and the envi-ronment, and sanitary pads. Ecologically minded parents are frequently extolled to consider the energy that goes into wash-ing cloth nappies against the necessity of putting used dispos-ables into landfill waste-disposal sites. The ecological option in terms of sanitary protection is much clearer: rubber devices like the Mooncup are completely reusable and produce no waste at all. And yet we hear very little about this very simple green step that many women could make. The taboo placed by Leviticus still holds its sway.

PART THREE

An Intimate History of the Living Room

It's time to enter the public areas of the house, where life is lived on display.

Once, all rooms were living rooms. Like stage sets, they'd be quickly dressed or furnished for different activities. That's why, up to the eighteenth century, the chairs in a room would be pushed back against the wall unless in use. Best behaviour and boredom were to be found in many living rooms when guests were present, as well as laughter and tears at great events like proposals, wedding breakfasts and funeral feasts. Intended to be seen by visitors as well as family, living rooms illustrate the art of putting on a show.

Why did living rooms eventually develop their different specialisations — drawing room, parlour, morning room, smoking room and so on? One argument suggests that ideas about courtesy caused change: gradually it became unseemly to perform certain activities in front of other people. In the seventeenth century, for example, the word 'disgust' was coined to describe a new revulsion that people felt towards tainted food or unpleasant odours. They started to think that eating was inappropriate in a living room, and that dining should have its own separate space. Then there was the growing fondness for solitude. Renaissance gentlemen liked to read and study, activities requiring quiet and private spaces. Thirdly, there was the emergence of a consumer society. As people began making things instead of growing them for a living, a multiplicity of new products and gadgets for the home appeared. And as they bought more possessions, homeowners needed more rooms to put them in.

The middle classes, both creators and creations of the industrial age, made a real cult of furnishings. By Victorian times, the desirable upper-middle-class home had several rooms of reception, in which weird little conventions and rituals marked out men and women of respectability from the unfortunate families who could only afford one communal space in which to live. The living room had reached its apogee. Throughout the twentieth century it would gradually become less formal once again, so that now, if you live in an open-plan house, you probably treat your living room rather like the flex-ible, adaptable, all-purpose medieval hall once again. Perhaps guests are even to be found sleeping on your sofa; certainly they are upon mine.

25 – Sitting Comfortably

The common sitting room [is] an Englishman's
delight to show his wealth.

Robert Southey, 1807

At the heart of living-room life is the chair: whether for resting,
writing (a much more important part of everyday life before
the telephone), reading or talking. In a medieval house, only
the lord or owner was allowed to sit down, while everyone else
stood and watched.

The book of poems by Charles, Duc d'Orléans, written while
he was a prisoner in the Tower of London after his capture at
the battle of Agincourt in 1415, contains an excellent illustration of a medieval living room (plate 21). The *duc* sits in the
best place, before the fire, while his retainers await his orders
(his chaplain in red). The floor of the room is beautifully tiled;
its walls have been hung with the tapestries which hide an inter-
loper or eavesdropper in many a tale from the Middle Ages.

This was medieval life for the grand: the temporary occupation of an endless succession of draughty castles, each furnished
quickly but luxuriously for the occasion. It's almost like camp-
ing: each night the whole set-up could be recreated somewhere
new. A medieval king moved around his realm constantly to
show himself to his subjects, physically maintaining law and

order, while his aristocrats peregrinated round their estates in order to consume upon the spot the annual proportion of the crop owed to them as landlords. King Edward III (1312–77) and his wife Philippa had such a nomadic life that their numerous children were born variously at the Tower of London, Windsor, Woodstock, Antwerp, Clarendon, Ghent, Hatfield, Langley and Waltham in Essex.

This is why the French still call their furniture *mobiliers*, or 'removables': many pieces did indeed follow their owners round the country from castle to manor. Many surviving examples of medieval furniture are either easily movable or demountable.

Perhaps the classic furnishing item for the mobile household was tapestry. It served several purposes. Tapestries are portable and flexible, able to eliminate the draughts from spaces of different size and shape. Secondly, they can convey iconographic messages through their design, sending out signals about their owners' erudition or aspirations. Henry VIII favoured a set telling the biblical story of Abraham, for example, which is about an ageing man's ultimately successful search for a male heir; Henry himself took encouragement from this. Thirdly, tapestry is a wonderful form of conspicuous consumption, especially if woven with gold or silver thread. Cardinal Wolsey had a closet hung with cloth of gold, and had more than 600 tapestries in his collection. A Venetian ambassador was amazed to describe how, when visiting the cardinal, 'one has to traverse eight rooms before one reaches his audience chamber, and they are all hung with tapestry'. Even more impressively than that, the tapestry displayed was 'changed every week'.

The great hall of a medieval house was essentially the only living room for its lower servants, and we already know that it also served as their bedroom. Any leisure time would be spent there, playing dice or singing. The floors of medieval halls were made cosier with cut rushes, a kind of disposable carpet. (The scholar Erasmus, visiting England, complained that the rushes were useful for soaking up 'spittle and vomit and urine of dogs and men, beer that hath been cast forth and remnants of fish and other filth unnameable'.) The dirty rushes would be thrown out and renewed as a household moved from house to house.

Over time this all-purpose medieval living room began to lose some of its functions. Sleeping and sex went off to the bedchamber, as we've seen already. Late medieval houses had a 'solar' or sitting room, separate from the common hall, where the family's ladies would sit, eat or sew. Then, as the defensive requirements of a manor house declined with the ending of the Wars of the Roses, grand houses began to acquire extra rooms purely for the purpose of receiving important guests.

In the royal palaces this led to the development of a chain of elegant reception rooms: the presence chamber, the privy chamber, the withdrawing chamber, all leading one into another. In the first the king would receive honoured strangers. The 'privy' or private chamber was for his intimate friends. In the 'withdrawing' chamber he could withdraw from company altogether. (This is the origin of the term 'drawing room'.) By the seventeenth century, the snug 'parlour' (for a *parlez*, a parley, or a private conversation) had developed even in more modest homes. Parlours were furnished with the new 'falling' or gate-leg table: flexibility in the furnishings was still required.

Lower down the social order, the specialised living room developed more slowly than the bedchamber or kitchen, because those whose lives were dedicated to work had no need of a leisure space. The living room's purpose was decorative, social and seemingly superfluous, but its presence indicated high social status. While it has a less obvious 'function' than the bedroom or bathroom, it has an even more subtle and interesting story to tell about contemporary society.

With the increasing peace and wealth of the Tudor age, aristocrats felt the need for more and different rooms for sitting around in and spending the hours. In a grand Elizabethan house like Hardwick Hall, there were three gigantic rooms: a great chamber, a long gallery and a withdrawing chamber, all of which could be described as living rooms.

The first, of great height and beauty, was used for receiving guests, for ceremony and formal entertainment. Here, on high days and holidays, its owner, Bess of Hardwick, Countess of Shrewsbury, would sit in state on a throne-like chair under a canopy, receiving compliments. The enormous long gallery next door was for gentle exercise and the display of family portraits (thirty-seven of them at Hardwick). A gallery was for 'pastime and health', and Thomas Howard found himself filled with 'delight' as he walked up and down his own, admiring the pictures of his 'honourable friends' that he'd hung there. They were a daily reminder of the excellence of his connections. The gallery also had another use: for getting out of earshot of the numerous members of an Elizabethan household. It was the only place in the entire house where one could be sure of holding a private conversation.

But the withdrawing chamber at Hardwick was a slightly more exclusive space. Here, members of the family could 'withdraw' with favoured guests for a more intimate party, and they might spend their own leisure time here when not in their bedchambers. Eventually, impractically large and showy Elizabethan rooms like the great chamber would die out, and it was the withdrawing chamber that would survive to develop into the drawing room of the Victorian house.

Hardwick Hall sees the beginning of the specialisation of the living room, but the process reached new heights in the eighteenth century. The music room, the library and the saloon all became desirable appurtenances, while the nineteenth century saw the rise of the smoking or billiard room for gentlemen, the morning room for ladies, and the conservatory for both.

The all-purpose reception room would eventually make something of a twentieth-century comeback, in the form of the knocked-through drawing/dining room in a terraced house or the modern open-plan lounge. The earliest indication of this trend came in the 'studio apartment', invented for New York's artistic community around 1900 but quickly adopted by other city dwellers. 'Mrs Apartment Seeker has been to a tea or reception at Mr Artist's studio apartment,' ran an article in the *Brickbuilder* magazine of 1912. She found it:

such an attractive place for his 'soirée' and so appropriate for the display of his pictures and work. How lovely it would be for her to give such teas and musicals, how effective. She immediately starts looking for one.

Common to all these living or reception rooms was the fact that they would be laid bare to the potentially disparaging eyes of guests. So they had to look as good as possible.

If the king, queen or other grand personage came to stay in a Tudor house, the owner would vacate the best rooms, happily handing them over to those placed above him in society. The decoration of the living rooms therefore got grander and grander as you went deeper into the house, and only the most important guests would get to see the innermost and most expensively decorated rooms. In later, more democratic times, when there were only one or two reception rooms, resources would be concentrated in the outer or more public rooms at the expense of the inner. That's why the most expensive item in a Tudor house – quite possibly more expensive than everything else put together – was the master's marital bed, while today it is the sofa or dining table that costs the most.

Below the peers in the Tudor hierarchy (there were only about fifty-five of them in the sixteenth century) came the gentlemen, the citizens, the yeomen and the labourers. William Harrison in 1577 described these four divisions in society, and their respective roles: the labourers and servants, for example, had 'neither voice nor authority'. Each person knew exactly where they fitted in, and would attempt to decorate their own living rooms appropriately.

The great change of the seventeenth century was the rise of the citizen class: town-dwellers growing prosperous through manufacturing, trade, printing and banking. In due course, these people began to think that they too should have the luxury living rooms of their betters.

Of course, expressing the fact that you had lots of money through the design of your reception rooms was nothing new: at Hardwick Hall, and other great houses of the sixteenth and seventeenth centuries, the emphasis had been on creating an impressive, overwhelmingly rich and colourful interior. What was new in the Georgian age was the idea that 'taste' could separate the discerning from the ignorant among the increasingly large number of people with cash to splash upon their living rooms. Anybody could have luxury, the argument went, but luxury without refinement was mere bling. To spend your money wisely, you needed an expensive education. 'No one can be properly stil'd a gentleman, who takes not every opportunity to enrich his own capacity and settle the elements of taste,' we hear in 1731.

So a new elite was created, with a sense of style based on knowledge rather than just upon wealth. From the eighteenth century onwards, the drawing room was the canvas upon which the new accomplishment of 'taste' was expressed. 'Of all our favourite words lately, none has been more in vogue, nor so long held its esteem, as that of taste,' claimed *The Universal Spectator* in 1747.

By the eighteenth century, the builders of aristocratic pleasure palaces had much more influence than previously upon the less well-off but eager to learn, because their houses were more accessible. Kedleston Hall in Derbyshire, for example, was a rare statement of astoundingly high design values. Sir Nathaniel Curzon tore down his grandfather's house and moved a village in order to build the new mansion, which was completed in 1765.

For its interiors he employed Robert Adam, who was then a relatively unknown young Scot recently returned from study in Rome. Adam was delighted with Curzon, a client 'resolved to spare no Expence, with £10,000 a year, Good Temper'd and having taste himself for the Arts'. Adam's brief extended from the plaster ceilings to the door handles, and the whole house was made into a (somewhat impractical) monument to ancient Rome. (Dr Johnson thought the house pompous and grandiloquent, and that it 'would do excellently for a Town Hall'.) The family themselves lived in a separate wing, and the main reception rooms were intended for great political parties.

As soon as the house was finished, tourists were keen to see inside. Mrs Garnett, 'a well-dressed elderly Housekeeper' and 'a most distinct Articulator', had the job of showing them round. She even found it worth her while to produce her own guidebook. Her customers were looking for amusement, but also for inspiration for their own reception rooms at home.

Kedleston's state rooms were planned to facilitate big political parties, and they also had the benefit of facilitating this new kind of visitor tour. Instead of visitors penetrating one doorway after another in an increasingly exclusive hierarchy like at Hardwick Hall, the living rooms here are arranged in a ring. They still increase in grandeur from music room to drawing room to library to saloon, but it is possible to make a complete circuit through them all, enjoying the paintings and furniture. Georgian houses like this are often described as being 'social' in design, intended for guests of all ranks to mingle rather than remaining in the room appointed for their own particular status.

Kedleston's visitors could see some of Britain's most amazing furniture. Among the house's greatest marvels are the drawing-room sofas made by the London cabinet-maker John Linnell (plate 25). (Unfortunately the sofas did not enjoy a smooth journey to Derbyshire: upon their arrival, a local workman had to be paid for 'glueing bits' back on.) In their sky-blue silk, with languid gold sea gods supporting their sides, they look more like masque scenery than furniture. The sofa itself was a novel imported Arabian idea. Upon it one could lounge, lean back and spread out one's skirts, a much more elegant and casual posture than it was possible to adopt in an upright seventeenth-century chair. These sofas were social pieces of furniture, made for two people to sit together. Earlier aristocrats, who sat in stately solitude upon a dais, would not have dreamed of this.

Once the aspiration to this kind of luxury, and the money and leisure time to pursue it, had filtered down the social scale, new 'styles' appeared in drawing rooms on a regular basis. There were successive crazes for the Chinese, Grecian, Etruscan, Neo-Pompeiian and Tudorbethan, new looks emerging at what seemed to be shorter and shorter intervals.

Perhaps none of these styles had a strong relationship to the time and place they were intended to recreate, but this didn't matter. Successive historical revivals were simply excuses to go shopping for a whole new set of possessions. A desirable interior would strike the eye as novel, exotic and fresh, preferably referencing some distant world like China or ancient Rome to add a touch of class and erudition. This is what impressed a serial country-house visitor like Mrs Lybbe Powys. At Eastby, the destination of one of her many days out, she noted that 'the Chinese bedroom and dressing-room in the attic storey is excessively droll and pretty, furnish'd exactly as in China'.

The owners of middle-class urban drawing rooms did not, of course, adopt the full-blown, gilded-sea-god splendour of Kedleston. Toning down avante-garde taste to make it palatable to a wider audience was part of the skill of the manufacturer of drawing-room furniture and fittings. Josiah Wedgwood junior, for example, once rejected a striking design for a black vase. 'We are not bold enough to adopt at once anything that is new and beautiful,' he explained, 'but require the sanction of fashion to give it value.' To shop successfully was a skill, and the errors of pretentiousness and garishness were all too common.

Decorating the drawing room was one of the duties, or pleasures, of the newly married wife. In his 1745 book *The Pleasures and Felicities of Marriage*, Lemuel Gulliver lists the items that a woman will look forward to acquiring upon marriage: 'costly Hangings, Venetian Looking-Glasses, enamel'd China, Velvet Chairs, Turkey Carpets, Capital Paintings, Side-board of wrought Plate, curious in-laid Cabinets'. The historian Amanda Vickery notes that in Jane Austen's novels, a female character shown around a single man's house is practically being given permission to assume that a proposal is forthcoming. In *Sense and Sensibility*, Mrs Jennings is shocked when an engagement does *not* follow on from Marianne's tour of her prospective husband's house. 'No positive engagement indeed!' her friends expostulated. 'After taking her all over Allenham House, and fixing on the very rooms they were to live in hereafter!'

So decorating a drawing room was a social obligation, as was holding merry parties in it once it was complete. Indeed, gatherings in Georgian living rooms had a new levity and effervescence unknown in earlier centuries:

> No more the Cedar Parlour's formal gloom
> With dullness chills, 'tis now the Living Room
> Where Guests, to whim, or taste, or fancy true
> Scatter'd in groups, their different plans pursue.

This new world of tasteful informality, cheeky chat and lovely curtains was worlds away from the hierarchic splendour of Hardwick Hall.

In the nineteenth century, though, the history of the living room was about to enter a darker phase.

26 – A History of Clutter

Have nothing in your house that you do not
know to be useful, or believe to be beautiful.
William Morris

The difference between Victorian living rooms and their predecessors lay in three main areas. Firstly, in the grandest Victorian
houses living rooms proliferated yet again. Increased specialisation led to morning rooms, front parlours, billiard rooms and
libraries, all different variations on the same theme. Secondly,
their colour schemes were plunged into murk and gloom. Rich,
dark colours replaced the light, bright Georgian tints, largely
because of changes in heating and lighting technology, which
we'll investigate in the next chapter.

But thirdly, and most importantly, Victorian living rooms
contained more *stuff* than ever before. Some of this clutter
was familiar from living rooms of the past, reborn into modern form. Edith Wharton, the American novelist, decoded the
language of the nineteenth-century drawing room in a scene set
in Victorian Mayfair. The contemporary equivalent of a long
gallery full of portraits expressing a family's noble relatives,
the room

was crowded with velvet-covered tables and quaint corner-shelves, all
laden with photographs in heavy silver or morocco frames, surmounted

by coronets, from the baronial to the ducal – one, even, royal (in a place of honour by itself, on the mantel).

Because it was so much easier to collect photographs of your friends than it was to commission painted portraits, it was no wonder that such things multiplied.

Much of the stuff in a Victorian drawing room was showier than ever before; some of it could even be described as vulgar. An 1870s advert for a suite of drawing-room furniture makes grandiose claims: it contained 'six well-carved chairs upholstered in rich silk, centre table on massive carved pillar and claws, the top beautifully inlaid with marquetry, large size chimney glass in handsome oil-gilt frame . . . pair of handsome ruby lustres'. Such 'rich', 'handsome' and 'massive' objects were Victorian must-haves. The sea-god sofas at Kedleston were rather overwhelming, but they were placed in an enormous room where few other pieces competed with them for attention. In the Victorian living room, variety was queen.

Its owners also wished to display the fruits of their industry and their empire. The Great Exhibition of 1851 inspired people to bring the whole world into their living rooms. Lucy Orrinsmith, author of *The Drawing Room, Its Decoration and Furniture* (1878), suggested that one's ambition ought to extend beyond a coal scuttle decorated with a picture of Warwick Castle and a screen showing 'Melrose Abbey by Moonlight'. Instead, homeowners should look out for quirky, exotic flourishes for their best room: 'a Persian tile, an Algerian flower-pot, an old Flemish cup, a piece of Nankin blue, an Icelandic spoon, a Japanese cabinet, a Chinese fan . . . each in its own way beautiful and interesting'.

This craze to possess had in fact started long before the nineteenth century. The late-seventeenth-century invention of shops and shopping by an urban middle class who lived by trade was mirrored by the growth of a new type of domestic space. What might be termed the 'middle-class' living room was full of superfluous objects, chosen for ornament rather than use yet cheap and not truly beautiful: a barricade of possessions intended to stabilise a precarious position in the world.

For those without the resources of the Curzons of Kedleston, wallpaper was an amazing material for a quick and cheap living-room makeover. When it first appeared in the seventeenth century, wallpaper was purchased at stationers' shops. As it was so inexpensive to put up, it's not surprising to find that between 1690 and 1820 there were more than five hundred stationers and paper-hanging businesses in London. In 1712, wallpaper became popular enough to attract a special tax. In 1836, the tax was repealed, and an even more marvellous world of choice was opened up: a visitor to the Sanderson Company's wallpaper showroom in 1901 found 'papers of a magnificence, a beauty, such as we had never imagined even in our wildest dreams of marble halls'.

Yet wallpaper was deceptive: it literally covered up problems. The business of making and selling it also attracted deceivers. A lively trade developed in counterfeits of the date stamps applied by wallpaper-tax inspectors to the backs of rolls. By 1806, the punishment for being caught creating these phoney stamps was increased to the death penalty. Wallpaper could even be hazardous to health: some inks contained arsenic, and when people went on holiday to the seaside, they felt better simply because they were no longer breathing in poisonous fumes from their drawing-room walls each day.

Despite its cheerfulness, wallpaper was sometimes *too* cheap, and looked tawdry. In nineteenth-century novels, a wallpapered room became a metaphor for a shallow, duplicitous character who overvalues appearances. In Thomas Hardy's *Far from the Madding Crowd* (1874), the untrustworthy Sergeant Troy is displeased by the casements and dark corners of an 'honest' old farmhouse: 'my notion is that sash-windows should be put in through-out . . . the walls papered'.

The literary scholar Julia Prewitt Brown argues that the first ever of these 'bourgeois interiors' (the crowded and slightly shoddy living rooms of the socially insecure) to be created in literature was situated on a desert island. In Daniel Defoe's novel of 1719, the adventurer Robinson Crusoe was taught by his father to aspire to belong to the 'middle state' of society, and he was taught that honest industry would lead to a life of well-earned ease. After his shipwreck Crusoe is trapped on his desert island. Being a good member of the 'middling sort', he devotes himself to the archetypally bourgeois pastime of inventorying and protecting the stores and tools salvaged from the sea. He fortifies a cave to protect his possessions from ravenous beasts, and is rarely to be seen outside it without his umbrella and his gun.

Robinson Crusoe was followed by a horde of successors: everyone can recognise the overcluttered, stuffy, uptight living room of a truly anxious status-conscious person with neither the ease of aristocratic riches nor the genuine restrictions of poverty. This phenomenon reached its apogee in an imaginary Victorian living room forever damned by Henry James and smothered in

. . . trumpery ornament and scrapbook art, with strange excrescences and bunchy draperies, with gimcracks that might have been keepsakes for maid-servants . . . they had gone wildly astray over carpets and curtain; they had an infallible instinct for disaster.

From the late nineteenth century, two new design movements began to blow the cobwebs out of the overfurnished living room. The Arts and Crafts Movement, and then the twentieth-century Modernist Movement based on the minimalist aethestic of the factory and the machine, were both in their own ways reactions to the tide of clutter.

It was Oscar Wilde (1844–1900), travelling the world to give his renowned lecture on 'The House Beautiful' to packed halls, who began to get the Victorians to throw away their junk. Some of them went on to become patrons of the Arts and Crafts

Movement, which combined a love of craftsmanship with a devotion to the dignity and beauty of labour. The idea was to banish the machine-made, meretricious or the modern from the Victorian home and to return to an age of simplicity, authenticity and beauty.

One of Oscar Wilde's listeners went on to create the ultimate Arts and Crafts house, Wightwick Manor near Wolverhampton. The teetotal and Congregationalist Theodore Mander made his fortune from his paint business, and in 1884 he attended a performance of Wilde's 'The House Beautiful' in Wolverhampton. Mander made careful notes, including the celebrated dictum that your house should contain nothing 'which you do not know to be useful or think to be beautiful' (a phrase which Wilde himself had cribbed from the designer William Morris, 1834–96).

Full of enthusiasm for this new way of thinking, the paint magnate began work on a brand-new house, which would nevertheless appear to be terribly old. Wightwick had all the modern conveniences, yet might at first glance be mistaken for a Tudor manor. Mander's architect, the appropriately named Edward Ould, intended that its timber frame should 'soon pass through the crude and brand-new period' to become a timeless, misty-eyed memory of a pre-industrial age. To furnish his house, Mander inevitably turned to William Morris, whose company produced entire interiors inspired by medieval colours and designs.

The items in the William Morris Company's range complemented each other, and whole interiors could be put together, conveniently, by mail order. This is how Theodore Mander decorated his house, by choosing items out of a catalogue. And the irony of the olde-worlde, hand-made splendour of Wightwick is that the house was the dream of an industrialist who'd made his money shipping tins of ready-mixed paint around the world.

The Arts and Crafts Movement saw rich people paying

craftsmen to produce by hand items which were well beyond the purses of the working classes themselves. Thorstein Veblen, the Norwegian-American historian of conspicuous consumption and a biting critic of the American economy, points out the strange desirability of imperfection:

The ground of the superiority of hand-wrought goods . . . is a certain margin of crudeness. The margin must never be so wide as to show bungling workmanship, since that would be evidence of low cost, nor so narrow as to suggest the ideal precision attained only by the machine, for that would be evidence of low cost.

These contradictions between the hand-crafted and modernity are still to be found at the Sanderson wallpaper factory in Loughborough, where William Morris's original wallpaper blocks remain in use today (plate 26). Some designs involve passing the paper through the printing press by hand up to twenty-two times. The result – highly wrought and very slightly flawed – remains an extremely desirable, and expensive, backdrop for a living room. (I have tried printing wallpaper myself using an original Morris block. I thought it would be easy, but I can vouch for the fact that it is a job requiring skills which must be honed over many years of experience.)

Many of the same features of the Arts and Crafts story are likewise to be found in the twentieth century, when housebuilders had to pay sky-high prices to achieve the effortlessly minimal look. The modern houses of the 1930s were supposed to be pared-down, simplified machines for living:

the home is no longer permanent from generation to generation; family ties, inconsistent with freedom of living, are broken. We demand spaciousness, release from encumbrances, from furniture and trappings that overload our rooms, possessions that tie us and tools that are obsolete.

And yet houses in experimental materials and designs came at a cost. One-offs like Amyas Connell's 1929 High and Over, near Amersham, are like ships sailing through the countryside, full of light and air, white-painted and beautifully clutter-free. These values remain so strong that many people today pay good money to de-cluttering specialists who help them throw away their junk.

Having passed through all these minefields of potential errors of taste and judgement, you can only sit comfortably in your living room if the lighting and temperature are likewise under control.

27 – Heat and Light

On winter days in London ... the smoke of fossil coal
forms an atmosphere perceivable for many miles, like
a great round cloud attached to the earth.
                    Louis Simon, a French-American
                        visitor to London, 1810

More than any other room in the house, a room for reception is
supposed to feel comfortably warm. Heating is part of the basic
hospitality that householders should extend to servants and
strangers alike. This is why the great hall at Hampton Court,
built in the early sixteenth century, was constructed upon the
ancient model with a central open hearth. There's no evidence
that it was ever actually used, but that fireplace nevertheless
formed the symbolic heart of the household.

Until the seventeenth century, the fires of great lords and
lowly cottagers alike consumed wood. It was always a valuable
commodity, and especially so if you had to forage for it yourself.
Yet, just like plumbing, the history of domestic technology has
not been governed purely by a rational desire to reduce the consumption of resources. Heating and lighting involve emotion as
well as economics.

The expression 'by hook or by crook' is often said to come
from the peasants' right to enter their landlord's forest to see

what resources they could glean. They were not allowed to cut down trees for firewood; those remained their master's property. Using either a shepherd's crook or the billhook of a reaper, though, they might grab dead branches. A wood was a carefully managed asset, and the source of much wealth and pride to its owners. One of the great distresses of the English Civil War and the associated social upheaval of the seventeenth century was the felling of forests that had been carefully managed over centuries.

The need to heat a house gave rise to perhaps the greatest architectural invention of the past millennium: the chimney. Houses without chimneys may be warm, but cannot avoid being horribly smoky and dirty as well. Chimneys began to appear in the thirteenth and fourteenth centuries to carry smoke out of the house and to provide an updraught to tickle the flames.

With the chimney, the modern house was born. Now it began to be possible to produce buildings of several storeys. The central stone or brick chimney would anchor a structure, as well as providing heat to chambers on several floors. Even if they lacked their own fireplaces, rooms would still gain warmth from the chimney stack. This allowed houses to become multi-roomed, with specialised spaces for cooking or sleeping or leisure. Among them was the living room.

When such rooms for sitting around in began to win an increasing proportion of a household's budget, the art of soft furnishing was born. In the earliest parlours or withdrawing rooms Tudor and Stuart carpets were laid upon tables or cupboards, not upon the floor, where rushes provided rudimentary warming for the feet. In the late seventeenth century, a random selection of tapestries for the walls began to be replaced by a suite of matching hangings *of the same colour*, intended for use in one room only. The idea of furnishings en suite, which would culminate in the red velveteen three-piece suite of my grandmother's sitting room, was born around 1660.

Interiors made softer and more welcoming with textiles

A rushlight in its holder. For a brighter light
(lasting half the time), you 'burn at both ends'

would have seemed even more so by
the soft light of rushlights or candles.
Rushlights were the poor person's light
source of choice. They were made by
coating rushes in hot fat, building up
the layers until the rush itself formed
the wick of a rather scrawny candle.
These long, gently curving lights could
be thrust through and balanced in
the holders still found in the walls of
ancient houses. To provide twice the
light, they could be lit at both bottom
and top ('burning the candle at both
ends'). The twenty minutes for which
each rushlight burned became a famil-
iar unit of time. Neighbours often pooled their resources, taking
turns to gather in each other's houses for night-time sewing and
mending by the eked-out glimmer. Rushes were such a cheap
and reliable way of providing light that they were found in the
poorest homes right into the twentieth century.

It's also worth mentioning that firelight was the most common source of light, and people were simply quite used to dim-
mer light conditions than today. They were able to perform
many tasks without any light at all. Matty Jenkyns, a character
in Elizabeth Gaskell's *Cranford* (1851), economises upon candles, and in winter was to be found 'knitting in the darkness by
the fire'. Lacking the light to read was not a problem in illiterate
rural societies: singing and reciting ballads passed the time just
as well.

Only the rich could afford a profusion of candles. The
expression 'the game's not worth the candle' makes it clear that

candles were economic units, and to burn a candle gave the sensation of burning money itself. Sometimes they were lit just to give exactly that feeling of profligacy: the beeswax candles imported from Venice or Antwerp for church festivals made a proud statement that the place and occasion were special. When in 1731 Sir Robert Walpole entertained the Duke of Lorraine at his Houghton mansion in Norfolk, guests were astonished by the 130 wax candles lit in the hall, with fifty more in the saloon. It was widely put about, in compliment to the Duke, that the cost of the lighting alone for his reception was £15. Beeswax candles, which burned clearly and didn't need much trimming, were the preferred choice for hard-to-reach light fittings like chandeliers.

As everyone knew the value of candles, a daily ration was often included in employment conditions. In the royal household, an allowance of candles accompanied the issue of firewood and food to individual members. The fate of leftover candle ends was hotly disputed: in larger households, they were the preserve of certain servants, who would sell them on to supplement their wages.

The government, too, decided to cash in upon the need for domestic lighting. In 1709, a deeply unpopular tax was introduced on wax candles at the rate of fourpence a pound. So, in Georgian living rooms, the knowledge that candles were being lit for guests *despite the tax* made it a greater compliment still.

There was a cheaper alternative to the expensive beeswax candle, which was nevertheless far superior to the humble rushlight: the tallow candle made out of animal fat. The ideal tallow candle would be made out of 'half Sheep's Tallow and half Cow's', because 'that of hogs . . . gives an ill smell, and a thick black smoke'. Tallow candles had a horrible brown colour and made a dreadful meaty stink: 'those horrible scents and pernicious fumes that old tallow sends forth when it is melted'. Despite the nastiness, desperate people would in times of famine eat tallow candles for the calories they contained. The art of creating the best blend was a valuable one, and in 1390 tallow candle-makers were listed among the crafts (called 'misteries') to be found in London. In 1462, the Worshipful Company of Tallow Chandlers was granted its Royal Charter.

Apart from the unpleasant smell, the great downside of tallow candles was the need to snuff. Every few minutes the wick had to be trimmed to avoid gutters and to stop the burning wick from smoking. So the candle-snuffer was a vital living-room implement until, in 1820, the French invented the plaited wick, which burned successfully without snuffing.

Of course, in an age of candle and firelight accidents were common. The London wood-turner Nehemiah Wallington had several lucky escapes from being burned to death, a fate not uncommon in his crowded parish of St Leonard Eastcheap in the City of London. Once, Wallington's servant, Obadiah, strictly contrary to instructions, had taken a candle up to his bedchamber. There it fell over and burnt 'half a yard of the sheet and the flock bed'. But the quick-thinking Obadiah woke up a fellow servant, and 'both of them start up and *pissed* out the fire as well as they could'.

Across town in a much grander house, Lady Russell (whose family gave their name to Russell Square) was once shocked almost out of her skin by a 'hissing fire' which ran all over the floor of the closet where she sat reading. She was at first totally mystified about what had caused it. Finally, a sheepish servant 'beg'd pardon' and admitted 'having by mistake given [her] a candle, with a gunpowder squib in it, which was intended to make sport among the fellow servants on a rejoicing day'.

Interiors lit by candlelight were designed to make the most of the limited light available. In prosperous Georgian drawing rooms there was silver and sparkle everywhere. The gold rims on plates, the silver of keyholes, even the metallic embroidery on waistcoats: all were intended to reflect and maximise the effects of candlelight. In fact, a lady's court dress woven with heavy silver thread had the effect of making its wearer gleam in candlelight.

A second tax upon the light was the hated yet long-lasting 'window tax', a 'tax upon light and air', as its detractors called it. Before 1696, the basic tax upon a household was levied upon the number of its hearths. But the 'hearth tax' was difficult to collect because tax inspectors needed to enter people's houses to check the number of fireplaces. Clearly they weren't going to be welcome visitors.

When in 1696 a new tax was levied instead upon windows, the inspectors had only to walk round the outside of the house and count. Initially there was a basic charge of two shillings upon all houses, which doubled to four shillings for houses with between ten and twenty windows. Changes to the banding of window tax helps to explain the mysteriously bricked-up windows in some Georgian city streets. In 1747, the bands were altered so that a house of ten windows or more had to pay six-pence per additional window. Several houses in Elder Street in London's Spitalfields had one or more openings blocked up at this point so that they would just slip under the ten-window level. (The neat idea that the window tax is the origin of the expression 'daylight robbery', though, is regrettably no more than speculation.)

While it was good for government finances, the downside of the window tax was this darkening of people's homes. 'A proper ventilation of inhabited houses is absolutely necessary for the public health,' thundered M. Humberstone in *The Absurdity and Injustice of the Window Tax* (1841). 'It is like a demon of darkness spreading immorality and wretchedness in its path.' The idea that a stuffy, unventilated house was unhealthy was further heightened by the continued belief in the concept of miasma.

Another annoying feature of the window tax was the lax and

When the rules
about window
tax were changed,
the owner of
this house in
Spitalfields
bricked up several
openings to avoid
the higher band

piecemeal fashion in which it was collected. Mobs sometimes attacked window-tax inspectors who suddenly reappeared after several years' unexplained absence, and the 1750s saw William Sinclair's epic and glorious battle with his local window-tax inspector in Dunbeath, Scotland. 'As to Mr Angus, the Caithness Collector,' he admitted,

I shall honestly tell you the reason I was not civil to him. In the year 1753 he came here and surveyed my windows and reported them to be

28. The next half year he came and surveyed them and found them to be 31 when there was none either added or taken away. In June 1754 he . . . left a list showing my windows to be 47 and gave that number to the tax man. I appealed and was charged at 31. The last time he came he said there was 34, and I fell into a passion and swore him that I would be revenged.

Because of these difficulties the window tax was eventually repealed in 1851.

In the late seventeenth century, coal began gradually to replace wood as the commonest household fuel. At first it was something of a luxury, as it burned hotter and for longer than wood. But it quickly caught on, and of course caught the government's eye as something which could be taxed. It seems somehow just that the City of London, destroyed by fire in 1666, was rebuilt partially with the proceeds of the new tax imposed upon coal.

In Georgian towns the ashes created by coal fires would be stored in people's cellars until the twice-yearly visit of the urban 'dustman'. In fact, dust and cinders originally formed the main business of the dustman's life before he branched out into collecting other forms of refuse too. Even today old dustbins might be found marked with the words 'no hot ashes'.

For your fire to burn successfully, you needed to keep your chimney swept. Until 1855, when they were outlawed and replaced by the 'humane sweeping' of chimneys with bendy brushes, nimble chimney boys were sent up the flues. An open fire, though, is a fairly inefficient means of heating because much of the warmth escapes up the chimney. The late-Georgian Count Rumford (he was American, his title awarded by the Bavarian government) transformed home heating when he fitted his revolutionary stoves into fireplaces. Now the fuel could be burned more effectively under better regulated conditions. His motive was fuel efficiency: 'more fuel is frequently consumed . . . to boil a tea kettle than with proper management would be sufficient to cook a dinner for fifty men', he claimed.

However, the eighteenth century's great innovations in heating took place in hospitals, prisons and cotton mills (where thread was more elastic at higher temperatures). When water-based central heating began to penetrate the domestic sphere, it was more often than not to be found in the greenhouses and kitchen gardens of great estates, where delicate plants and pineapples required hot-water pipes and stoves to be stoked all night by a sleepless gardener. Some of Britain's earliest domestic hot-water radiators were installed in 1833, and can still be seen at Stratfield Saye House in Hampshire today. But they heated the corridors only: in the abundant aristocratic manner, the living rooms retained the wasteful open fires that were nevertheless so pleasant for their owners. And indeed, why would you bother to install such conveniences in your home if you could afford housemaids to empty the grates before you woke each morning?

A fourteen-year-old housemaid named Harriet has left a heartbreaking letter from the 1870s, describing the heavy work she had to do when the weather turned cold in the autumn:

I have been so driven at work since the fires begun I have had hardly any time for anything for myself. I am up at half past five and six every morning and do not go to bed till nearly twelve at night and I feel so tired sometimes. I am obliged to have a good cry.

At Chatsworth House parties in the 1920s, fifteen fires still burned in the living rooms, each requiring fresh coal four times a day: a total of sixty bucketfuls for the footman to carry.

Yet 'to the English a room without a fire is like a body without a soul', observed Hermann Muthesius in 1904.

The many advantages the fireplace is deemed to possess . . . not least its aesthetic advantages . . . so completely convince the Englishman of its superiority to all other forms of heating that he never even remotely considers replacing it with the more efficient and more economical stove.

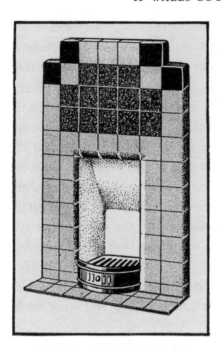

A tile fireplace from the twentieth century. For emotional reasons, the fondness for open flames persisted even after central heating had arrived

In an age of smoke, housemaids had many tricks for cleaning hangings, carpets and furnishings. To freshen a tapestry or hanging, the author of *The Complete Servant* (1830) recommends that you should 'blow all the dust off with a pair of bellows. Cut a stale loaf into eight pieces. Beginning at the top of the wall, wipe lightly downwards with a piece of the bread.' Likewise, food could cleanse a carpet: 'shake well, spread over it with a brush some grated raw potatoes. Brush clean and leave to dry.' A list of instructions for housemaids made in 1782 recommends strewing tea leaves upon the carpet and then sweeping them up, and also gives an insight into dusting: 'books are not to be meddled with, but they may be dusted as far as a wing of a goose will go'. These cleaning tasks were endless in Victorian London, where people even thought it worth thrusting a cloth into their front-door keyholes to help prevent the dirty air of a poisoned city from seeping into their homes.

Living rooms got even dirtier when oil lamps began to replace candles in the later eighteenth century. 'I have seen houses almost filled with the smoke from lamps, and the stench of the oil,' a footman recollected. In a large establishment lamps required a separate new room for the cleaning of their glass shades. The Duke of Rutland, at his home, Belvoir Castle, had a trifling 400 lamps for his hard-working servants to polish. They hated it. 'Lamps were often neglected,' reveals *The Footman's Directory* of 1825, 'especially in households where servants changed jobs quickly, since everyone thought they would last their time.'

But the oil lamp would soon be superseded by gas, which had long been exploited by human beings, and possibly provided the source of the perpetual flames in Greek and Roman temples. It made its appearance in modern Britain in factories, asylums and theatres long before it penetrated the home. This was coal gas, produced by baking coal. Today our gas is natural, piped from pockets beneath the sea, and it burns much more brightly than the coal gas used between late Georgian times and the 1970s.

William Murdoch, a Scottish engineer working in the Cornish mining industry, was the greatest innovator in the field of gas lighting, employing it in 1792 to illuminate his offices in Redruth. His name is less well known, though, than Frederick Windsor's, the man who organised a public demonstration of this new lighting for George III's birthday in 1807, and who set up the first public gas-supply company. A showman by nature, Windsor was a great proselytiser for his new product, which was mysterious and rather frightening. People marvelled at the properties of this 'illuminated air', but remained fearful of explosions and fires. Windsor (somewhat unconvincingly) reassured potential clients that coal gas was even 'more congenial to our lungs than vital air'.

In 1812, the Gas Light and Coke Company set up the first

gasworks in Britain. Gas was piped across towns by plumbers, the people whose skills seemed best suited to this new task, so its vocabulary is identical to that of water: 'mains', 'taps', 'flow', 'pressure' and 'current'. At first gas was mainly used for street rather than domestic lighting. Westminster Bridge was illuminated by gas as early as 1813, and there would ultimately be more than 60,000 gas street lamps all over London. One thousand six hundred still remain today, in Westminster and around St James's and Buckingham Palaces. They are maintained by six gas-lamp attendants employed by British Gas, a remnant of the once vast pool of lighters who went round cities at dusk with their long torches.

I've had the pleasure of using one of these torches in the company of Phil Banner, who's spent forty-two years with British Gas. He showed me how his works: you squeeze a rubber bulb at one end, which forces a gust of air upwards, and the flame burning at the other end leaps out like a dragon's tongue and ignites the gas. (The remaining lamps are usually lit today by a clockwork timer rather than a torch.) Lighters like Phil were once familiar figures on the London streets. Prostitutes might pay them *not* to light the lamps in corners convenient for their business, and those needing to rise early might ask the lighter to knock on their doors during the dawn round when the lamps were extinguished.

By the 1840s, supplies were working well enough for gas to make a tentative appearance in the urban home. From this point on, any British town with more than 2,500 inhabitants usually had a gasworks, and gas lighting became a must-have in middle-class living rooms. One writer in the *Englishwoman's Domestic Magazine* even recommended that parties 'must always be given by gas light . . . if it be daylight outside, you must close the shutters and draw the curtains', the better to show off your gasoliers.

But the inexpensive and slightly lowbrow connotations of gas meant that it was still shunned by the upper classes: they stayed loyal to candles. At the same time, billing remained a quarterly affair, placing it out of the reach of the truly poor. It was only in the 1890s that the gas companies, worried about losing business to their new rivals selling electricity, introduced the 'penny in the slot' meter. One Victorian cartoon shows a desperate father trying to commit suicide by sticking his head in the gas oven. His concerned family beg him to put off the deed until the cheaper evening gas rate starts.

Gas must have provided a quite stunning improvement in light levels and, therefore, in people's ability to entertain themselves in the evenings. It nevertheless had many drawbacks. There were frequent explosions and fires; it was not uncommon for gas leaks to be investigated by the light of a match. Also, gas consumed the oxygen in a room's air, replacing it with black and noxious deposits. The aspidistra became such a popular plant because it was one of the few that survived in oxygen-starved conditions. The reason that Victorian ladies have such a reputation for fainting is partly because of tight lacing, but also because of the shortage of oxygen in gas-lit drawing rooms. In 1904, Hermann Muthesius still noticed 'a widespread dislike of gas-lighting', and its confinement to 'halls and domestic offices for fear of the dirt caused by soot and the recognition of the danger to health that arises from piping gas into the room'. (Clearly the health of the servants working in the domestic offices was a lesser concern for homeowners.)

The arrival of the cleaner but more expensive electricity in the 1880s gave householders a choice. Some people started to have their gas pipes and fittings converted to take electricity instead. Yet a light bulb cost the same as the average week's wages, and you needed to have your own generator. The armaments manufacturer Sir William Armstrong was a prominent pioneer of electric light and installed a small hydro-electric plant in his Northumberland home, Cragside. His innovation was rivalled across the Atlantic by several Fifth Avenue millionaires who also built their own small generators in 1880s New York. In 1881, Mrs Cornelius Vanderbilt even went to a ball dressed as an electric light. But these early adopters ran the risk of accidents. After her electrical system at home caught fire, Mrs Vanderbilt panicked and had it taken out.

The widespread adoption of electricity was delayed for many years because each generator produced a different level of output. This meant that different towns, or even individual houses, had their own currents. Manufacturers were therefore reluctant to invest in developing fittings because there was no national market for their products. It would take the creation of the National Grid in the 1930s to allow electricity to achieve ubiquity.

The other twentieth-century transformation in living-room light levels was the use of glass on a scale not seen since the huge windows of the strangely proto-modern Hardwick Hall. Natural light was worshipped by twentieth-century architects, who liked to blur the boundaries between indoors and out. 'The spaciousness of the modern sitting-room is not limited by the enclosing walls, but is extended to the garden and distant landscape by means of large openings – windows, loggias or sun-porches,' wrote F. R. S. Yorke in a round-up of the latest architectural developments in 1934. He was describing one-off, architect-designed houses for the rich, but these values would also be seen in post-war affordable housing. The influential SPAN houses produced by Eric Lyons from the 1950s, for example, have their own enclosed garden courtyards separated from the living room merely by glass, and are full of natural light. 'The convenience and simplicity, and indeed much of the charm of the modern interior are due to open planning,' Yorke added, describing a trend which defined the twentieth-century living room.

Oddly, the modern open-plan house represents a return to medieval times, when houses had a central, flexible and spacious hall. The difference lies in the absence of people: today a quarter of American households consist of just one person, and a further 50 per cent of them consist of couples living without children.

This leads us on to the biggest-ever change in the history of home life: the disappearance, in the early twentieth century, of the servants.

28 – 'Speaking' to the Servants

No relations in society are so numerous and universal
as those of Masters and Servants ... so it is proportionally
important that they should be well defined and understood.
Samuel and Sarah Adams, *The Complete Servant*, 1825

Our review of living-room technology has very quickly revealed
that pre-twentieth-century houses of any pretension whatsoever
simply could not operate without their servants to carry coal
and to clean. Perhaps the biggest difference of all between then
and now is the absence of this particular variety of intimacy in
the home. People in the past took it completely for granted that
they'd have non-family members living cheek by jowl beneath
their roof.

In Tudor and Stuart times, between a quarter and a half of
the entire population were employed in domestic service at some
point in their lives, and the bond between master and servant was
one of the most important social relationships. Being a servant
wasn't something of which to be ashamed: you gained protection
and honour by association with your own particular lord. You
would be glad to wear his badge or even a cloak in his household
colour, a uniform called a 'livery' because it was part of a living
allowance that also included bed and board. People were proud
to serve the man who in return met their physical needs.

Clearly this attitude was long gone by the beginning of the twentieth century, but in 1900 domestic service remained the single largest source of female employment, and liveries were still worn. Henry Bennett, a footman who started work at Chatsworth House in 1928, was issued with several sets: a state livery, 'one semi-state and a black suit yearly, and a black mackintosh, and a white coat and cap for car work . . . we had to breech when over six for dinner'. Yet Bennett was a living anachronism; domestic revolution was on its way. In the most significant upheaval in a thousand years of domestic history, by 1951 a mere 1 per cent of households had a full-time residential domestic servant.

Once upon a time masters and servants were more than used to each other's company. In the medieval house with its common hall they simply couldn't escape from each other, and ate all their meals together. In such crowded circumstances servants were constantly enjoined to discretion, sobriety and the avoidance of gossip. The members of Henry VIII's privy chamber, his most intimate servants, were instructed to be 'loving together' and not to ask questions: 'they must leave enquiry where the King is or goeth, not grudging, mumbling or talking of the King's pastime, late or early going to bed, or anything done by His Grace'.

These people close to a great nobleman, serving him in even quite menial ways, were themselves well-born. One Elizabethan, noticing that his fellow gentlemen were less and less willing to work as servants and that the ties linking households were loosening, deeply regretted the passing of the great medieval household. He mourned for the 'decay of Hospitality and Good House-keeping' in elegiac terms: 'The Golden world is past and gone.'

Yet even 350 years later, a houseful of servants could find a sense of community and pleasure in each other's company. Stanley Ager, a butler, remembered his first day of work as a 'hall boy' at a Worcestershire country house in 1922. Although he was the lowest of all forty servants working there, 'everyone was friendly'. Gradually he climbed to the lofty position of butler. In his retirement, he wrote: 'I still miss the staff. They fought among themselves and they always caused me far more trouble than the Lord and Lady – yet I miss them most of all.'

The decline in the status of household service was linked to the growing requirement for privacy on the part of the family, and gradually servants began to spend less time with their masters. In the seventeenth century, this took architectural form: the backstairs, the servants' separate dining hall and the bell to summon service all made their first appearance in the home. In the medieval house there had been no need for bells: you simply shouted for a servant who would have spent all of his or her time well within earshot.

In the 1760s, Hannah Glasse advised young housemaids to become soundless, like ghosts: 'learn to walk softly, and not disturb the family'. Hers was the century in which the green baize door appeared as a potent symbol of the division between above and below stairs. Its green felt covering was intended to eliminate any noise from the servants' quarters. By 1864, the Victorian architect Robert Kerr could write that 'the family constitute one community, the servants another . . . each class is entitled to shut its door upon the other, and be alone . . . on both sides this privacy is highly valued'.

In class-conscious Victorian times, these attitudes led eventually to hideous extremes, such as the fifth Duke of Portland insisting that his servants turn to face the wall as he passed (though he did also have a personality disorder). His household at Welbeck Abbey was most unusual, remaining almost medievally huge and male-dominated: even in 1900 it still contained 320 staff, including four 'royal' footmen to wait on the family, two 'steward's room' footmen to wait on the other servants, a 'schoolroom' footman, a valet, a wine butler, under-butler, master of the servants' hall, two pageboys, a hall porter, two hall boys and six odd-job men.

When it came to the relations between family and servants, the views of Mrs Beeton, household manager extraordinaire, grate upon modern ears. 'A servant is not to be seated', she wrote, 'in his master's or mistress's presence; nor offer any opinion, unless asked for it; not even to say "goodnight" or "good morning", except in reply to that salutation.'

No wonder servants throughout the nineteenth century became increasingly demoralised and unhappy in their roles. Eric Horne, a retired manservant, gave a welcome glance into the heart that beats beneath the butler's impassive waistcoat when he described his discouragement: 'I felt that I was gradually going into a net, and losing all liberty in life: the constraint became almost unbearable, but what could I do? . . . I knew nothing but gentleman's service wherewith to get a living.' The head butler at Cliveden House in Berkshire, Edwin Lee, likewise remembers a lonely life:

It may seem strange for me to say that when I was surrounded by so many people, but I was like the captain of a ship, there was no one to whom I could go with my problems . . . I received little praise if things went well. I remember once saying this to her ladyship.
  'What do you expect me to do, Lee, keep patting you on the back?'
  Given an answer like that I never laid myself open again.

Lower down the social scale, economics still dictated a much closer proximity between employer and employee. In the parsonage where the Brontë sisters grew up, there was just one servant, old Tabby. Charlotte, aged twelve, described a typical morning at Haworth: 'Tabby the servant is washing up the breakfast things, and Anne, my youngest sister . . . is kneeling on a chair, looking at some cakes which Tabby has been baking for us. Emily is in the parlour, brushing the carpet.' This communal, almost medieval mingling of family and servants brought them all very close together. When Tabby broke her leg in 1836, the three sisters insisted that she stay in bed while they looked after her and did her work.

Among the many different specialist roles to be found in a large establishment, the footman's duties are particularly interesting because they are quite hard to define. His job was essentially to look impressive and add grandeur to the household. In the early 1900s, former footman Eric Horne recalled 'an old titled lady in Eaton Place who was very proud of her two tall matching footmen. When she was engaging them she would make them walk backwards and forwards across the room to see if she liked their action, just as though she was buying a horse.' Footman Henry Bennett was required to change his own name (Ernest) to Henry, for the convenience of his employers. He was replacing a man named 'Long Henry' who had been an impressive 6 ft 2 ins tall. Records of footmen's wages show that those over 5 ft 6 ins often received a higher wage than their shorter colleagues.

The footman passed many of his working hours enduring the mind-numbing tedium of 'waiting'. Being in waiting meant standing, smartly, ready to take a message or bring a tray or open a door as people came through. In 1905, Diana Cooper described an aged footman at Belvoir Castle whose job was to beat the dinner gong, 'feebly brandishing the padded-knobbed stick with which he struck it. Every corridor had to be warned and the towers too, so I suppose he banged on and off for ten minutes, thrice daily.'

This must have provided nothing like the job satisfaction of making a meal or producing a pile of clean clothes. 'The life of a gentleman's servant is something like that of a bird shut up in cage,' wrote footman William Tayler in 1837. 'The bird is well housed and well fed, but deprived of liberty, and liberty is the dearest and sweetes[t] object of all Englishmen.'

But to describe their duties as entirely demeaning and nebulous is to underestimate the sense of theatre, excitement and occasion that footmen brought to their employers' lives. Jonathan Swift, writing in the eighteenth century, confirmed that the footman was 'the fine gentleman of the family, with whom all the maids are in love'. In the previous century, we hear that the 'running footman' who delivered urgent messages or ran alongside his master's coach was always a fine physical specimen, and that 'the waiting-woman hath the greatest fancy to him when he is in his close trousers'. With Gordon Grimmett, third footman at Longleat House in Wiltshire,

it was the theatre of service which appealed to him, the dressing up in livery with almost period movement and big gestures . . . the throwing of the voice when announcing the guests, their beautiful clothes and jewels, the style, the grace.

This is a theme often returned to in footmen's memoirs. Even in the twentieth century they express a nostalgic fondness for the pageantry of the past:

There's something artistically satisfying in wearing full livery and carrying it well. It encourages graceful movement and gesture and adds a bit of theatre and glamour to the occasion. With the shift towards the ordinary and the tawdry we could well do with a bit of it in our lives today.

In due course, though, industry and retail, with their higher wages and increased social stimulation, became increasingly attractive to the kind of young men or girls who would once have thought to become servants. Mary Hunter, who started work at Cragside House in Northumberland in 1920, had an intimate insight into the dramatic decline in household service. When she joined the household as a fourteen-year-old under-parlour-maid, there were twenty-four servants. When she left it, seven years later, she was one of only three staff remaining.

By modern times servants were no longer treated with the respect they'd received when they were often young members of minor branches of the master's own family. The Victorian cook Hannah Cullwick bitterly resented having to ask for 'every little thing' she needed out of the family's locked larder: 'it's inconvenient – besides I think it shows so little trust & treating the servant like a child'. Mrs Beeton, on the other hand, made it quite clear that mistresses *ought* to treat servants as inferior beings: 'a lady should never allow herself to forget the important duty of watching over the moral and physical welfare of those beneath her roof'.

So, in the living rooms of a house, orders were given and received. The morning room, however, was the place particularly used for chastisement or praise. Here servants were interviewed for a position, and givings-of-notice and sackings took place. It's a room that witnessed many tears as futures were made and broken. And this was often women's work. In her marriage, the woman was clearly supposed to be subordinate. As William Cobbett put it in 1829, a husband 'under command' of his wife was 'the most contemptible of God's creatures' – in fact, he might as well kill himself. A wife, though, had the duty to command the household's servants. Even the put-upon fifteen-year-old addressed in *Le Ménagier de Paris* had this responsibility: 'you must be mistress of the house, giver of orders, inspector, ruler, and sovereign administrator over the servants . . . teach, reprove and punish the staff'. As Mrs Beeton put it, more than 350 years later, 'As with the COMMANDER OF AN ARMY, or the leader of any enterprise, so it is with the mistress of the house.'

At one time the heads of the departments of a great medieval household had been men of status and dignity. The few women employed were in very lowly positions indeed. A fourteenth-century reference to a 'servant-woman' recommends that she be 'kept low under the yoke of thraldom', and be given only 'gross meat' to eat. Yet as household sizes declined, women took over their management. In one sense eighteenth-century housekeeping was slowly losing status and becoming quite separate from the all-important sphere of public life. 'Female Virtues are of a

Munificent mentor or terrible tyrant? The mistress of a household might perform either role. Here a lady presents her maid with a cook book, and another servant receives instruction in the art of carving

Domestic turn. The Family is the proper Province for Private Women to Shine in,' insisted a writer in *The Spectator*. At the same time, though, to remember that women were the managers of domestic enterprises is to accord them more power and respect than many would recognise from a cursory glance at life in the Georgian age. Women had the power to hire and fire. 'People acquire and get rid of servants just as they do Horses,' runs one account of household management written in 1850. Women made purchasing decisions and commissioned contractors to provide cleaning or fumigation services (such as that offered by Mr Tiffin, 'bug-destroyer to Her Majesty'). A slap-dash housewife might be duped into significant loss of cash or face by duplicitous servants: 'merits greatly exaggerated – defects studiously concealed – ages falsified by the Servants themselves'.

Part of the modern misperception of housewives as tame, use-less creatures stems from the idea that women were supposed to disguise their managerial status and powers. US First Lady Letitia Christian Tyler ran the president's household almost invis-ibly in the 1840s: she 'attends to and regulates all the household affairs', but most commendably, 'all so quietly that you can't tell when she does it'. And despite their low profile, Letitia and her contemporaries actually had considerable authority over the behaviour of their families and dependants. 'A clean, fresh, and well-ordered house exercises over its inmates a moral, no less than a physical influence,' wrote one Victorian parson, 'and has a direct tendency to make the members of the family sober, peaceable, and considerate of the feelings.'

By the nineteenth century the woman was perfectly well estab-lished as this hard-working but unruffled 'angel in the house', beneficent, caring, all-controlling. Her cares were to be kept to herself rather than shared with her busy, important, money-earning husband. In her drawing room, the Victorian wife was advised to talk to her husband about what she'd read in the newspaper rather than bother him with problems with the serv-ants or the sickness of their children.

In that sense the living room was a place of repressed feelings. And so it remains today, as families struggle to answer the con-tentious question of who should do the housework.

29 – So Who Vacuums Your Living Room?

You will find, my young friends, that great care is necessary
to clean furniture, and make it look well.
Thomas Cosnett, *The Footman's Directory* (London, 1825)

The house-proud but depressed heroine of *The Women's Room*
(1978) has conflicting feelings about housework, enjoying it and
hating it simultaneously. In her kitchen, 'clean china pieces . . .
gleam and reflect. The beauty was her doing.' But she worked
endlessly to achieve it: 'cleanliness and order were her life, they
had cost her everything'. She eventually presented her husband
with a bill for all the services she had rendered him, and ran off
to study literature at Harvard instead.

The rise of the working professional woman in the late twentieth century has brought the mistress–servant relationship
back into existence in many middle-class homes after a hundred years. Both parties in the relationship are usually female
now. In the Tudor royal household, though, before the fall in
the status of such work, it was male scullions who swept the
courtyards twice a day, removing 'corruption and all unclean-
ness out of the King's house' because it was 'very noisome and
displeasant unto all the noblemen'. The 'sweeping of houses
and chambers ought not to be done as long as any honest man
is within the precincts of the house', advised the Tudor doctor,

Andrew Boorde, 'for the dust doth putrify the air'.

Keeping your house clean was essential for health, but also part of presenting the right image to the world. 'The entrance to your home . . . must be swept early in the morning and kept clean,' wrote the author of the fourteenth-century *Ménagier de Paris*. The difficulty of cleaning up after a huge household was one of the things that kept great medieval noblemen on the move, trekking from residence to residence every few weeks. During the reign of Mary I, the court became trapped at Hampton Court Palace because the queen was suffering a phantom pregnancy and could not travel. While Mary endured the 'swelling of the paps and emission of milk', the courtiers gathered for the expected birth. The squalor grew; the garderobes overflowed into the moat. The conditions grew so foul that tension between the English courtiers and the Spanish supporters of Mary's husband Philip reached boiling point. Philip had to threaten that the first Spaniard to draw his sword would have his right hand cut off. Cleaning could therefore be a fraught, important issue, whereas today it consumes so much less of a household's time and energy that we tend to give it little thought.

Of course, the economics of the labour market meant that right up into the twentieth century it was simply cheaper to employ humans to do many household jobs. The Royal Society was presented with the idea of a washing machine (for 'rinsing fine linen in a whip cord bag, fastened at one end and strained by a wheel cylinder at the other') by Sir John Hoskins as early as 1677, but the first patents for such machines were not filed until more than a hundred years later. So those who could afford it sent their clothes out to an industrial laundry.

It was a woman, Melusina Fay Peirce, who first proposed the concept of co-operative housing in 1869, and her motivation was to abolish the burden of individual cooking, washing and sewing. Living communally should minimise 'all the waste of ignorant and unprincipled servants and sewing women, all the dust, steam and smell from the kitchen, and all the fatigue and worry of mind caused by the thousand details of our modern housekeeping'. Unfortunately, though, the experimental communal laundry she set up in Cambridge, Massachusetts, collapsed for want of efficiency.

When it did take off, co-operative living was inspired by convenience, not by high-minded ideas like Peirce's. The Ansonia on Broadway became America's most advanced 'apartment hotel', expensive but ultra-convenient. As well as enjoying their own flats, residents could use the swimming pool, Turkish baths, storage facilities, car-repair shop, grocery store, barber, manicure studio, safe-deposit boxes and cold-storage room for furs in the basement. They could eat in their shared dining room on the seventeenth floor, and the whole building was linked by a remarkable system of pneumatic tubes.

But living in a hotel to eliminate the housework didn't really catch on outside the biggest and richest cities. In fact, the 'big bold twentieth-century boarding house' of Jazz Age New York was criticised by the *Architectural Record* as being inimical to proper family life, 'the consummate flower of domestic irresponsibility'. If a woman wasn't going to clean her own house, the *Record* argued, what on earth was she going to do instead? The apartment hotel was 'the most dangerous enemy American domesticity has had to encounter'.

Few people would make such a claim today, so there must be some other reason for the inescapable fact that throughout Western society households have been shrinking, not growing, in recent centuries. Households in the West have declined from an average of 5.8 members in 1790 to the current 2.6 in America today. It's partly because labour-saving devices have made economies of scale in cooking, washing and cleaning less and less attractive. But there's something else to consider as well.

The Harvard legal scholar Robert C. Ellickson points to 'transaction cost' as an alternative explanation for these relatively small-scale units. This is the notional cost incurred every time an extra body is added to the household, as newcomers need to invest time and effort in acquiring the knowledge that allows the organisation to run at its financial and emotional optimum. In larger groups decision-making becomes more costly and complicated. Only in times of upheaval and danger does an extended household present an advantage, hence the enormous resident entourages of medieval warlords or the kibbutzim in Israel's early years. (The kibbutz still exists, yet, significantly for Ellickson's argument, its members now demand less communal dining and more private space.)

And so each small household today sees to its own vacuuming or laundry or rat-catching, and men and women argue constantly about whose gender bears the heaviest burden. Maybe, as the world becomes a more hostile place with shortages of water and oil, we will return to the larger units of living favoured in dangerous medieval times. And perhaps then the basic activities of cleaning and preparing food will rise in status once again.

30 – Sitting Up Straight

When we rejoined the ladies in the drawing room, Princess took me by the arm and hand and led me into a corner. Most intimate and cosy. Is flirtatious. I tried not to press her hand back, lest *lèse-majesté*.

James Lees-Milne on meeting Princess
Michael of Kent, 23 August 1983

When there are guests in your living room, there's always been a tension between paying respect – which means keeping at a suitable distance from another individual's personal space – and offering intimacy. As a form of flattery intimacy trumps respect, because it implies the dropping of barriers and the creation of trust. Hence the informal barbecues for world leaders that George W. Bush used to host at Camp David.

Henry VIII would likewise drape an arm round the shoulders of a favoured ambassador or courtier. But then – just like a lion – he could round upon and maul a man just as soon as he became overfamiliar: the king 'could not abide to have any man stare in his face when he talked with them'.

This knife-edge that has to be walked between respect and intimacy creates another danger: manners that are simply too nice. Then as now, being overly well-mannered is unmanly and debilitating. In a Stuart snuff shop full of fops, 'bows and cringes of the newest mode were here exchanged twixt friend and friend, with wonderful exactness'. It's a recognisable description of high camp. Behaviour books from every period recommend striking a balance between manners and brutality, but no one can ever define exactly what that balance should be. Learning it at the knee of one's mother is the mark of a true gentleman, and the pretenders who have to read about such things in books never quite catch up.

In his classic *Über den Prozess der Zivilisation* (1939), Norbert Elias made a striking link between fancy manners and political absolutism. He traced a path through history which saw societies dominated by independent warriors, or knights, gradually give way to courtly ones, in which a single dominant figure lords it over everyone else. The knights were uncouth and violent – as they had to be, to win power. They used brute physical force to seize the food and land to which they felt entitled. The courtiers of an absolutist king did not win their power through force, because the physical needs of the upper classes were now met by a taxation system. Instead, they competed with each other through their exquisite, nuanced and civilised behaviour.

If we follow in Elias's footsteps from the medieval to the modern period, we can chart the arrival of new concepts such as 'shame' or 'embarrassment', emotions that had a much weaker hold on medieval psyches. Elias describes 'shame' as 'a fear of social degradation . . . which arises characteristically on those occasions when a person who fears lapsing into inferiority can avert this danger neither by direct physical means nor by any other form of attack'. Bowing, hat etiquette, proposing toasts, dancing: all provided a Tudor or Stuart with new means of humiliating his enemies or winning admiration from his friends.

In the grand, formal and stately great chambers of Hardwick Hall, or its seventeenth-century successors, one was expected to behave in a grand, formal and stately manner. It was unthinkable for a servant on duty in these rooms to address his master without making a bow. Good servants were expected to be:

> so full of courtesy as not a word shall be spoken by their masters to them, or by them to their masters, but the knee shall be bowed . . . their master shall not turn sooner than their hat will be off.

And this kind of behaviour was not just for servants. The fifteen-year-old wife addressed in the advice book *Le Ménagier de Paris* is told, literally, not to look at another man, or even another woman:

> Keep your head upright, eyes downcast and immobile. Gaze four *toises* (about 24 feet) straight ahead and toward the ground, without looking or glancing at any man or woman to the right or left, or looking up, or in a fickle way casting your gaze about.

In the reception rooms of a Tudor house, it would be equally unthinkable for two people of different rank to be seated in the same kind of chair: inevitably the more elaborate chair, placed nearer to the fire, would be occupied by the more senior person. Even walking up and down the long gallery had its own terms of engagement, described in this essay called *Rules to be Observed in Walking with Persons of Honour* (1682):

> If you walk in a Gallery . . . be sure to keep the left hand; and without affectation or trouble to the Lady, recover that side at every turn. If you make up the third in your walk, the middle is the most honourable place, and belongs to the best in the company, the right hand is next, and the left in the lowest estimation.

And yet it's worth remembering that all this was a performance for the benefit of others. When alone, people could, and did, behave more naturally. Off duty, you might 'loosen your garters or your buckles, lie down upon a couch, or go to bed, and welter in an easy chair . . . negligences and freedoms which one can take only when quite alone'. Queen Elizabeth I, always very conscious of her image, would never allow herself to be seen in an un-queenly state. She had the windows overlooking the Privy Garden at Hampton Court blocked up so that on cold mornings, when she liked to lollop about vigorously in the gardens 'to catch her a heat', she could do so unobserved.

Britain's political revolution of the seventeenth century caused another revolution: in body language. Charles I was defeated in battle and eventually executed by his own subjects for pushing his royal prerogative too far. During the period after his defeat, when the English Commonwealth replaced monarchical rule, a new form of greeting began to appear that reflected the fact that the social hierarchy had been destroyed. The doffing of the hat to one's superior was replaced by a form of greeting which assumed that both parties were equals: England's new, democratic rulers prided themselves upon refusing to bow, insisting instead upon shaking hands.

Once absolute political rule began to decline, the most extreme excesses of courtly behaviour and manners also lay in the past. Even after Charles II had been 'restored' to England's throne, a series of further revolutions saw the power of the Stuart kings eroded in the much more limited job descriptions of the Hanoverian kings. Likewise, the new, sociable age of the eighteenth century was less formal than the previous one in its behaviour. The Georgians aimed to create an atmosphere of relaxation rather than stern stateliness: as Lord Chesterfield put it, 'one ought to know how to come into a room, speak to people, and answer them, without being out of countenance, or without embarrassment'.

Chesterfield still paid serious attention to body language, but now the emphasis was on elegance rather than formality. 'I desire you will particularly attend to the graceful motion of your arms,' he recommended, in 'the manner of putting on your hat, and giving your hand'. Conduct was even more relaxed across the Atlantic. 'Formal compliments and empty ceremonies' did nothing for Martha Washington, chatelaine of the US's presidential household from 1789. 'I am fond only of what comes from the heart,' she said.

Clothing also dictates body language, and for women the wearing of stays encouraged a stiff and upright carriage. It's handy to have something to do with the hands placed on display by the wearing of hooped skirts, so Georgian accessories were brought into service: 'snuff, or the fan supplies each pause of chat'. The French today are much bigger kissers than the English, but this was not so in the eighteenth century. Then, a Swiss visitor wrote home from England: 'let not this mode of greeting scandalise you . . . it is the custom of this country, and many ladies would be displeased should you fail to salute them thus'.

In the nineteenth century, though, a certain pursing of the lips occurred, and the free and easy Georgian manners began to be seen as vulgarly uninhibited. Ironically, it was partly the medical advances of the Enlightenment which seemed to push women back into a more ceremonial age. The realisation that women were fundamentally different from, rather than a weaker version of, men led to the idea that ladies were fragile things needing constant protection. This was achieved by turning attention to decorum and manners. Ladies were considered to have mislaid the ability to make jokes, or even to walk; thus the now-lost art of leaning upon a gentleman's arm was born. This new morality

Hints on how to bow, from *A Complete Practical Guide to the Art of Dancing* (1863)

brought to an end the kind of entertainments that had enlivened Georgian drawing rooms. There was no more dubious gambling or dancing. 'Waltzing is so dangerous', wrote the anonymous author of *Advice to Governesses* (1827), 'that I wonder how a prudent mother can tolerate the amusement.'

In the late Victorian period, America and Europe clash in Edith Wharton's historical novel *The Buccaneers*. 'The friendly bustle of the Grand Union, the gentlemen coming in from New York . . . with the Wall Street news' were sadly lacking in the cold, aristocratic British drawing rooms which a group of young American heiresses nevertheless wish to conquer. The young conquistadors found themselves 'chilled by the silent orderliness' of the British household. The maid-servants were 'painfully unsociable', and they 'were too much afraid of the cook ever to set foot in the kitchen'.

This makes British drawing rooms sound stiff and retrograde, but they had at least become the part of the house dominated by women. Once, the master of the house had controlled his family's social life, just as he did its financial or reproductive plans, but somewhere along the way men relinquished their role as hosts. In 1904, Hermann Muthesius explained that

the Englishwoman is the absolute mistress of the house, the pole round which its life revolves . . . the man of the house, who is assumed to be engrossed in his daily work, is himself to some extent her guest when at home. So the drawing-room, the mistress's throne-room, is the rallying-point of the whole life of the house.

Muthesius also noted that the woman 'keeps an eye on all exchanges with the outer world, issues invitations and receives and entertains guests', and this is the topic of the next chapter.

31 – A Bright, Polite Smile

Everyone complains of the pressure of the company,
yet all rejoice at being so divinely squeezed.
François de La Rochfoucauld
on London parties, 1784

Everyone has seen the bright, polite and slightly false smile pasted upon the lips of a host and hostess. Now we move on to the actual hour of a living-room performance, from the amazing conspicuous consumption of the Stuart masque to the formal Victorian fifteen-minute call.

Being sociable has always been something of a duty, and the line between the convivial and the tedious is a fine one. Eleanor Roosevelt calculated that in the year of 1939 she had shaken hands with 14,046 people. 'My arms ached,' she recollected, 'my shoulders ached, my back ached, and my knees and feet seemed to belong to someone else.' But the people whose hands were shaken were doubtless pleased with their experience. Generosity, gift-giving and hospitality are essential for holding society together.

How to entertain your guests? Well, Tudor or Stuart guests might have been treated to a formal masque, a kind of dramatic and musical entertainment involving professional and amateur performers alike. Henry VIII thought it amusing to appear in disguise at one of Cardinal Wolsey's parties, and to make the ladies dance with him. On another court occasion, Anne Boleyn made her debut in a masque called '*Le Chateau Vert*' in the character of 'Perseverance' (this turned out to be most appropriate in light of the subsequent lengths to which she would go to bag the king). Singing or musical entertainments were always popular, and Henry VIII poached some of the best singers from Cardinal Wolsey's boys' choir for his own. Masques continued into the next century, getting more and more lavish or even debauched: at one performance for the rather seedy James I, the actress playing the Queen of Sheba smeared cream and jelly all over the drunken King Christian of Denmark. The two ladies supposed to be playing Faith and Hope drank too much and were found spewing behind the scenes.

Francis Willoughby's seventeenth-century *Book of Games* is full of bright ideas for cheaper parties, describing the rules of backgammon and 'ticktack' and giving instructions for playing cards, beginning with the very manufacture of the cards themselves: take '3 or 4 pieces of white paper pasted together and made very smooth that they may easily slip from one another, and be dealt & played. If they grow dank, they must be dried and rubbed one by one to make them slip again.'

As well as creating a lot of labour, the open fire led to a whole lost slice of life: the art of amusing yourself while warming yourself in low light levels. Indeed, there is a whole genre of caricature which might be described as 'person caught in the undignified position of warming their naked backside against an open fire'. In such a place, at such a time, the intimate art of storytelling thrived, as did silly games like the 'Laughing Chorus' described in the *Young Ladies' Treasure Book* (1880). To be played 'round a good fire in the long winter evenings', 'the person in the corner by the fire says, "Ha!" and the one next to him repeats, "Ha!" and so on . . . No one who has not played this game can realise its mirth-provoking capacities.'

Francis Willoughby suggests simpler seventeenth-century

games suitable for firelight conditions, such as capping rhymes. He commemorates one quick-witted Mr Booker, who, when challenged to find a rhyme to 'porringer', came up with 'The King had a Daughter & he gave the Prince of Orange her.' Now, one might play such a brain game in the car, but not at home, as the modern living room is packed with other, less effortful forms of stimulation.

In the noble great chambers of houses like the Elizabethan Hardwick Hall, the parties generally remained stiff and formal, with people staying in their proper places. As we've already seen, though, the mid-eighteenth century saw London townhouses like Norfolk House acquire state apartments planned upon a circuit rather than a straight line and which were thrown open for processional parties. The mingling of different ranks in an informal manner became more common as the eighteenth century passed. Sitting upon chairs arranged in a perfect oval for a measured discussion, a formation central to the drawing rooms of the baroque age, fell out of fashion. 'All the ladies sitting in a formal circle is universally the most obnoxious to conversation,' claimed a character in a novel of 1817, 'here I am like a bird in a circle of chalk that dare not move as much as its head or its eyes.'

So great became the drawing room's emphasis on sociability that by the nineteenth century some visitors were bored almost senseless by the long, relentlessly chatty days common to nineteenth-century house parties. 'This day we have been all sitting together in the drawing room going on with our various little employments,' wrote Maria Edgeworth in 1819. These entertainments included making puppets, copying pictures and sorting ribbons, but there was the frustrated 'Fanny in the library by her recluse philosophical self for some time – Then joining the vulgar herd in the drawing room'. Likewise, Prince Pückler-Muskau, who visited England between 1826 and 1828, found that he couldn't even go to his own room to write a letter because it was 'not usual, and therefore surprises and annoys people'. And so it went on, in sociable country houses, into the twentieth century. Here's James Lees-Milne visiting Wallington, in Northumberland:

After dinner I am worn out, and long for bed. But no. We have general knowledge questions. Lady T. puts the questions one after another with lightning rapidity . . . all most alarming to a tired stranger.

The art of conversation received a blow in the twentieth century. 'The amount of time in the home has in recent years been much reduced through such innovations as the cinema, cheap travel, playing and watching games, careers for women, crèches, and so on,' wrote F. R. S. Yorke in 1937. For those still spending the occasional evening at home, the valve radio became the new focus of the living room (plate 30). Now the 'host' of the evening's entertainment might not even be present in the room, but presiding over an event recorded elsewhere.

The British Broadcasting Corporation was created in 1922 from a consortium of the six biggest wireless manufacturers, including Marconi and General Electric. The transmission of nightly BBC programmes provided people with a social, not a solitary, experience, as they listened with friends and family. By 1925, there were 1.5 million licence holders. The BBC published pamphlets on topics such as how to form a 'radio circle', or listening club; on 'How To Conduct a Wireless Discussion Group'; and even 'How to Listen'. 'Listen as carefully at home as you do in a theatre or concert hall,' its author instructed the would-be listener. 'It is just as important to you to enjoy yourself at home as at the theatre.'

The first regular television broadcasts were made in 1932, a year in which seventy-six half-hour programmes went out. But no one was sure how many living rooms they reached. In 1933, viewers were asked: 'The BBC is most anxious to know the number of people who are actually seeing this television programme. Will those who are looking in send a postcard marked "Z" to Broadcasting House immediately?'

And TV was much slower to catch on than radio had been. It was the Coronation of 1953 that brought the set into many living rooms, as many people bought theirs especially for the occasion. People rushed round to their neighbours' houses (and those who had attempted to keep up with the Joneses by installing an aerial on their roofs to suggest that they too had TV were caught out). The *Radio Times* for Coronation Day devotes only a very small box to television programming, with radio programmes taking up nearly all the space. From 1952, however, the number of radio licences issued finally began to fall, while in the same year TV licences reached 1.5 million. In 1955, the launch of ITV brought adverts into people's living rooms, and also, with the introduction in the 1960s of *Coronation Street*, working-class culture.

The television would change eating habits, bringing them firmly out of the dining room and into the living room. Sofas from the 1950s often had plastic trays clipped onto their arms to hold food or drinks, biscuit manufacturers brought out 'television assortment' tins, and people began to consume their 'TV dinners' in the front room with only forks in their hands, the knives left behind in the drawer.

The television appears to be a supremely modern device, but in fact it takes on the role of the community storyteller or minstrel. Sitting down after the day's work to hear the news, a song sung or a story told is something we have in common with the users of a medieval great hall. Computer games are often blamed for individuals becoming isolated or withdrawn, but multiplayer games are the modern equivalent of the Victorian 'laughing chorus' or the rhyming games which promoted mental agility in the living rooms of the seventeenth century.

Entertaining guests is not necessarily about fun. But without the preparation, trepidation and strain we wouldn't have the most basic social bond of all outside the family: that created by hospitality. First and foremost, it's forged in the living room.

32 – Kissing and Courtship

'Did you ever kiss a boy?'
'You mean really kiss? On the lips?' I asked.
'Yes,' Nancy said impatiently. 'Did you?'
'Not really,' I admitted.
Nancy breathed a sigh of relief. 'Neither did I.'
    Judy Blume, *Are You There God?*
    It's Me, Margaret, 1978

To kiss is not necessarily a romantic act. In medieval times, men exchanged kisses of great portent: of peace, fealty or ceremony. Likewise, a more modern monarch had his or her hand kissed incessantly by supplicants or people accepting honours, right up to the twentieth century. But everyone knew that a medieval man caught kissing a woman who was not his wife had something quite different in mind.

Living rooms from the grand medieval solar to the humble Edwardian boarding-house parlour formed the backdrops to tense but semi-public moments in a person's life. Until the First World War, many young females were not mistresses of their own destiny but had to wait, tense and expectant, while their prospective suitors asked a father's permission before making a proposal. Before that stage was reached, the living room was often the stage for the display of female accomplishments advertising their suitability as potential wives: singing, playing and needlework.

There have always been tales in literature of star-crossed lovers who would have married for love but were parted by fate or society. Even the much-married Henry VIII himself was on an endless, disappointing quest for the one perfect woman with whom he would achieve a blissfully happy ever after. He idolised Anne Boleyn for seven long years before he got her to commit, and was fond of telling people that 'he loved true where he did marry'.

Having said that, though, the king was in a position to make a choice, and most other people were not. The idea that love is the best reason for marriage is quite a modern idea, and one quite specific to the Western world. Historically, in Europe and America (and even today in many cultures elsewhere) marriage usually began as a property arrangement, in its middle part was mostly about raising children, and ended up with love. John Boswell, a historian of homosexuality, notes that on the contrary, marriage in the West today is the other way around. It begins with love, moves on to children, and often ends in disputes about the ownership of property.

Until the Enlightenment, people were supposed to place religious duties above marital ones. A neighbour was worried, Mehitable Parkman told her husband in Salem, New England, in 1683, because 'she fears I love you more than God'. Well-born young ladies of the seventeenth and eighteenth centuries were certainly not allowed the luxury of feelings. Like puppets in a play, they waited placidly while dynastic marriages were sewn up for them by their parents. Elizabeth Spencer, on the other hand, seems unusually proactive and mercenary in outlining her requirements to her fiancé in 1594:

I must have two footmen . . . I would have twenty gowns of apparel . . . I would have to put in my purse £2000 and £200, and so, you to pay my debts. Also I would have £6000 to buy me jewels.

Edmund Harrold, the diary-keeping wig-maker of Manchester, left only nine months between his first wife's death and second marriage, and began courting his third wife only three months after the second wife died. He felt obliged to marry quickly, having been advised to do so by his doctor, by a sermon he heard in church and by his consciousness of his own weaknesses: 'It is every [Chris]tian's duty to mortify their unruly passions and lusts to which ye are most prone. I'm now beginning to be uneasy with myself, and begin to think of women again.' To marry was everyone's duty, except for the aged: 'Of all the passions the old man should avoid a foolish passion for women,' wrote Dr Hill in *The Old Man's Guide to Health and Longer Life* (1764).

Sometimes the occasional heiress took independent action, ran off and entered into a clandestine marriage. The brilliant and scandalous Georgian Lady Mary Wortley Montagu took matters into her own hands like this: 'I tremble for what we are doing. Are you sure you will love me forever? Shall we never repent? I fear, and I hope.' But that was behaviour for the back door and garden gate, by night, not the living room. Her suitor was taken for a highwayman because of his suspicious lurking about outside the house. Given Lady Mary's tremendous and praiseworthy zest for life, it's disappointing to report that her secret marriage did not work out well.

And yet love and emotion need not be entirely absent from our picture of upper-class drawing rooms. Even the macho James Boswell admits that a Georgian male lover may sigh, cry or whimper without shame: 'it is peculiar to the passion of Love, that it supports with an exemption from disgrace, those weaknesses in a man which upon any other occasion would render him utterly contemptible'. Such sighing and crying, though, would be quite inappropriate after a marriage. While he might well be 'supple enough' to kneel and beg for a woman's hand, a proper Englishman would bluster that he could 'never get the muscles of [his] knees to give way afterwards'.

The nineteenth century saw love entering the equation more often, even for the highest in society: Queen Victoria famously proposed to Prince Albert, having made her uncle (who'd proposed the union years before) wait until she was good and ready. Theirs was framed as a love match, and after Albert's death Victoria mourned him for the rest of her life.

Society's lower ranks had the freedom to indulge in a more companionate idea of marriage, and until the seventeenth century weddings were rather informal. They only required a fairly hazy verbal agreement between the two parties to be reached in front of witnesses, followed by sexual consummation. Civil marriage was one of the new and revolutionary practices introduced by the English Commonwealth in the seventeenth century (previously ecclesiastical law had trumped the common law concerning marital relationships). The Puritans of New England were likewise enthusiastic proponents of the idea that marriage was a contract between two people, not a sacrament, and their court records show that women, not men, were more likely to sue for divorce on the grounds of adultery, neglect and cruelty. It seems that the state was a better protector of their rights than the church had been.

By 1694, the English state had decided to make money out of marriage, and a tax was introduced. Clandestine marriage, a ceremony performed in secret so that anyone objecting to the union was given no chance to speak, was gradually stamped out. The Marriage Act of 1753 tightened things up further, with weddings allowed only between 8 a.m. and midday, as part of the Sunday service. This explains why a wedding meal is still known as a 'breakfast': for centuries it took place in the morning.

Although he lived in the age when love was supposed to play a part, Charles Darwin took a scientific and pragmatic view of a marriage proposal. Despite the annoyance of losing the 'freedom to go where one liked' and the 'conversation of clever men at clubs', and of having 'less money for books &c', he decided that 'a nice soft wife on a sofa with a good fire' would be good for his health. So, he concluded, 'Marry Q.E.D.'

33 – Dying (and Attending Your Own Funeral)

My dearest dust, could not thy hasty day
Afford thy drowsy patience leave to stay
One hour longer: so that we might either
Sit up, or go to bed together?
Lady Catherine Dyer's epitaph for
her husband William, 1641

These last chapters have described how people's homes intersected with the great wide world outside. That relationship between public and private life continues even after a person's death.

The age at which people can expect to die has been gradually creeping upwards since Norman times. The median age of everyone in Britain today is thirty-eight, whereas in fourteenth-century society it was just twenty-one. Only 5 per cent of fourteenth-century individuals made it to the advanced age of sixty-five. People in the past therefore were considered to have reached maturity much more quickly. Boys as young as seven were expected to work, and could from that age be hanged for stealing. Youthful societies tend to be more violent, more brutal – but maybe, also, more vigorous and more creative.

But there are also some surprising continuities between today and the past. Even in the Tudor and Stuart periods old age began at fifty or sixty, probably a greater age than one might expect given that children became adults much sooner. We've been misled by the figures for average life expectancy into thinking that everyone expected to die at about forty. They didn't. While people were used to their fellows dying at a young age, this was considered unfortunate. 'Threescore years and ten' was the perceived 'natural' length of a life. Even then the elderly were a significant consumer group, and purchasers of a variety of age-related paraphernalia. Henry VIII had 'gazings', or spectacles, with lenses of rock crystal from Venice, and also a couple of wheelchairs ('chairs called trams').

The sufferings of old people sound similar throughout the centuries, while the complaints about them sound ever thoughtless. The Jacobean Thomas Overbury ranted about the 'putrified breath' of old men, their annoying habit of coughing after each sentence, and of 'wiping their drivelled beards'. 'Elderly gentlewomen are useful persons to make tea, and take snuff, and play low whist,' and not much else, complained the magazine *John Bull* in 1821.

Old age was clearly not only a physical problem but a social one too. Lady Sarah Cowper in the early 1700s sounds remarkably modern when she complains: 'I seem to be laid by with all imaginable contempt as if I were superannuate at 57 past conversation.' Yet she was also (inconsistently) contemptuous about her contemporaries who sought to look younger than their years. One acquaintance

affects the follies and airs of youth, displays her breasts and ears, adorns both with sparkling gems while her eyes look dead, skin shrivell'd, cheeks sunk, shaking head, trembling hands, and all things bid shut up shop.

Women have always been affected more by old age than men. A lifetime of heavy labour and poor diet would have made the effects of the menopause – decreased bone density, excess hair and the loss of teeth – even more exaggerated, so a Tudor woman would have quickly passed from youthful desirability to a witch-like appearance. The medical theory of the four humours worked against them too: once they were no longer producing milk or monthly blood, their bodies were thought to be 'drier' and therefore more like men's. They were considered, 'under the stopping of their monthly melancholic flux', to have turned into second-class men, without men's strength or reason.

After your death your intimate history was still not quite over: you had to experience your own funeral. There was an average of seven days between death and burial, for example, for those buried in the eighteenth-century Christ Church in Spitalfields, London. That final week would be spent in your own living room, and family and friends would come to visit. The Stuart wig-maker, Edmund Harrold, described what happened after the sad death of his wife 'in my arms, on pillows'. His community helped him to make heartbreaking small decisions about her clothing – 'I have given her workday cloth[e]s to mother Bordman and Betty Cook our servant' – and the big one about what to do with her body: 'Now relations thinks best to bury her at [the] meetin[g] place in Plungeon Field, so I will.'

The passing of a medieval earl required the turn-out and line-up of all his friends, servants, supporters, tenants and hangers-on. The remnants of that tradition could still be seen in play at the death of Andrew Cavendish, eleventh Duke of Devonshire, in 2004, when scores of servants lined up along the drive at Chatsworth House to salute his hearse. If you had no friends, your heirs could buy them for you. A staggering 31,968 people attended the funeral of the Bishop of London in 1303; many were paid to turn up. In remote Hertfordshire the ancient custom of 'sin-eating' endured in the 1680s. Poor people would be hired to attend and 'to take upon them all the sins of the party deceased'.

From 1660 it became illegal to be buried in anything other than a woollen shroud. The law was passed to support the British wool industry against the slave-serviced and aggressively expanding cotton industry. The profession of undertaker

The trade card of one of the earliest professional undertakers. They undertook to co-ordinate the coach-hire firm, upholsterer and apothecary, all of whom had previously been commissioned separately

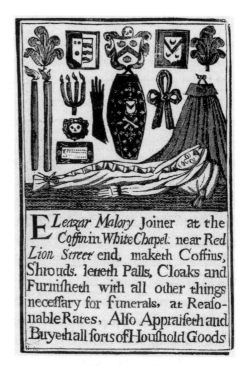

ELeazar Malory Joiner at the Coffin in White Chapel. near Red Lion Street end, maketh Coffins, Shrouds. letteth Palls, Cloaks and Furnisheth with all other things neceffary for funerals, at Reafonable Rates, Alfo Appraifeth and Buyeth all forts of Houfhold Goods

developed in the late seventeenth century to co-ordinate the activities of the coffin-maker, coach-hire company and upholsterer; previously all had been commissioned separately by the dead person's family. The upholsterer was required to hang the living rooms of a house in mourning with black fabric; your heirs might also order a 'funerary hatchment' from the College of Arms (a painted diamond showing your family's arms) to hang over the front door. The 1666 funeral directions for Sir Gervase Clifton, of Clifton Hall, Nottinghamshire, illustrate how his living rooms were decorated for the occasion:

The hall to be hanged with a breadth of black baize
The passage into my lady's bedchamber to be hanged with a breadth of baize
The great dining room, where the better sort of mourners are to be, to be hanged with a breadth of baize.
The body to be there.

Undertakers obviously had an interest in encouraging people to put on a show, and eventually, as a super-successful Victorian profession, they became subject to ridicule for their pompous and overbearing attitudes.

The display of the corpse of an important personage was a hugely important ritual. But sometimes grand funerals could take several weeks to arrange. The actual body would have rotted before then, so a wax or wooden image or 'representation' was used to stand in for it. The tail end of this custom can be seen in the display at Westminster Abbey of the curious waxworks representing Charles II, William III and Mary II, and Queen Anne. Making these funerary figures was the origin of Madame Tussaud's business.

The early embalming of bodies was a very inexact science, and if it went wrong the build-up and explosion of gases in the coffin could be spectacular and damaging. Charles the Bald, the Holy Roman Emperor, died away from home in 877. His attendants 'opened him up', 'poured in such wine and aromatics as they had' and began to carry his body back towards St Denis. But the stench of the putrefying corpse caused them to 'put him in a barrel which they smeared with pitch'. When even this failed, they carried him no further and buried him at Lyons.

Removing the internal organs was a wise precaution against putrefaction: this is why Jane Seymour's viscera are buried at Hampton Court Palace (where she died) rather than at Windsor Castle (where she was officially buried). It was said that Henry VIII's body exploded as it lay overnight in its coffin at Syon Abbey, a staging post on his final journey towards his own burial at Windsor, and that dogs licked up matter dripping onto the church floor. (We might add that dogs also licked up the blood of the biblical Ahab as a punishment for falling under the influence of his pagan wife Jezebel. So perhaps this story was spread about by the supporters of Katherine of Aragon, still trying to get Henry back for his treatment of his first wife.)

Elizabeth I, famously virginal, lost her final battle to prevent her body from being penetrated by a man. Her Privy Councillors, well aware of her wish not to be autopsied, had their attention distracted by the business of proclaiming James I as her successor. Contrary to her orders, Secretary Cecil gave 'a secret warrant to the surgeons', let them into her chamber, and there 'they opened her which the rest of the council afterwards passed over, though they meant it not so'.

These surgeons removed her entrails, but the techniques for preservation were still inadequate. Elizabeth's body was stuffed with herbs, wrapped in cerecloth, nailed up in a coffin and left at the Palace of Whitehall to be watched over by her ladies-in-waiting. But that night Lady Southwell, sitting up in vigil with the dead queen, was horrified to experience the 'body and head brake with such a crack, that [it] splitted the woods'.

A century later, embalming was more effective when Mary II met her death from smallpox in 1694. 'Rich gums and spices to stuff the body' kept her safe from the worst ravages of decay until her funeral. Charles I's corpse also survived well after his execution in 1649. When his coffin was opened in 1813, his body was discovered to have been

carefully wrapped up in cere-cloth, into the folds of which a quantity of unctuous or greasy matter, mixed with resin, as it seemed, had been melted, so as to exclude, as effectually as possible, the external air.

This had been so effective that, when it was unwrapped, 'the left eye, in the first moment of exposure, was open and full, though it vanished almost immediately'.

The surgical advances made by Dr John Hunter in the eighteenth century included a new expertise in preserving cadavers which rendered the wax representation obsolete. One of Dr Hunter's associates, a Dr Martin Van Butchell, had his own dead wife's blood vessels injected with carmine and glass eyes inserted. He kept her in his sitting room and introduced her to visitors to the house. It was only the second Mrs Van Butchell who finally insisted that her predecessor should leave.

Meanwhile, those lower down in society put up with burials that ranged from pragmatic (plague victims dissolved in pits of quicklime) to the ignominious (an unmarked mass grave created after a battle). But a dead person of any pretension would commonly lie in their living room while mourners were summoned by the tolling of the parish church's 'passing bell' to pay their respects, bringing sprigs of rosemary or rue.

It's true that the increasing intricacy of mourning dress and the petty rules regarding its timing began to make the Victorian cult of grief appear overblown and insincere. But the great advantage of the funeral-with-a-cast-of-thousands was its cathartic, crowd-pleasing quality. Now our corpses are shuffled off quietly to the cemetery or incinerator, and we're embarrassed by loss and sorrow. If this book can teach us anything, though, it'll be the fact that this might change yet again.

A person's final appearance in his or her own living room: in an open coffin

Charles, duc d'Orleans, as a prisoner in the Tower of London. He occupies a grand medieval living room, with tiled floor, hangings on the walls, his attendants all standing while the duke is seated.

A later living room, but still with very little furniture, and that very portable. Queen Elizabeth I is receiving ambassadors. Her chair has arms and is placed under a canopy as a mark of her royalty.

The Long Gallery at Hardwick Hall. Its use was three-fold: for displaying portraits of relatives, for exercise and for private conversation. Eavesdroppers could not creep up unobserved in such a big room.

The classic country cottage. This house at the Weald and Downland Museum dates from the early seventeenth century. Its brick-built chimney, a novelty, separates the two main rooms downstairs, and upstairs one bedroom leads into another.

A marvellous gilded 1760s sofa at Kedleston Hall (top left). Decorated with golden mermaids and sea-gods, the sofa was novel for its informality. It allowed two people to sit and chat as equals.

One of the William Morris Company's original wallpaper blocks. Morris's designs involved passing the paper through the printing process up to twenty-two times.

Wightwick Manor, in the West Midlands, furnished with the medieval-inspired products of the William Morris Company.

The middle-class drawing room of Jane and Thomas Carlyle in Chelsea (1857). It was the nerve centre from which Jane struggled to run her household. She ran through thirty-two servants in thirty-four years.

A crowded Victorian sitting room. Creators and creations of an industrial age, Victorian householders prided themselves on their cosy, cluttered – and, to modern eyes, claustrophobic – drawing rooms.

Cleaning the living room was an endless task when open fires and gas lighting constantly produced soot and dirt. But the relative cheapness of Victorian labour meant that machines replaced humans unexpectedly slowly.

Now the radio (top left) or television opened the door to a world outside the home. The fire had finally lost its prime place as the focus of the living room.

'Tea', the *drink*, was a novelty of the late seventeenth century, and was thought rather racy and dangerous. 'Tea', the *meal*, was invented in the nineteenth century to fill the gap between lunch and an ever-later dinner hour.

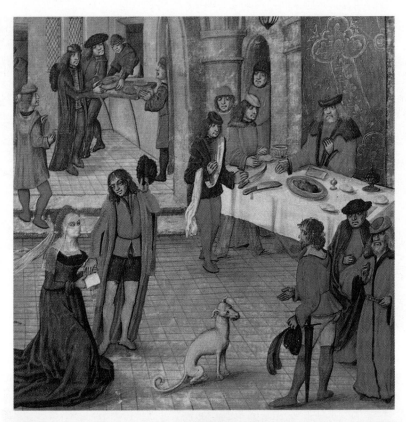

A medieval dining hall. The master eats alone because no one else present was grand enough to sit and share his table. His servants, probably young men from good families, bring dishes to the table from a serving hatch.

The cooks in a royal kitchen were nearly all male. Like a posh restaurant today, the kitchen at Hampton Court was like a high-pressure food factory turning out meals to tip-top standards.

This is 'Whiskey', the last of the spit-dogs. Specially bred, with long bodies and short legs, spit-dogs ran inside a small treadmill which revolved a roasting spit over a fire.

A Georgian table (top left) with a sugar sculpture. It represents the tail end of the history of 'subtleties': decorative models of flowers, fantasies or even buildings made in sugar, which feasted the eye as well as the belly.

The kitchen at the Carlyles' house in Chelsea, both bedroom and workplace for their cook. Dank, dark and gas-lit, the Victorian kitchen crammed into the basement of a tall terraced house seemed worlds away from the airy drawing room above.

A 1930s refrigerator party. Fridge owners invited guests to novelty meals consisting entirely of cold food (and cocktails).

The 'English Rose' kitchen (top right), designed immediately after the Second World War, was intended to use up stock-piled aluminium set aside for the building of Spitfires.

'Back-to-back' houses. More houses backed onto these street-facing ones, surrounding a courtyard that contained everyone's shared privies and the 'brewhouse' or laundry house.

Beddington Zero Energy Development (BedZED) in Surrey contains houses designed to minimise the use of heat and water. The 'chimneys' on the roof are for ventilation and heat exchange, rather than for burning fossil fuels.

PART 4

An Intimate History of the Kitchen

Early censuses didn't count people or houses, they counted 'hearths'. In medieval times, the cooking fire was the essential, central point of a household. For the next few centuries, though, the kitchen was banished, shunted off to an outbuilding or down into a basement, relegated to servants and shunned by the family. Only recently has it come back to take its place at the heart of the home.

Another journey, taking place within the kitchen itself, is from the raw to the cooked. Today we like to have an intimate relationship with our food. We prefer to know where it's come from, and we certainly aim to minimise the length of its journey from nature to mouth. We know that raw food and fibre are good for us. Until very recently, though, humanity longed for easily digestible, highly proc-essed food. For centuries people went to great lengths to avoid eat-ing raw fruit or vegetables. Trading patterns with other nations have also affected our diets – did you know that Henry VIII ate coconuts, and the Georgians enjoyed mangoes and Bologna sausages?

Technology has also shaped kitchens: open fireplaces gave way to ovens and eventually to ranges; coal and coke replaced wood before being superseded themselves by gas and electricity.

Above all, though, kitchens are conservative places. Cooking involves routine; cooks are the guardians of traditions. Their recipes order the world. 'Empires, kingdoms, states and republics are but puddings of people differently made up,' wrote the author of *A Learned Dissertation on a Dumpling* in 1817.

Food is therefore political, and the kitchen has been the scene of vicious class and gender battles.

34 – Why Men Used to Do the Cooking

The cook was a good cook, as cooks go; and
as cooks go she went.

Saki, 1904

A feast was, and remains, an incredibly important signal that
all is well within a family, household or place of work. Such set-
piece meals have now migrated out of the domestic realm into
the hotel or restaurant, but they once took place in the home.

That's why the Lord Steward used to hold one of the great
offices of the realm. It was his job to make sure that the king
and all his servants had plenty to eat. In any great household,
not just a royal one, the Steward was in charge of an extensive
and vital department of servants responsible for supplies, cater-
ing and cleaning; all the functional (as opposed to ceremonial)
arrangements. Clearly this was an important and responsible
post, always held by a man, and it was also very honourable.

Beneath the overall guidance of the Steward came the Master-
Cook, another masculine job. Most of the many people beneath
his management were male as well. One of the very few women
allowed at Henry VIII's court was Mrs Cornwallis, 'the wife
who makes the King's puddings'. (She was rewarded for her
work with a house in London.)

This all-male kitchen, serving food to be eaten by the crowds

An eleventh-century royal kitchen staffed by men, redrawn from the Bayeux Tapestry

of servants in the great hall, was a powerful and desirable image throughout the medieval period. The combination of warmth, security and food was made even more attractive by the camaraderie of the household. 'Think of all the times we boasted at the mead-bench, heroes in the hall, predicting our own bravery in battle,' reminisced an Anglo-Saxon warrior.

The male domination of the highest-status kitchens only began to change in the seventeenth century. Then ambitious young men started to want to become doctors or lawyers rather than domestic servants, and the status of household service began to fall. Towns rather than households became the building blocks of society. Women would take over domestic cooking, and the art of haute cuisine, practised by professional males, would go off into the public arena of the restaurant.

But the ideal of a well-staffed, mostly male kitchen, like those to be found in the great palaces of the nobility and church, had no place lower down in society. In the small farmhouses and cottages of medieval England women had always done the cooking. King Alfred went on the run from the Vikings in 878, 'living a restless life in great distress amid the woody and marshy places'. Later legend claims that he took refuge in the hut of a swineherd. Here, the swineherd's wife gave him the task of watching the cakes baking, which Alfred – notoriously – neglected, and he got an ear-bashing from the humble housewife as a result. The story has several possible meanings. Perhaps the cooking king demonstrated praiseworthy humility, or perhaps he'd wrongly neglected his kingdom (the cake) so that the Vikings could burn it. Or it might even have been a warning to other housewives against letting men into their kitchens.

The beginning of the end for the communal meal can be seen much earlier than the seventeenth-century handover of the cooking from men to women in the grandest houses. It can be placed right back in the fourteenth century. (Or at least that's when the rhetoric began. It's amazing that people are still complaining about this to this very day: when they criticise families for eating in front of the television, they're echoing sentiments which have been heard for six hundred years.) The fourteenth-century *Vision of Piers the Plowman* describes how the lord and lady had decamped to 'a privy parlour' to 'eat by themselves', in order to 'leave the chief hall/ That was made for meals, for men to eat in'. With the departure of the master of the household from the common dining hall, the separate and private dining room was born.

Back in Britain's medieval great halls, though, architecture continued to develop just as if the lord and lady really did dine there every night according to the nostalgic ideal. Carved panelling was introduced, high windows were added, and a dais appeared to hold the top table used when the lord did make one of his occasional appearances. (You can still see this in an old-fashioned Oxbridge college today, where the fellows eat on a platform raised above the students in the body of the hall.) An oriel, or bay, window provided the dais with extra light. Often the 'upper' end of the hall where the top table stood had plastered, whitewashed walls. The light from the oriel window, bouncing off the bright walls, would illuminate the master and his family, as if they were actors upon a stage for the rest of the household to admire and emulate.

In a modest house, the table, or 'board', might have been provided with stools for guests but just the one chair with arms, which was reserved for the household's head. The original 'chairman of the board' was literally so, seated on a chair while everyone else was on a stool, presiding over his dependants and his dining table. The notion that those in charge have the best seats is so powerful that judges still have 'benches', professors hold 'chairs' in their subjects, and those promoted to the board of a company will take a 'seat' there.

This top table had to be laid with extreme punctiliousness. 'Look that your napery be sweet and clean . . . your table-knives brightly polished, and your spoon fair washed,' runs one book of medieval advice to waiting staff. 'Do not pick your nose or let it drop clear pearls, or sniff, or blow it too hard, lest your lord hear.' The Elizabethan Earl of Montague recommends that the waiter should even bow as he places each napkin, knife and spoon upon the board.

At the bottom end of the hall an elaborately carved screen was constructed to hide the entrance to the kitchens. It disguised the doors to the buttery (for storing drinks) and the pantry (where bread was kept). The pantry was the workplace of the pantler, who handed out bread to the household. John Russell's fifteenth-century book of advice for young servants recommends that three knives are kept in the pantry: one to chop the loaves, another to pare them, and a third, 'sharp and keen', 'to smooth and square the trenchers'. 'Trenchers' were slices of old bread which acted as throwaway plates. They were formed from the burned and blackened bottoms of loaves. The more desirable top crust was eaten at once by the master and guests, hence the enduring term 'upper crust' for something posh.

Yet even as it reached its architectural apogee, the great hall was slowly dying. Lords and servants alike sloped off to eat elsewhere. Only in some very remote country places did its practices persist. An extraordinary glimpse of history is found in the recollection of an aged Derbyshire farmer in 1898. In his youth,

the master and his family sat at a table near the fire, and the servants at a long table on the opposite side of the room. First the master carved for his family and himself, and the joint was passed on to the servants' table . . . the men sat next to the chair in order of seniority, and were very particular about keeping their proper places.

The farmer was describing a long-lost hierarchical but harmonious world.

In due course the great hall became such a potent symbol of Merrie Old England that the Victorians – distressed by modernity, sweatshops and pea-soup fogs – reinvented it. However, they used their great halls for displaying antiques and for afternoon tea, not for entertaining their servants to dinner.

Once cooking had become women's work, the status of the kitchen and its staff embarked upon a slow and steady decline. The late seventeenth century saw a burgeoning of feminine roles in the household, as men went out to seek their fortune in the professions instead. *The Compleat Servant Maid* of 1677 lists ten different jobs for women, from waiting-woman, housekeeper, chambermaid, cook and under-cook to nurserymaid, dairymaid, housemaid, laundress and scullion.

This was the shape of things to come: more numerous and more specialist female servants, rising to a zenith in the nineteenth century. By the twentieth century, though, a combination of psychological and economic circumstances brought 'the servant problem' to an acute pitch for middle-class employers. The more extreme Victorian absurdities of household specialisation came to an end with an increasing scarcity of labour. Chefs became 'cooks general'; housekeepers became 'working housekeepers'; and the footman was replaced by the 'female chauffeuse-cum-companion'.

Society was no longer based on deference, and rightly so. Shame and frustration were increasingly the emotions of the kitchen, where the servants who did the dirtiest work were treated the worst by their employers. Pity the kitchen maid who complained that among her fellow servants 'everyone was called by their surname but as I was never seen or spoken to by anyone outside the kitchen, I didn't have a name at all'. Eventually such women voted with their feet and left domestic service for good. As supply dwindled, there would be a gradual increase in the status of domestic servants, exemplified in their modern, less demeaning name of 'staff'.

Monica Dickens was an upper-class debutante who for a lark became a not-terribly-efficient cook-general in the 1930s. She published a book about her amusing adventures in other people's kitchens in 1939. This was the point at which the middle classes felt entitled to servants, but couldn't understand why they couldn't keep them. Dickens's employers were usually in a state of some desperation, but she managed to disappoint even their low expectations through some calamity or breakage. At first she enjoyed acting out the unaccustomed role, but refused to dress for the part, deciding that 'it was rather the modern idea for maids to revolt against wearing caps'. Dickens turned cooking into comedy, but the type of people who employed cooks must have found the joke rather dark.

The second half of the twentieth century saw the kitchen's story split along two rival paths. According to one version, the woman of a household takes responsibility once again, just as she did in a medieval cottage, and produces simple meals from scratch for a small family unit. In the other, the kitchen falls completely out of use, and people eat food produced by other people outside the home, or even in other countries. Takeaway outlets providing hundreds of meals a day, or a meal service which brings a calorie-controlled portion of food to your door, fill the bounteous function of a great lord's household kitchen.

We have yet to see which will come to dominate twenty-first-century life.

35 – The Kitchen Comes in from the Cold

The centre point of interest in a house is the
kitchen with the adjacent Pantry, and round
those apartments must range the other rooms.
R. Briggs, *The Essentials of a Country House*, 1911

In a medieval peasant's cottage, the only room of the house
was its kitchen, which served as bedroom and living room as
well. The kitchen would eventually return to prominence in
twentieth-century house design, but during the intervening centuries it was sent out, and away, to be as far distant as possible
from the living rooms.

The kitchen might have been central to the lowly cottage,
but in the grander houses of medieval England it was placed in
a separate block. The Anglo-Saxon 'thane' was quite a significant landowner, as he possessed at least five hides of land. (A
'hide' was the amount of land required to grow enough food
for one family.) Your average thane aspired to having a separate
bakehouse and kitchen buildings, set at a short distance from
his home's main rectangular hall. The fear of fire meant that a
kitchen had to be semi-sacrificial; it was much more likely to
burn down than the rest of the house.

At Hampton Court Palace, too, the kitchen was originally
detached from the main hall. Over time, other smaller kitchens

and related offices sprang up around the Great Kitchen, so that now it looks like a whole small town, stuck like a monstrous disorderly carbuncle onto the side of the grand courtyards of the palace proper.

One thousand five hundred meals a day were prepared in this complex of more than fifty separate rooms. The Boiling House was a room containing a boiling copper for stock and soup. The Pasty House was a room where pie cases were made. The servants of the Spicery provided fruit as well as spices. The confectioners worked in an upstairs room where they produced delicate sweets and comfits on chafing dishes. The Wet Larder contained fish, the Dry Larder stored grain, and there was a further Flesh Larder for meat.

Because grand houses were the economic centres of estates, they were almost like factories for processing food and needed many different specialist workshops. Larders, ice houses, dairies, brewhouses and bakehouses were all additional outposts of the kitchens, housed in outbuildings. 'On the south side of the house', ran a survey of Montacute House, Somerset, made in 1667, 'there is a large woodyard and necessary buildings of dairies, washing, brewing and baking' as well as 'a pigeon house'. Households would often be rightly proud of the products made in these outbuildings. Here animals were slaughtered, beer brewed, napkins laundered.

This ideal of the kitchen being in a semi-separate building persisted into the eighteenth century, when the increasing gentility of the upper classes made them ever less tolerant of the dirt, smells and noise of food preparation. When Kedleston Hall was designed, the kitchen was placed more than thirty metres from the main guest dining room, and separated from it by a long curving corridor. The family's own dining room, for private use, was more than twice as far distant.

This begs a question: did the owners of grand houses always eat cold food? At first it seems likely, with the distance that the food had to travel, and considering the lengthy ceremony with which it was served. But in fact there were many tricks to minimise the loss of heat on the journey from kitchen to table. Food was only plated up in the dining room, travelling along the corridors in a heat-conserving tureen. Cloths and mufflers were used to keep the serving dishes warm as they made their way along the corridors.

Then there were the skills and physiques of the servers to be considered. In a really grand house, the job of serving-man was exclusively male. In numerous paintings of medieval halls, you can see servers carrying big dishes of food from a hatch near the kitchens towards the dining tables. These would be fine young men, quick and powerful, who would take pride in getting food to the table fast. Vigorous, fleet-footed footmen would have run with the dinner along the curved corridors of Georgian Kedleston. In a well-regulated house, where cooking and serving worked like clockwork, everybody enjoyed hot dinners.

In the nineteenth century, the idea persisted that kitchens ought to be remote from the polite areas of the house. There would be tradesmen calling, rubbish to be collected and other noisy activities to be kept distant from the master and his family. But in busy cities, with space hard to come by, the kitchen had to be squashed down into the basement of the house rather than set off to the side.

So the lofty, spacious, airy, echoing kitchens of the eighteenth-century country house were transformed into airless, lightless underground bunkers. In Virginia Woolf's childhood home, 22 Hyde Park Gate, the six or seven maids were banished from the main storeys of the tall terraced house. They were relegated to a basement kitchen of almost 'incredible gloom', or to the boiling hot attics where they slept. One of these young women once let her true feelings slip out. The young Virginia overheard one of her mother's maids describing her workplace: 'It's like hell.'

The First World War and the collapse of the kind of economy

in which one third of the country had worked as the domestic servants of another third brought about change. When the mistress of a household finally entered her own kitchen and was forced to learn how to cook, kitchen conditions inevitably improved.

Of course, in working people's houses there had been no such distinction between kitchen and living rooms: they remained one and the same. The National Trust's 'back-to-back' houses in Birmingham represent a housing type once found all over the Midlands and north of England. These houses, one backed against another to save bricks, had two bedrooms, one often shared by a whole family, the other let to a couple of lodgers. In the downstairs room, perhaps nine people would spend their leisure and eating time, and even their working hours. The front room/kitchen of one of the houses now on display was used by a glass-eye-maker as his workshop as well.

Over the course of the twentieth century, though, open-plan living became acceptable even in expensive homes. No longer was the kitchen squeezed into the smallest possible space and made a second-class room; it returned to being a social space, where family, not servants, would spend much of their time.

In the later twentieth century, Terence Conran once again demonstrated an unerring instinct for making money out of a major domestic shift (just as he had done with his duvets). His shop Habitat provided cheap but stylish products for young couples remodelling the traditional Victorian terraced house to their new and Swinging Sixties needs, as they ripped out the walls between sculleries, kitchens and dining rooms. 'You may well find', he wrote in 1974, 'it's worth combining the living/dining-room or kitchen/dining-room so that the dining space can be of use all day.'

Habitat spaghetti jars, wooden salad servers and chunky mugs (instead of cups and saucers) were the chosen utensils of mothers who worked all day and did their own cooking in the evenings as well. The robust yet cheerful 1970s kitchen was 'central to entertainment, as well as to tasks like homework, and there was a certain homespun air that went with the potted herbs and the use of "honest" building materials such as brick, stone and wood'.

Since then, a rejection of 1970s country-cottage kitchen kitsch has seen sleek and streamlined interiors with slate worktops and handle-less cupboard doors dominate style magazines. But you can't really imagine cooking in a kitchen designed by Porsche, for example, and its owners are more likely to be found eating out in restaurants.

Today the aroma of dinner cooking in a warm, bashed-about room, with children's pictures taped to the fridge, has come to symbolise home and security for many people. But the idea that cooking produces an attractive scent is another very modern idea. Throughout the previous centuries it wasn't just fear of fire that kept the kitchen so remote for so long. It was also a dread of smell.

36 – The Pungent Power of Pongs

The taste of the kitchen is better than the smell.
Thomas Fuller, *Gnomologia*, 1732

We live today in an age of deadened senses. People in the past could be shocked or transformed by a smell, something that rarely even registers in our sanitised world.

Perfume in the past was much more important than it is today, not least to disguise the odour of an unwashed body. A beautiful smell was considered rarer and more valuable, and the concept of 'miasma' as the bearer of disease meant that a bad smell was thought to be positively harmful. Smells were believed to be so powerful that a tiny baby born without breath would have onions placed under his nose, and only if this failed would a midwife take the (much more effective) action of blowing into his mouth to inflate his lungs.

Today pregnant women are told to avoid smoking, drinking and uncooked eggs, but early modern women had instead to avoid the upsetting smells, sounds or even sights that might damage the foetus. In 1716, Liselotte, Duchess of Orléans prided herself upon her unusual ability to carry a child to term despite strong scents: 'If I hadn't been able to stand perfumes I should have been dead long ago. Every time I was lying in Monsieur [her husband] came to visit me, wearing perfumed Spanish gloves.'

Unpleasant tastes were not remarked upon nearly so often as unpleasant smells or sights, and the word 'disgust' (literally 'unpleasant to the taste') only entered the English lexicon in the early seventeenth century. 'Disgust' is a modern concept: only when food is relatively abundant can people afford to overlook certain forms of nutrition on the grounds of nastiness. In lean, mean times no one found any type of food disgusting.

Once the concept of 'disgust' had arrived, though, people began to find various forms of food potentially offensive, and to think that cooking smells should to be eliminated. So, when new houses were designed, this was another reason for kitchens to be hustled out of the main part and preferably placed into a separate block.

The architectural writer Roger North did his best to persuade people to eject kitchens from the new 'compact' houses or 'piles' of his century, the seventeenth. To include a kitchen in a compact house was an error, he thought, because 'all smells that offend, are a nuisance to all the rooms, and there is no retiring from them'. An important strand running right through the history of house design thereafter is concerned with vanquishing the smell of drains or cooking alike. In 1773, Robert Adam wrote that dining rooms, 'instead of being hung with damask, tapestry &c', should be 'always finished with stucco . . . that they may not retain the smell of the victuals'.

When the open fire was replaced by the enclosed kitchen range in the early nineteenth century, it actually made the problem of cooking smells even worse. Before this, the open chimney and its updraught had acted as a ventilation system, but not even royalty could escape from the unfortunate consequences of the range. 'The Queen remarked that you ought to be thankful that in your house you have no smell of dinner,' recollected a servant named Joshua Bates of a conversation overheard while he was waiting upon Queen Victoria during a visit to his employer's home. 'It is because I am constantly shutting doors,' was her host's reply. 'And so am I,' remarked Prince Albert, 'but I can't prevent it.'

The idea that the smells of cooking should be eliminated from the home remained in place throughout the nineteenth century, and only in the twentieth century did it begin to break down. In the 1980s, a new subculture was born: the 'foodie'. This epicurean but amateur cook had existed previously, but a work published in 1984 by Paul Levy and Ann Barr, *The Official Foodie Handbook*, really marks the term's coming of age. 'Foodies' are interested in where their food comes from and what it tastes like; to them, the smell of a chicken roasting or a cake baking is central to ideas of home.

However, nobody wants their house to reek of fish the morning after the night before, and what really allowed the twentieth-century open-plan kitchen and living room to function was the invention of the extractor fan. Placed in the cooker hood, it sucked the cooking smells out of the room. It was an invention of the 1930s, but only really came into use in domestic (rather than restaurant) kitchens in the 1960s, when kitchens, dining rooms and lounges began to blur in function.

It took these two vital developments – a new pleasure to be taken from good smells, and bad ones to be removed with the extractor fan – for the kitchen to become not just a room for cooking, but a room for living.

37 – Stirring and Scrubbing and Breaking Your Back

– 'You're very faddy, Mrs. Rawlins!'
– 'Perhaps I am, Mum, but it's them as has to do
the work knows what's best!'
Housekeeper Mrs Rawlins insists on using
Robin starch, advert in *Good Housekeeping*, 1928

Although it sounds like rather a dry topic, the ergonomics of kitchen design has had a tremendous impact on the lives of men and especially women throughout the centuries. Badly designed kitchen products could even kill: the lead leached from pewter vessels mistakenly used to store vinegar was poisonous, as were copper pots once their protective tin coatings had worn off.

The first and most basic of cooks' needs is flame. Intense heat is required to produce the 'Maillard reaction', the process which causes the savoury browning of food. Its effects are clearly visible in bread crusts, chocolate, dark beers and roast meat. The other, sweeter type of browning is the caramel effect of burnt sugar. Either needs a high temperature; both are high-status forms of cooking.

Stewing food (essentially cooking it in water) requires less heat, but fails to produce the intense bitter or sweet chemicals of the two browning processes. To quote Mrs Beeton, stewing 'is

the cheapest method . . . little fuel is used. Nothing is wasted . . .
the cheapest and coarsest meat can be used.' Having understood
the economics of both cooking processes, it's not surprising to
find that browned, intensely cooked food has been eaten by
preference by richer people from Tudor times until the present
day, from the spit-roast chicken of Henry VIII's kitchen to the
seared tuna steak consumed by today's health-conscious billion-
aire after his second heart attack.

The one-room medieval peasant's dwelling contained a central open hearth. A hearthstone – a flat rock – provided the
base for a fire. Fires sometimes burned for years, even decades,
without being extinguished. They were nursed carefully because
it was no mean feat to ignite a fresh flame. Over fires hung iron
pots with rounded bottoms. Although it can't be stood on a
table, a round-bottomed pot has many advantages: it's easy to
make, to nestle into a sandy floor or to sit upon an iron tripod.
To stir your pot without getting burnt you needed a very long-
handled wooden spoon.

This was very simple technology, but it was extremely effective. You could throw any food that came to hand into your pot
to make the soup called 'pottage', which cooked all day without
too much attention. Pottage was the ubiquitous dish of medieval
England. You could even cook numerous items simultaneously
in a single pot, wrapped in cloths or separated by wooden divid-
ers. In early-twentieth-century Oxfordshire, the rural family
described in Flora Thompson's *Lark Rise to Candleford* (1939)
still eat a whole dinner cooked in a cauldron: a small square of
bacon; boiled vegetables; and a pudding in muslin. So the open
fire reigned supreme for centuries.

The oven, however, which represented a significant financial
investment, was located outside most people's homes. Early
ovens work quite differently from modern ones, where heat
is provided continuously throughout the cooking process. A
stone- or brick-lined oven is heated *before* the food goes in, by

the burning inside it of bundles of twigs called faggots. Then the ashes are raked out, loaves are shovelled in, the door is closed, and the bread is left to bake in the slowly cooling oven.

When I used the bread oven at the Weald and Downland Museum, we stopped the oven's opening with a wooden door previously soaked in water to prevent it from catching fire. We sealed the gaps round the door with a strip of uncooked dough. When this dough was baked, we knew that the bread inside it must be finished too. After the baking of the bread, the oven still contained just enough heat to bake a second round of cakes or biscuits. The very word *bis-cuit* means 'second-cooked'.

Part of the skill of the cook lay in judging just how hot the oven was. There were tricks such as placing inside it a big white stone that would change colour as it heated. These simple thermometers were called 'wise men' in Buckinghamshire kitchens. A cookbook from 1882 reveals that even then cooks had to use a mixture of observation and guesswork to deduce the temperature of their ovens:

If a sheet of paper burns when thrown in, the oven is too hot.
When the paper becomes dark brown, it is suitable for pastry.
When light brown, it does pies.
When dark yellow, for cakes.
When light yellow, for puddings, biscuits and small pastry.

Clearly, if you were going to all this trouble to heat up a large oven, it was sensible to bake a considerable quantity of loaves for all your neighbours, and baking was most efficiently done outside the home. In rural areas, many leases dictated that tenants pay for the use of the lord's mill and bakehouse for their bread. It made sense to share facilities in cities as well.

In fact, city dwellers have always been reliant on takeaways, and many foods are more conveniently cooked in bulk by the shopkeepers who make it their business. A *Description of London* (1183) mentions an early pie shop on the banks of the Thames selling 'coarser flesh for the poor, the more delicate, for the rich, such as venison'. Not only pies but even stews prepared at home might be sent out to baking shops near by and returned cooked.

In the homes of the great, where fresh meat was available to be roasted over the open fire, the spit was a very labour-intensive device that needed constant turning. The sweaty and dirty turnspit boys of the Tudor royal kitchens were commanded to smarten up, no longer to 'go naked or in garments of such vileness as they do now . . . nor lie in the nights and days in the kitchen or ground by the fireside'. And yet the turnspits at least had a warm place to sleep, and they could snack on the meat. They 'lickt the dripping pan and became huge lusty knaves', wrote John Aubrey.

But the days of the human spit-jack (a 'jack' is simply a man who does an odd job) were numbered once a mechanical alternative was invented. Some mechanical jacks worked by clock-work; others relied on the heat rising from the flames to turn a fan. One amusing technological dead end, quickly abandoned, was the dog-turned spit, in which a specially bred 'turnspit' dog from Pembrokeshire was employed. Bred to have long bodies and short legs, these turnspit dogs looked a little like sausage dogs (plate 36). Charles Darwin commented on their shape as an example of genetic engineering. They worked in teams of two, taking turns to run inside a wheel linked by shafts and chains to a spit. But the dogs were not completely reliable. In 1723, the tycoon William Cotesworth of Gateshead gave up on his dog-wheel and demanded its removal 'to keep the dog from the fire, the wheel out of the way and the dog prevented from shitting upon everything it could'. The poet John Gay had another common complaint – lazy dogs who simply scarpered:

> The dinner must be dish'd at one
> Where's this vexatious turnspit gone?
> Unless the skulking cur is caught
> The sirloin's spoiled, and I'm at fault.

But a naturalist noted in 1853 that 'the invention of automaton roasting-jacks has destroyed the occupation of the Turnspit Dog' and 'almost annihilated its very existence'. In due course the turnspit dogs died out completely as a breed, but you can see one (stuffed) at Abergavenny Museum, Wales.

The grandest medieval kitchens also contained the equivalent of a hob, a brazier over which gentler, pan-based cooking could take place. In the eighteenth century this device was known as the 'stewing stove'. The burning charcoal was placed beneath iron grids supported from a brick structure. Noxious charcoal fumes, inhaled during a lifetime spent bent over his signature delicate sauces, destroyed the lungs of the Regency 'celebrity chef', Antonin Carême. His epitaph from a fellow foodie described Carême as being 'burned out by the fire of his genius and the charcoal of the rotisserie'.

The Industrial Revolution was followed by the invention of a new 'science': domestic economy. Fresh from creating more efficient factories and industrial processes, various innovators now turned their attention to the centuries-old habits and equipment established in the nation's kitchens. 'Nothing can be more preposterous', expostulated Charles Sylvester in 1819, 'than the prevailing construction and management of a gentleman's kitchen.'

By 1864, the architect Robert Kerr could write that efficiency had become the chief consideration below stairs. 'The Family Apartments have to be contrived for occupation,' he wrote, 'but the Offices for work . . . every servant, every operation, every utensil, every fixture, should have a right place and no right place but one.'

The writer H. G. Wells had personal experience of domestic service, having grown up 'below stairs' at Uppark in Sussex, where his mother was the housekeeper. He dramatised the problems facing servants in old, inconvenient houses in his novel *Kipps* (1905): 'They build these 'ouses . . . as though girls wasn't 'uman beings . . . It's 'ouses like this wear girls out. It's 'aving 'ouses built by men, I believe, makes all the work and trouble.' It's also exasperating to observe that the maids depicted in adverts for household appliances and detergents all wear perilously impractical high heels. Footmen suffered too: one calculated that in his own London place of work there were 'eighty stairs from top to bottom, sixteen stairs to answer the front door, thirty-two to the drawing-room with tea'; and a colleague calculated he'd walked eighteen miles, indoors, during a single busy day's work.

'The first thing to be considered in a plan for the kitchen is saving steps,' wrote Laura E. Lyman in *The Philosophy of Housekeeping* (1869). Catherine Beecher, the American Victorian kitchen guru, was impressively prescient in imagining how the different elements of the kitchen could interplay more effectively. She recommended a sliding door between the kitchen and dining room, for example, demonstrating a new attention to ergonomics. Catherine and her sister Harriet went on to design, among other futuristic things, moveable screens and cupboards on wheels. The multifunctional spaces they envisaged in their ideal *American Woman's Home* (1869) looked both backwards to medieval flexibility and forwards to the twentieth century's Modern Movement open-plan house.

The industrial age also brought with it the seismic shift from open fire to enclosed kitchen range. Steps along the way included the American Count Rumford's eponymous 'stove': the neat grate and enclosed iron surround that could be introduced into wide and wasteful hearths. While it could hold several pots, Rumford's original design was too big for many homes. But it held the germ of the idea of the kitchen range. In due course, this ubiquitous piece of iron equipment contained a fuel-efficient stove, an oven, a boiler to provide continual hot water and a hot plate, all in one. Every range had its own quirks and needed careful handling to limit its fuel consumption to the

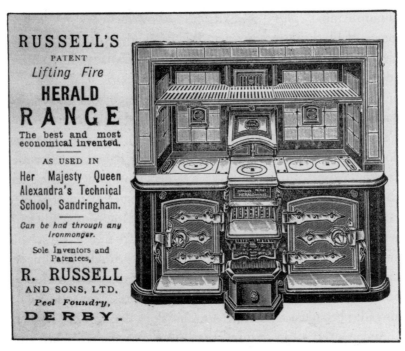

RUSSELL'S
PATENT
Lifting Fire
HERALD
RANGE
The best and most economical invented.

AS USED IN

Her Majesty Queen Alexandra's Technical School, Sandringham.

Can be had through any Ironmonger.

Sole Inventors and Patentees,

R. RUSSELL
AND SONS, LTD.
Peel Foundry,
DERBY.

The arrival of the kitchen range revolutionised cooking, slashed fuel consumption, standardised recipes and encouraged the use of the saucepan

recommended monthly half ton of coal. 'Each housewife should study the draughts . . . so that she may be able to direct the cook how best to get good results from the amount of coal burned,' advised the *Ladies' Home Journal* in 1897. Operating a range was like performing on the organ: 'only to be played by one who knows the stops'.

Like the expensive and finely tuned instrument that it was, the range needed careful cleaning and maintenance. It required 'blacking' twice a week, first thing in the morning, a process that took about ninety minutes. The 'black lead' polish was brushed into the iron surfaces, then buffed up to a shine. A recipe for this noxious polish, given in *The Footman's Directory* (1825), requires 'two quarts of small beer, eight ounces of ivory black, three ounces of treacle, one ounce of sugar candy, half an ounce of gum Arabic', plus 'oil of vitriol'. I know from my own experience of blacking the range at Shugborough Hall that it takes a week for traces of the polish to work its way out from underneath the fingernails.

With the range, more efficient kitchen design was now on its way. But progress came in fits and starts: the range represented a significant financial investment, and there was still an emotional attachment to the welcoming, leaping flames of the wide hearth. 'Would our Revolutionary fathers have gone barefooted and bleeding over snows to defend air-tight stoves and cooking-ranges?' asked Harriet Beecher Stowe during the American Civil War. Indeed no, she said: the 'great open kitchen fire' was their motivation; the memory of it kept 'up their courage' and 'made their hearts warm and bright with a thousand reflected memories'. Indeed, even in the 1930s America's president would call his radio broadcasts his 'Fireside Chats'.

And conservatism ensured that kitchens remained places of standing, scrubbing and stirring, with only rare glimpses of comfort. The Victorian household expert Mrs Panton recommended that kitchen servants might possibly be allowed to lay 'a rug, or good square of carpet' down on the floor, but only after their work was done and if they were very careful with it. Likewise the architect J. C. Loudon suggested in a mealy-mouthed manner that 'a small looking glass might promote tidiness of person and a piece of common carpet would add to the comfort of the room'.

But the seemingly endless labour of feeding, firing, cosseting and cleaning the range would not last for ever. Gas cookers – marketed as 'wageless servants' – were among the items displayed at the Great Exhibition of 1851, and by 1898 one in four homes had both a gas supply and a cooker. Many people hired their cookers from their local gas company, rather than buying them outright.

In 1923, an extraordinary invention appeared: the 'Regulo'.

This was a thermostat for a gas oven, so that for the first time meals could be cooked at a known temperature over a measured length of time. This turned cooking from an art into a science. Adverts trumpeted the Regulo as an 'inestimable boon to our wives and daughters, enabling them to prepare for us, with the minimum of attention, a repast cooked with automatic precision'.

The electric Belling 'Modernette' cooker of 1919. The gas and electricity companies waged all-out war for customers

While gas had the advantage of cheapness, electricity would challenge it as Britain's favourite kitchen fuel in the late nineteenth century. The great drawback to early electrical supplies was the wild variation between the voltages produced by different plants in different towns. This meant that no electrical appliance could be made and sold nationally. This eventually began to change in 1926 with the laying of plans to create the National Grid, and in 1930 a group of manufacturers finally managed to agree a set of common standards for cookers. The electricity companies vigorously proclaimed the benefits of electric as opposed to gas cookers: they were easy to use, safer and cleaner. Even so, in 1939 a mere 8 per cent of British homes had electric cookers, and 75 per cent stuck with gas.

In 1908, Ellen Richards calculated that an eight-room house required eighteen hours of cleaning time a week just to remove dust. Washing the windows and walls would take the total up to twenty-seven hours a week, even before the clothes-washing, bed-making and cooking began. This was simply unsustainable after the two world wars removed the huge infrastructure of servants who had done such work in the past. Now there began to be a real necessity for efficient, labour-saving kitchens. Books for the newly servantless middle classes began to appear, with tactful titles such as *Cook's Away. A Collection of Simple Rules, Helpful Facts, and Choice Recipes Designed to Make Cooking Easy* (1943). This particular volume teaches novices how to break an egg, and advises them not to chop onions with raw hands because the smell will linger and spoil the enjoyment of a later cigarette.

'There cannot have been any time in the history of our country', wrote Lady Beveridge in 1945, 'at which the attention of all people has been so much engaged by the problem of housekeeping without tears.' She rightly explained that 'it is not only that so many houses have been destroyed' by war, 'but also that the remainder have been discovered to be all too frequently designed for a social system which is a thing of the past'.

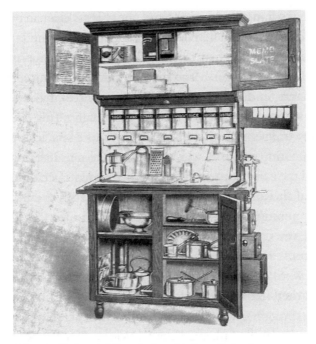

After the Industrial Revolution, kitchen design became
a matter for scientific study. This multipurpose cabinet
represents a step along the way to the fully fitted kitchen

The history of post-war housing leads us towards prefabrica-
tion, standardisation and an ever greater squeeze upon space
as Britain filled up with people. The fitted kitchen was in fact a
German invention, first appearing in 1926 in a Frankfurt social
housing project. Ten thousand of these so-called 'Frankfurt
Kitchens' were installed. They were inspired by the narrow gal-
ley kitchens of railway trains, and the space they contained was
tight but very well-planned. Shockingly modern to contemporary
eyes, they had work surfaces which pulled out like drawers and
draining boards on hinges which could be folded away. In them
the housewife was conceived as an engineer, quickly and efficiently turning out meals; in fact, the design was partly intended
to free up time which could be spent instead in Germany's factories. But the design's drawback also lay in its tiny size. Women

ended up working in there all alone, unable to keep an eye upon their children or to be helped by the rest of the family.

The Frankfurt Kitchen might have become more popular in Britain if it had not been for the Second World War. After the war, Britons tended to look west not east, seeking inspiration for new kitchen designs from their American allies. The large, luxurious fridges and kitchen units of a more spacious and less war-torn country became post-war desirables in Britain.

One of the early home-grown British fitted kitchen designs was 'The English Rose' of 1948, intended to use up the industrial-strength aluminium which had been stockpiled for building Spitfires. You could quickly fit out an entire kitchen by choosing various units and cupboards from the standard range. The work surfaces were covered with the new melamine, which could be wiped rather than scrubbed clean. It was quite an upmarket product, though, and if you couldn't afford it, there were col-ourful sticky-backed plastics like Fablon or Stix-On to brighten up shelves or tabletops instead.

The extractor fan was perhaps the greatest mechanical devel-opment of the twentieth century, as it allowed kitchens and living areas to become one single space. The most recent trans-formation, though, has been the arrival of online services allow-ing you to order any food, raw or cooked, from anywhere, and to have it brought to your door.

A very cheeky 1970s billboard for Kentucky Fried Chicken read simply 'Women's Liberation', and the production of food has now been transferred from the domestic to the public realm. What the Tudors used to call 'dressing victuals' is now broken down between extremely specialist producers all over the world. With many people today using their ovens as extra cupboards and their microwaves instead of their hobs, looking at the his-tory of the kitchen is like surveying a lost realm which holds less and less meaning for us.

But perhaps with global financial chaos this is beginning to change. Only a couple of years ago it seemed that 'foodies' were the few people who still cared about their kitchens. Apartments in New York were being built without kitchens at all, for people who order in every meal. Yet a slight movement in the direction of back-to-basics is apparent in dining habits, partly as a result of the efforts of the chef turned public-health expert Jamie Oliver. In 2003, only 24 per cent of Britons said that they 'always cooked from scratch', but today this has risen to 41 per cent.

Perhaps our recent recession has driven people to examine more carefully what they eat, and put a bit of life back into their kitchens. Now that cooking is no longer a matter of stirring, scrubbing and breaking your back, there is a dignity, beauty and generosity in putting time and effort into making something to eat.

38 – Cool

To ice CREAM. Take Tin Ice-Pots, fill them with any
Sort of Cream you like, either plain or sweeten'd . . .
you must have a Pail, and lay some Straw at the Bottom;
then lay in your Ice, and put in amongst it a Pound of
Bay-Salt; set in your Pots of Cream, and lay Ice and
Salt between every pot . . . set it in a Cellar where
no Sun or Light comes.

Mrs Mary Eales's Receipts, 1718

There's no question that kitchens smelled bad in the past. Before refrigeration, seasonal food was not a desirable, it was a necessity. Even hours counted: one Victorian housewife insisted upon 'an early dinner today' because the salmon, green-pea soup, chickens and jellies she had ordered were going off in the hot weather. All cooks knew that putting charcoal in with tainted meat would absorb something of the putrid smell, and horse-radish grated into milk would help it limp on for another few hours without turning.

How on earth, it's tempting to wonder, did people store fresh food before the days of refrigerators? Actually, a stone larder is an astoundingly simple yet effective invention. A thick marble slab remains cold on a hot day, and fish and meat would be laid directly upon it. Then there was the ice house, a wonderful invention, first heard of at St James's Palace in 1666. Called the 'snow-well', this one was sunk into the ground and given a roof of straw. It was most convenient to build your ice house near your lake, if you had one, so that in winter it was easy to carry in frozen lake-water and pack it in straw for the summer season. In a dark, underground room of a constant temperature, ice could last nearly the whole year.

Ice cream was a Georgian delicacy, as the recipe above from 1718 indicates, and artificial refrigeration was first seen in 1748 when William Cullen gave a demonstration at the University of Glasgow of a freezing machine that worked by the turning of a handle. As so often, though, he was too far ahead of his time, and no one saw the commercial possibilities in his idea. Only in 1834 did Jacob Perkins make the first proper refrigerator. But most people went on using ice houses, ice bought from roving ice wagons, and in their kitchens, simple iceboxes to keep their food fresh. The latter was a kind of wooden cupboard, well insulated with cork, lined with tin or zinc, and filled with food and lumps of ice. Ice was considered one of the items necessary for a picnic by *The Girls' Own Paper* in 1880: 'wrap the ice in a blanket and put it under the seat of the wagon'.

Victorian ice cream was quicker to make than its Georgian predecessor: you used a purpose-made churn. A drumful of cream was placed in an outer chamber packed with salt and ice. You turned a handle to agitate the cream, while the intense cold surrounding it gradually caused crystals to form.

In the late 1880s, the refrigerator finally became a practical business proposition. Fridges were among the new electrical devices to be found in go-ahead kitchens. They were initially rather glamorous possessions, and in the 1930s their owners might invite their friends to a 'refrigerator party' where each course was pre-prepared and then whipped from its own shelf in the fridge. Cookbooks from the period show guests in evening dress gathered in the kitchen to enjoy the novelty of eating an entire meal of cold food (plate 38).

Not everyone appreciated how refrigerators worked. In Monica Dickens's account of her life as a debutante cook in the 1930s, it was the gas man who finally gave her the answer to the mystery of 'why the ice in the refrigerator was always melting. He roared with uncouth laughter when he realised that I didn't know that one had to keep the door shut.'

People also didn't realise that pre-1929 refrigerators employed a noxious combination of gases as coolants. After leakages of ammonia and methyl chloride had caused several deaths, attempts were made to find safer alternatives. Einstein was among the scientists who turned their skills towards solving this particular problem, but his was not the most commercially successful solution. After research by a consortium of refrigerator manufacturers, the dangerous gases were replaced, in the 1930s, with freon, a chlorofluorocarbon. Again, this happened without anyone realising the danger freon itself posed, this time to the Earth's environment. Freon and other CFCs have since been banned because of their deleterious effect on the ozone layer.

Twentieth-century advertising campaigns for fridges – and indeed all the new electrical appliances – were aimed at women, tempting them with the prospect that they could go out and play golf rather than slave away in the kitchen, if only they would invest. The Magnet company invented a character called 'Miss Magnet', and in 1927 presented 'Miss Magnet's Ideal Home'. It came complete with vacuum cleaner, stove, iron, fan, washing machine and even electrical cream separator. The earliest electric kettles, dating from around 1900, were plugged into light fittings and took a lengthy twelve minutes to boil.

The provision of electricity was nationalised in 1947, and the post-war relaxation of the hire-purchase rules made it much easier to buy expensive gadgets. By 1959, Britain was recovering from its wartime austerity. 'Money doesn't chink these days,' reported *Queen* magazine, 'it crackles louder than a forest fire.' Much of this newly available money was spent on the kitchen, and by the mid-1960s 61 per cent of London households had a refrigerator.

Frozen food and the fridge gradually eased the daily pain of having to go to the shops for fresh supplies. '*La dolce vita* did not come packed with the detergent inside the new washing machine,' wrote Marilyn French in her feminist novel of 1978, 'but for women especially, the new washing machine or dryer or freezer really was a little release from slavery. Without them and without the pill, there would not be a woman's revolution now.'

The ultimate post-war gadget of desire, though, was the Kenwood mixer. Kenneth Wood, who gave his own name to his products, was a former RAF engineer who'd worked on the development of radar. In 1947, his new venture, an electrical firm, produced its toaster, and in 1950 his Kenwood 'Chef' or mixer was launched at the Ideal Home Exhibition. Harrods sold out within a week, and by 1968 Wood had sold more than a million of his Chefs.

Many people get more pleasure out of buying rather than using such a thing: today four in ten people in Britain admit that they possess kitchen gadgets they no longer use. The fridge, though, is not among them. More important even than the cooker, it's ended up as the one absolutely essential kitchen appliance.

39 – Peckish

One cannot think well, love well, sleep well, if
one has not dined well.
> Virginia Woolf, *A Room of One's Own*,
> London, 1929

When do you sense that gnawing in the stomach that can only be satisfied with a biscuit and a cup of tea? The times for feeling peckish have shifted over the centuries. The main meal of the day has gradually migrated from mid-morning to mid-evening, while breakfast and tea are relative newcomers.

Tudor people had a very different rhythm to their day, and indeed to their year, as their working hours were much shorter in winter than in summer. Breakfast was not a regular meal for them and was late to develop: the Great British Tradition of bacon and eggs dates only from the twentieth century. (But the dish itself is a classic medieval peasant combination, as chickens and pigs were the animals most likely to be owned by smallholders.)

Eating a snack of bread first thing, according to the Elizabethan William Harrison, was unusual, the action of a 'young hungry stomach that cannot fast until dinner-time'. Tudor people could happily skip breakfast, though, because they didn't have long to wait until lunch. As soon as enough time had elapsed for the household's cooks to rise at daybreak, get the fire started and the meat cooked, lunch was ready. The day's biggest meal was eaten mid- to late morning. The Tudors ate again, more lightly, in the evening.

The orders for the running of Henry VIII's royal palaces state that 'the first dinner' should begin 'at ten of the clock, or somewhat afore, and the first supper at four of the clock'. (The reference is to 'the first' because there were two sittings in the great hall for each meal. It was like a staff canteen for the several hundred court servants.) This main morning-to-midday meal might last two or three hours in a pretentious household: the nobility, according to William Harrison, might be found 'commonly sitting at the board 'til 2 or 3 of the clock at afternoon, so that with many, it is a hard matter to rise from the table to go to evening prayers'.

The increasing use of artificial light in the late seventeenth century saw the evening supper pushed back into the hours of darkness, but it would only be the eighteenth century and the Industrial Revolution that brought significant changes to mealtimes. Once people began to leave their homes to go out to work in factories, offices or shops, a midday meal was no longer convenient. Now the biggest repast for most came in the late afternoon, after the working day was over. At the same time, those rich enough to lead lives of leisure began to eat later dinners and suppers too, just to prove that they had no need to rise early in the morning. Richard Steele in the early eighteenth century recalled how 'In my memory the dinner hour has crept from 12 o'clock to 3.'

Throughout the eighteenth century, supper grew grander, and was nudged later and later into the evening hours. Eventually, by the 1840s, a new meal had to be introduced to fill the long gap between a light lunch and a night-time dinner now customarily at 8 p.m. The new meal, 'tea', quickly became an institution (plate 32).

Tea itself developed in two contrasting ways. The 'high tea' of working people included kippers, baked beans and other hot food, and stood in for dinner. Meanwhile, the aristocracy prided themselves on serving more refined food that wouldn't spoil a later dinner. James Lees-Milne in 1943 contrasted one solid, bourgeois spread – 'breads of different hue, jam, potted meat, biscuits, shortbread and cake, delightful but curiously middle class' – with Lady Cunard's ethereal and upper-class 'weak China and a thumb-nail of chocolate cake'.

The next step for the rich was to dissolve teatime into an American-style cocktail hour: in 1938, we hear that 'hostesses who only two years ago would have shuddered at the clink of tall glasses' now 'offered intoxicating drinks to those to whom the new-fangled afternoon tea seemed too reminiscent of the school-room'.

Another consequence of the Industrial Revolution was the need for workers to eat something substantial first thing. Since Georgian times breakfast for all had been standard, consisting of tea and toast. By 1810, people could say that 'next to water tea is the Englishman's proper element'. Foreigners were also intrigued by the phenomenon of toast: 'you take one slice after the other and hold it to the fire on a fork until the butter is melted . . . this is called toast'. It was 'incomparably good', thought a Prussian visitor in 1782. It might also be spread with what James Boswell called 'that admirable viand, marmalade'.

The light aristocratic breakfasts of the eighteenth century – tea and toast, coffee and rolls – were replaced by the heavier meals that Victorian gentlemen considered necessary to sustain them during a day at the office ('a malady of incurable character' might well result from going to work without the proper fortification). A journalist named George Augustus Sala compiled an awe-inspiring list of his regular breakfast dishes: 'a mutton-chop, or a rump-steak, or a good plateful from a cold joint, or a couple of eggs broiled in bacon, or a haddock, or a mackerel, or some pickled salmon, or some cold veal and ham pie or half a wild duck'.

Higher up in society, though, the peculiar tradition persisted that an aristocrat somehow didn't need a breakfast. It was considered a middle-class meal, necessary only to wage slaves, and males made light of it by refusing to sit down while eating it. 'The men walked about to eat their porridge,' explained the narrator of the novel *The Go-Between*, set in the last days of Queen Victoria. 'This, Marcus told me, was *de rigueur*; only cads ate their porridge sitting down.'

Now, anything goes when it comes to mealtimes. Three meals a day and no snacks, or five small meals, or no carbohydrates after 5 p.m.: you will find dietary advice recommending any possible permutation imaginable. But there is a clear consensus that food is most usefully consumed early in the day. Medieval people seemed naturally to have known that a big meal in the morning is better for the body, so the food fuels a day of activity.

In the Middle Ages they got something else right too. With sugar, hydrogenated fats and chemicals missing in both cases, there isn't that much difference between the medieval and macrobiotic diets.

40 – Trying New Foods
(and Drinks, and Drugs)

When will this evil stop? Your very Chambermaids
have lost their bloom, I suppose, by sipping tea.
What an army has gin and tea destroyed!

Jonas Hanway, 1757

The single room of a medieval dwelling developed into a range
of spaces for different purposes. The medieval palate likewise
developed over time to take pleasure in an ever-growing smor-
gasbord of tastes. Each novel ingredient had consequences for
the kitchen because it required new utensils. Your own teapot
and wok are the result of Europe trading ever further eastwards,
while your sugar bowl and cocktail shaker are the effects of
reaching out west.

The Tudors served all the dishes of a meal at once, mixing up
sweet and savoury. They'd even happily combine the two in the
same dish. A desirable meat pudding, for example, might contain parboiled liver, cream, eggs, breadcrumbs, beef suet, dates,
currants, spices, salt and sugar. Perhaps their most important
flavouring was salt. It was taken by each diner, using his or her
own knife, from a common container. An expensive and decorative vessel known as a 'salt' was therefore always to be found
upon a medieval table. It was usually the first and most valuable

item to be placed on the board as it was laid. Because the salt stood in the middle of a trestle along which people would be seated in order of status, those who found themselves 'above the salt' could celebrate this as confirmation of their high position.

Salt was also the chief preservative. 'You must be careful that your Meat taint not, for want of good salting,' ran the instructions for a cook-maid in 1677. Butter and cheese were also much saltier than today to help prevent them from going off. The Bishop of Worcester used one pound of salt for every ten pounds of butter made on his estate in 1305.

Salted fish was also common, especially on Fridays when meat-eating was forbidden by the church. Of the usual medieval salted fish, cod remains familiar, but ling, hake and whiting less so. Then there were eels, of which 2,000 were caught annually at just two mills on the River Avon belonging to Evesham Abbey (a statistic recorded in the Domesday Book). In fish ponds were reared young bream, pike, roach, perch or trout. The networks for getting foodstuffs to and around medieval England were really rather efficient: fish was imported from Iceland, for example, and fresh sea fish is mentioned in the fifteenth-century market regulations even for landlocked Coventry. If you really hated fish, you could get away with eating puffins or barnacle geese on fast days or during Lent instead. These seabirds were classified as fish rather than flesh.

After salt in importance came spices: expensive, rare and worth going to war for. The Tudors had surprisingly strong connections to some very distant countries. Henry VIII had a cup made from a coconut, while ginger, mace, cloves, cumin, cardamom, nutmeg, saffron, cinnamon and pepper were all well known in his kitchens, along with forgotten exotica such as galingale, cubebs and 'grains of paradise'. Almonds, a staple of medieval cooking, were also imported in large quantities. Such was their rarity and value that spices were kept locked up: in 1597, the household of the Earl of Northumberland at Petworth

House, Sussex, purchased 'a little trunk to keep spice in the kitchen'. There's no evidence that spices were used to 'disguise' the flavour of bad meat, as you might often read. It seems that people simply liked the taste. One particularly popular Tudor dish was 'frumenty', named for the Latin *frumentum* (corn). Wheat was boiled in milk, spices were added, and the resulting sludge made an excellent side dish for venison.

The separating out of sweet from savoury was an important development of the sixteenth century. One step towards the breakdown of the communal household meal was the new Elizabethan practice of serving the sweets that now followed the main meat course in a different room.

Often a concert or play followed dinner in the great hall, so it was necessary to clear the tables away. The action of removing the dirty plates from the tables was in French called the *desert*, the creation of an absence (the same word used for the Sahara). This act of 'deserting' the table gave its name to the dessert or sweet course served elsewhere while the entertainers were setting up.

Dessert was eaten, then, in the parlour, or even in a specially constructed small room called a 'Banqueting House', a pleasant little chamber sometimes set upon the roof. A Banqueting House might even be a separate, fantastical little house in the gardens, a short, digestion-aiding walk away from the great hall.

The food at a banquet included confectionery, the sugar sculptures known as subtleties, or preserved flowers or fruits. Of course, sweet foods were known before sugar importation began, with honey doing sugar's job (and furthermore being used to make drinks such as mead and its spiced cousin 'metheglin'). 'Raisins of Corinth', figs and dates appear on medieval shopping lists to satisfy the sweet of tooth. But cane sugar also became available to the very richest medieval people. In 1288, the royal household used 6,258 pounds, and in 1421 'sugre candi' from Italy was for sale in London.

Sugar grew more common in the sixteenth century when the Spanish plantations of the West Indies provided fresh supplies. Elizabeth I was extremely partial to it, and a visiting German traveller was not surprised by her black teeth: 'a defect the English seem subject to, from their too great use of sugar'. Like most novel and expensive foods, sugar was initially plugged as an aphrodisiac. Indeed, a plateful of refined-sugar products such as subtleties and candies must have caused a very strange sensation. A person's first sugar rush, as experienced today by toddlers at birthday parties, is something akin to feeling drunk, and produces similarly excessive behaviour.

Sugar remained a luxury item into the seventeenth century, when traders' ships settled down into the 'triangular' pattern which sustained both the slave and sugar trades. They took guns from Britain to Africa, captured Africans to work the sugar plantations in the West Indian colonies, and brought back sugar to their starting point of Britain. In the years of the fight to get Parliament to outlaw slave-trading, abolitionist sugar bowls proclaimed their owners' commitment to serving sugar imported only from the non-slave-owning parts of the West Indies. One example in the Museum of London has the caption: 'East India sugar is not made by Slaves. By six families using East India, instead of West India sugar, one Slave less is required.'

Another novelty that changed social habits was Sir Walter Raleigh's double-edged gift of pleasure and danger. He brought tobacco, and therefore the pipe, back to England from Virginia. (Once, a new servant of Raleigh's saw smoke and assumed that his master had accidentally set himself on fire. He helpfully doused Raleigh with a bucket of water.) James I was another early friend to the prohibitionist lobby, making a strong stand against the habit of smoking on the grounds of health in his book *The Counterblast to Tobacco* (1604).

Yet smoking also had a practical function in a time of strong and noxious smells. Who can blame Samuel Pepys turning to tobacco as he walked down a plague-stricken Drury Lane? 'I was forced to buy some roll-tobacco', he said, 'to smell and to chaw.' Likewise, those who worked in the dangerous industries of gilding or hat-making, where they were likely to encounter chemicals 'offensive to the Brain', were ripe for seduction by the makers of 'Imperial Golden Snuff'. Snuff would 'bring away all Mercury which lodges in the head', it was promised.

The eighteenth-century fop, like cool people throughout the centuries, enjoyed holding 'a Pipe in his Mouth to make his Diamond Ring the more conspicuous', thereby showing off two consumer products at the same time. The desirable paraphernalia of clay pipes, wooden pipes, cigarette holders and jewelled and engraved cigarette cases would all find their way into smokers' eager hands. Eventually the specialist 'smoking room' was created in grander Victorian houses, after Edward VII as Prince of Wales had made tobacco (almost) respectable. Smoking rooms were elaborate, gloomily decorated places, often in the Moorish style, and required a new outfit: the frogged smoking jacket.

The sixteenth century had seen the introduction of numerous other novelties from the vegetable world. They included the 'apricock', from Portugal, the melon, from France, and the tomato. Arriving from Mexico, tomatoes, or 'apples of love', were grown merely as decorative plants until, in about 1800, people decided to taste them, and concluded that they were delicious.

The humble potato was also unexpectedly slow to catch on in Europe. Only after a good deal of promotional work by agriculturalists did it achieve favour as a cheap and nutritious crop. The tubers we read about in Elizabethan times may well have been sweet potatoes. John Hawkins, slave trader, brought back a vegetable called 'skyretts of Peru' from 'the coast of Guinea and the Indies of Nova Hispania' in 1564; it was probably the sweet potato. (Skirrets were an old root vegetable, rather like a parsnip, 'sweet, white, good to be eaten, and most pleasant in taste'.) Richard Hakluyt, the great traveller, certainly described sweet potatoes in his *Principal Navigations, Voiages, and Discoveries of the English Nation* (1589). He called them 'the most delicate roots . . . the inside eateth like an apple, but it is more delicious than any sweet apple sugared'.

The Spanish brought over the savoury potatoes that eventually became more common, but the British clearly preferred the sweet variety. In a precursor of the sweet-potato pies of American cuisine, a recipe from 1596 describes how to make a tart 'that is a courage to a man'. Sweet potato is mashed with quinces, dates, eggs, wine, sugar, spices and 'the brains of three or four cock sparrows'.

The arrival of nicotine and the potato in the sixteenth century would have a lasting effect upon English society. The comparably significant novelty of the seventeenth century was the caffeinated hot drink. While people drank hot possets and caudles in Tudor times, these were chiefly reserved for people who weren't feeling well. Coffee had been encountered by medieval crusaders in the Middle East, but they don't seem to have liked it enough to bring it back to England. Its first recorded British sighting was in the study of a Greek scholar in 1630s Oxford, the town which went on to open the first public 'coffee house' in 1652.

It's hard now to imagine that tea too was once a wildly novel and possibly dangerous drink, expensive, and therefore kept under lock and key. Samuel Pepys had his first 'cup of tee, (a China drink) of which I never drank before' in 1660. At first people simply didn't know how to make it: Sir Kenelm Digby thought it necessary to inform readers that the correct length of brewing was 'no longer than while you can say the Misere Psalm very leisurely'. This tea was usually drunk black. Before refrigeration, milk was much more perishable than it is today, and most was quickly made into butter or cheese, or reserved for invalids.

As tea became established, it brought with it a whole new category of kitchenware: the tea set. Tea leaves were locked in a caddy, like the 'Japan box for Sweetmeats and tea' owned by the seventeenth-century Duchess of Lauderdale and kept in her private closet at Ham House. Then cups were required. Initially these were the delicate, handle-less, Chinese porcelain containers known as 'dishes', imported from the Orient merely as a sideshow to the business of transporting tea leaves: the crates of china acted as ballast in the tea clippers. Tea dishes purchased in the seventeenth century rarely matched, and the idea that cups should form an identical set did not develop until home-grown British ceramic production took off in the eighteenth century.

Next, a small heater was required to heat the water, along with a teapot in which to stew the leaves. At first, the 'mote spoon', a spoon with holes in it, was used to fish stray leaves out of the tea dish, but in due course this would be replaced by the tea strainer. A tea table might complete the set-up for a tea party in a lady's drawing room.

Along with this new drink, a whole new social entertainment had been born. Tea-drinking was a welcome excuse to invite guests into your living room, where you would then show off both your purchasing power (through your tea set) and your good manners (through knowing how to serve the tea). Once the servants had brought everything in, the ceremony of pouring out would be performed by the hostess.

Yet tea's reputation remained somewhat dubious: it was alien, exotic and expensive. 'I can feel little or no abatement of my pain', wrote an anxious father to a sickening, tea-drinking son in 1731, 'till I hear you are finally determined to drink no more of that detestable, fatal liquor.' In turn-of-the-twentieth-century New York, the craving for strong tea still symbolises the sorry state of fallen woman Lily Bart in Edith Wharton's *The House of Mirth*. '"You look regularly done up, Miss Lily. Well, take your tea strong." Lily smiled faintly at the injunction to take her tea strong. It was the temptation she was always struggling to resist.'

Chocolate – mixed with eggs and spices to form a rich drink – began to appear at late seventeenth-century breakfasts. Samuel Pepys discovered it was a good cure for a hangover, relishing it especially when his head was 'in a sad taking thro' last night's drink'. William III's new palace at Hampton Court had a special private kitchen off 'Chocolate Court', the workplace of the king's own hot-chocolate-maker, the fortuitously named Mr Nice. I feel rather jealous of the newly married Lady Myddleton of Chirk Castle, who in 1686 received delivery of 'a box of Chocholett for my Lady weighing 37 pounds'. Yet chocolate could not be produced in a solid form until the nineteenth century, and Lady Myddleton's box would have contained a powder for drinking or cake flavouring.

Enjoying smoking, coffee, tea or chocolate with friends created new and intimate forums for conversation in the seventeenth century. Their eighteenth-century equivalent, the next novel drink to cause a social revolution, was gin. It had no such benign effect.

Because the craze for gin suddenly sprang up almost from nowhere, gin-drinkers had no notion that it was not a good idea to drink it by the pint as they did ale. Gin had such a marked effect on London's sobriety that people talked about it just as they might discuss crystal meth or any other dangerously addictive drug today. Henry Fielding, in his *Enquiry into the Causes of the late Increase of Robbers* (1751), accused gin of causing a crime wave: 'Many of these wretches there are, who swallow pints of this poison within the twenty-four hours; the dreadful effects of which I have the misfortune every day to see, and to smell too.'

The streets of 1730s London were littered with the bodies of the insensible, most memorably depicted in William Hogarth's print of *Gin Lane*, where mothers neglect their children and suffer all kinds of drink-sodden humiliation. There were many attempts to clamp down upon the sale of gin; informers were bribed to turn in unlicenced gin-sellers; there was much moralising. All these efforts were in fact in vain: the 'problem' of gin was only solved when macroeconomic changes and an increase in the price of its raw ingredients simply made it unaffordable for the poor.

It was often an innovation in ship technology that brought new foods and drinks to the English table, including citrus fruit. The sixteenth-century sailor John Hawkins made his men eat lemons to stave off scurvy, and oranges were well known to the Tudors. Cardinal Wolsey would go forth into early-Tudor London carrying one, its flesh removed and replaced with a sponge soaked in vinegar 'and other confections against pestilent airs'. Father John Gerard, a Jesuit priest kept prisoner in the Tower of London in the 1590s, used orange juice as an invisible ink to write letters to the friends who helped him escape. (A letter written in orange juice is illegible until it is heated in an oven.)

Limes and grapefruits began to appear from the West Indies in the 1680s. But the banana, first seen in London in 1633, was not regularly available in London's markets until the fast steamships of the nineteenth century were able to bring supplies over from the Indies before they rotted. In the late Georgian age, it was discovered that green turtles from the West Indies could be kept alive in tanks of fresh water long enough to make the journey to England, so turtle soup cooked 'in West Indian fashion' began to appear on fashionable tables. Mr Howse, the cook at Saltram House in Devon, was described as 'one of the most accomplished Turtle dressers of the Age'.

And the turtle remained the reptile of choice for aristocrats. 'Heat up some of the turtle soup', commanded the fictional detective Lord Peter Wimsey on his wedding night, in a novel published in 1937, 'and give us the *foie gras*, the quails in aspic, and a bottle of hock.' James Bond had a similar penchant for pâté de foie gras when he made his first appearance in 1953, and also for another exotic fruit: upon ordering 'half an avocado pear with a little French dressing', he is complimented by a maître d'hotel upon the excellence of his taste.

But even with novelties like gin, bananas, foie gras and avocado pears making their debuts, English taste remained resolutely retrograde. Part of the reason was religious. Since the Reformation, Protestant priests had condemned luxurious clothes, houses and food alike. The 'art of cookery, originated not in Luxury; but in Necessity', wrote Richard Warner in 1791. He, and many other British food writers, thought that cooks should confine themselves merely to 'rendering any food more digestible than it would be, in its natural, or simple state'. So the English stuck with their stolid tradition: a wedding feast at Charlecote House near Warwick in 1845 still saw 'every cottage on the estate . . . regaled with beef, plum pudding and good ale'.

Although British mainstream taste remained conservative, it was gradually but inevitably inched forwards by improvements in the technology of food production. Even the 'roast beef of old England' had once been a novelty. The ending of the Wars of the Roses and the peace imposed by the Tudors allowed herds of cows to be kept alive and fed throughout the winter for the first time. The Tudors evolved a system whereby cows made a one-way journey from their birthplaces in the high pastures of Wales and the north of England, down to the Home Counties for fattening, and then on to Smithfield in London for slaughter and sale. By 1539, Sir Thomas Elyot could write that 'Beef of England to Englishmen which are in health, bringeth strong nourishing', and, to the French, eating cow became symbolic of *les rosbifs* across the Channel.

In the seventeenth century, the growing dairy industry replaced curds with cheese as the most common form of preserved milk. The Stuart period was also notable for its use of butter, so much so that a visiting Frenchman thought English food 'swimming' in

the stuff, practically every dish being 'well moistened with butter'. While everybody had always longed for fresh meat, it was
only in the eighteenth century that it began for the first time to
become available to the lower ranks in society. A revolution in
farming saw turnips, swedes and clover introduced as fodder to
keep even more cattle alive throughout the winter. More cattle
led in turn to more manure to enrich the soil. In 1710, the average
ox sold at Smithfield Market weighed 370 pounds, but by 1795
creatures of 800 pounds were standard. It was in Georgian times
that the English confirmed their lasting reputation as carnivores.
A Swiss traveller wrote that he'd 'always heard' the British 'were
great flesh-eaters and I found it true. I have known people in
England that never eat any bread.' Indeed, people said that the
Duke of Grafton, 'who eats an ox a day', was planning a trip to
the spa at Bath, 'to enable himself to eat two'.

Until the nineteenth century, dishes tasted only roughly

In the eighteenth century, arable farmers became capable of producing the
fodder to keep animals alive all winter. Cows became much bigger, and
the golden age of roast meat dawned

similar each time they were made. About 1800, the modern idea of a standardised recipe appeared. Until then, recipes had been somewhat vague on quantities, length of cooking and temperature. They commonly began with instructions such as 'take four tame Pigeons' or 'take a swan'; nature, not a shop, was providing the ingredients. The quantities were usually described as 'proportionable' or 'meet', and cooking times were often along the lines of 'until well boiled'.

Eliza Acton is widely recognised as the inventor of the modern recipe book. Her innovation was to list measured ingredients at the start of each recipe before embarking on the instructions. So life was becoming better ordered and time divided into units that everyone could measure and recognise. Instinct was subordinated to experience; tastes were becoming more firmly fixed. But maybe, ultimately, food was becoming sterile.

The twentieth century has seen the world grow smaller and the cuisines of every region appear in our kitchens: French, Italian, Indian, Chinese, Thai, Mexican, Japanese and Californian. Ironically, though, the simultaneous removal of food production from the domestic to the industrial sphere has also tended to iron out regional and local quirks in cookery. There's certainly an argument that national television and magazine advertising, once it appeared in the 1950s, flattened out the individuality of what had previously been a set of lively local traditional cuisines in America.

Salt and sugar, the cheapest flavourings, still predominate. Ostensibly we have many more flavours than ever before, but many of them seem practically identical. So much so, in fact, that since transport is now good enough for anyone anywhere to eat anything in any season, some rich westerners are rejecting air freight in order to remain loyal to the local. Tudor and Georgian aristocrats, desperate for novelty, would have found this unimaginable, but the labourers upon their lands would have wholly understood.

41 – Chewing, Swallowing, Burping and Farting

We have brought chemistry into our kitchens, not as a handmaid but as a poisoner ... we have let the beer of the people disappear, and have grown ashamed of roast beef.

Mary Ellen Meredith, 1851

The history of chewing and digestion tells the story of the rise and rise of processed food. Until very recently, with our post-industrial desire to return to a more 'natural' way of living, raw food, roughage and vegetables were far from desirable.

Medieval people particularly prized food that they didn't have to chew. Tender young kid goats, lambs or birds were all delightful. Doves were reserved for the lord of the manor, thereby raising the status of small birds. The Tudor favourite was the melting meat of a young kid, 'praised above all other flesh', and devoured to celebrate the end of the gruelling Lenten fast.

But most of the population, if they ate meat at all, had to make do with tough, smoked or salted flesh. Medieval peasants were forbidden by law from hunting the deer and other tasty animals that were reserved for their betters. In 1066, the Normans introduced Forest Law to protect the areas where deer were husbanded for hunting. A forest was therefore defined by its legal status, not by its trees. Forest Law limited the hunting of deer to landowners only, and the punishments for breaking it were horrific: 'whosoever slew a hart, or a hind, should be deprived of his eyesight'. *The Anglo-Saxon Chronicle* tells us that William the Conqueror himself was personally concerned with the matter. He

forbade men to kill the harts, so also the boars; and he loved the tall deer as if he were their father. Likewise he declared respecting the hares that they should go free. His rich bemoaned it, and the poor men shuddered at it.

The character of Robin Hood, the outlaw, became so popular with the common people because he ignored the hated Forest Law. But unlike Robin, who took what he wanted from the forest, peasants never tasted venison unless they ran the high risks associated with poaching. If a peasant was lucky enough to own a cow, sheep or chicken, he would have valued it far too highly to eat it. Farm animals were for transport, milk, wool or eggs, not food. So the peasant's meat intake was largely limited to small and nasty creatures: squirrels, wild birds, hedgehogs ('hogs' or 'pigs' of the hedges). To cook a hedgehog you wrap it in clay and put the clay ball into the fire. A couple of hours later, you smash the clay, which pulls the prickles off the meat. Should a pig or sheep be slaughtered, every single scrap would be eaten, including snout, trotters and internal organs. Hams would be sewn up in hessian and hoisted into the smoky rafters above the fire for preservation.

Yet meat was readily available for those lucky enough to have a job at the royal court. Peasants could only dream of the pleasure courtiers and servants took in nibbling the finest juicy flesh, cooked for hours on a slow-turning spit. The concept of the desirability of soft 'roast' meat was incredibly powerful, so much so that we still use the word 'roast' to describe a joint that's merely been 'baked', in the technical sense, ever since the oven replaced the spit.

The fourteenth-century ploughman Piers described in *Vision of Piers the Plowman* did not set his sights as high as red meat. Instead, his fantasy foods included chicken, goose, salt bacon and eggs. He had to make do instead with lumpy green cheeses, loaves of beans and bran, 'parsley, leeks and many cabbages'. In fact, 76 per cent of the calories in the diet of a medieval peasant would come from bread and pottage. The shepherds in the fourteenth-century play that forms part of the 'Chester Mystery Cycle' likewise eat bread, bacon, onions, garlic, leeks, butter, green cheeses, oatcakes and a rather nasty-sounding dish of sheep's heads soused in ale and sour milk.

In hard times Piers or the shepherds might also have eaten indigestible crops really intended for animals. These included 'berevechicorn', a mixture of barley, oats and vetch, or 'bollymong' (oats, peas, vetch and buckwheat). People often sowed fields with a mixture of seeds – rye and wheat together, for example – so that even if one crop failed the other would provide at least something to eat. These crops produced the very roughest 'brown bread . . . having much bran', which 'filleth the belly with excrements and shortly descendeth from the stomach'. Root vegetables also kept the belly feeling full: carrots and parsnips were 'common meat among the common people, all the time of autumn', wrote Thomas Cogan in 1584.

That was the diet of shepherds and ploughmen, but towndwellers obtained similar foods from markets. Town authorities made great efforts to have bread and ale, the staple foods for everyone, sold at reasonable prices. They faced perennial problems, though, through the antics of the 'forestallers', unscrupulous dealers who bought up food before it reached the market stalls. They passed it on to private clients, literally 'forestalling' the general public.

One thing remained standard throughout the whole history of Britain: people ate lots of grain, whether in the form of pottage, ale or bread. A breakfast served to the Earl and Countess of Northumberland in the fifteenth century consisted of a two-pound 'manchet', or best-quality loaf, *each*, plus another 'trencher' loaf, pre-sliced, for use as their plates.

Medieval bread came in a variety of forms, from the desirable, refined 'manchet', or white rolls, to the rough, coarse 'cheat', or brown bread. A 'white baker' and a 'brown baker' carried out different tasks, and a brown baker was not allowed – by a regulation of 1440 – to possess a sieve. Why 'manchet'? Possibly from 'mayne', the name for the best quality of flour; maybe from *manger*, French for 'to eat'; or perhaps from *main*, French for 'hand', because manchet rolls were about the size of a fist.

The various soupy dishes called 'pottages' and 'slops' were Tudor mainstays. Andrew Boorde defines pottage as 'liquor in which flesh is sodden in, with putting-to of chopped herbs, and oatmeal and salt'. Alternatively, you might make 'pease pottage' from dried peas. You could keep your pottage on the go for months, topping it up each day, hence the nursery rhyme:

> Pease pudding hot
> Pease pudding cold
> Pease pudding in the pot
> Nine days old.

Vegetables were cooked so severely for fear of indigestion, and if they were found in grander dishes at all, they were hidden away as part of a meat hash or in a sauce. The inappropriate fart was a mainstay of medieval humour, and sometimes fart jokes were taken so seriously that they passed into legal documents. A thirteenth-century gentleman called Roland the Farter was forced to pay for his tenure of Hemingston in Suffolk by performing 'every year on the birthday of our Lord before his master the king, one jump, and a whistle, and one fart'.

Even the humble potato, upon its arrival from America, needed an image makeover before it was welcome because people thought it flatulent. As John Forster, potato promoter, wrote in 1664: 'If any shall Object; That this Bread is windy, I answer;

That it cannot be, for the Roots being first boiled . . . and afterwards baked, it is impossible they should be windy.'

The aristocracy preferred their food well-cooked partly to avoid wind, but also to dodge the danger of disease present in poorly washed greens. 'Beware of green salads & raw fruits for they will make your sovereign sick,' warned a cookbook in 1500. Surviving medieval recipes often involve cooking food twice. In microbiological terms these multiple and prolonged heatings made food safer to eat, something to which great importance was rightly attached. The late Stuart journalist, Ned Ward, described the horrors of tapeworm:

> Want of digestion, craving Drowth,
> Dull Eyes, dry lips, and feav'rish Mouth,
> Unsav'ry Belches after Drinking,
> Foul Stomach, and a Breath that's stinking,
> All these Symptoms, that will tell ye
> You've crawling Insects in your Belly.

Georgian sufferers from tapeworm could have tried medicines such as 'Dr Walldron's Worm destroying Cake'. One satisfied user (from Leeds) found that Dr Walldron's cure caused him to excrete 'upwards of three hundred worms, some of them of Uncommon Thickness'.

In fact, it's difficult to identify raw, as opposed to cooked, greens in people's diets until around 1600. From then on, though, we can begin to identify vegetables on upper-class British dinner tables. Surviving lists or inventories of silverware start to include containers for oil and vinegar intended for 'sallets'. Gervase Markham, writing around the turn of the seventeenth century, describes a sallet, or salad, of 'chives, scallions, Radish-roots . . . young Lettice, Cabbage-lettice, pursalane and divers other herbs'. Carrots, though, were still to be 'boiled'. On the whole he recommends 'boiled sallets', or else vegetables pickled in vinegar, as more easily digestible.

Fruit was treated with similar disdain. In the medieval forest peasants could also forage for apples, hazelnuts, wild strawberries and even wild honey, and also fruits less familiar to modern ears such as crab apples, sloes and bilberries, 'wont to be an extraordinary great profit and pleasure to poor people'. Medieval paupers ate a good deal more fruit than their lords and masters, who again feared disease and had no need to scavenge.

Diarrhoea was much more of a menace in an age before clean water. This explains the long-held fear of fruit in particular, which was considered a powerful and dangerous laxative (although Henry VIII was partial to strawberries). Fruits 'engender ill humours', warns a health manual of 1541. The medieval apples with their beautiful names (Costard, Pippin, Blanderelle) were therefore often stewed; likewise the apples mentioned by Shakespeare in the sixteenth century: Leather Coats (we'd call them russets), Apple-Johns, Bitter-Sweets. Lady Burlington in 1735 boasted that 'almost the whole house is ill of a looseness [of the bowels] excepting myself which I take to be owing to my not eating much fruit & that only what is good'. One feels almost sorry (a rare occurrence) for the bumptious Jonathan Swift, obliged to watch a friend gobbling the most 'delicious peaches, and he was champing and champing, but I durst not eat one'. Fruit makes rare appearances on Victorian menus, usually still stewed or made into a pie. The harmless grape, for Mrs Beeton, was an effective cure for even 'the most obstinate cases of constipation'.

Victorian menus intended for women and children still reveal a surprising absence of vegetables, and cookery books recommend some seemingly interminable cooking times. You should boil carrots for more than two hours, claims one, for ease of digestion, and even macaroni should have ninety minutes. The 1909 edition of Mrs Beeton's cookbook is quite explicit that the cook's goal is 'to facilitate and hasten digestion'. Her Digestive Time Table shows that pickled cabbage takes a regrettable four and a half hours to digest; much better to boil, as it then leaves the stomach after only three and a half hours.

There's a fascinating theory that Charles Darwin's well-known health problems were due to the worries he had (as a man of his time) about his digestion. Suffering from dyspepsia, he was prescribed 'Fowler's solution', a medicine containing arsenic. The nausea and tingling he experienced in his toes were taken as positive signs that the drug was working. Darwin did in fact exhibit twenty-one of the twenty-six possible symptoms of someone suffering from arsenic poisoning.

Only more recently, with the advent of almost instantly digestible types of convenience food, has this search for quicker digestion lost pace. After industrialisation, threats to health came not from dirty water and inadequately washed raw produce, but from processed, pre-packaged goods containing attractive-looking, quickly absorbed calories which were nevertheless devoid of any lasting nutritional benefit. Canned meat with preservatives is worse for you than fresh; biscuits are less nutritious than fresh bread.

Baking standards had been a matter of concern since the *Assisa Panis*, or Assize of Bread, of 1266, which first attempted to set standard sizes for loaves in response to short-selling. A pamphlet published in the 1750s with the title of *Poison Detected* exposed the tricks of unscrupulous bakers, who'd use lime, chalk and even alum to make their loaves bigger and whiter. According to the pamphleteer, they'd even employ the powdered bones of dead bodies to eke out their flour.

Parliamentary reports throughout the Victorian age revealed how much skulduggery still went on in this important industry. A report of 1862 described how in numerous bakeries 'masses' of cobwebs could be seen 'frequently falling into the dough'. But the greatest scam perpetrated upon poor housewives was the replacement of stone-grinding flour mills with roller mills. The new technique reduced the amount of vitamin B1 and iron in flour, and therefore bread. From about 1890 to the 1930s a generation of poorer children were anaemic as a result.

Tinned food had first appeared for army use in the Napoleonic wars, and 'desiccated' or instant soup was available from the 1840s. The makers of processed food encountered various problems. The canning concern of Stephen Goldner, for example, enthusiastically produced bigger and bigger containers of beef. Once their tins reached a colossal 2.7 kg in weight, though, the beef at the centre could not fail to be improperly cooked, and the tins would either explode or give people food poisoning. Other well-known wheezes perpetrated upon the city consumer included watercress grown in beds of horrible human sewage, or else a mendacious butcher who might 'wash your old meat that hath hung weltering in the shop with new blood' to make it look fresh.

Yet many people found processed food convenient and delicious, and ignored health concerns. It's been argued that Britain's early industrialisation, and its accompanying need for convenience food, explains the peculiarly British fondness for crisps, chips and sandwiches, which contrasts sharply with the Mediterranean tradition. When Crosse and Blackwell in 1855 introduced brown pickles to the British public, made without the poisonous green food colouring of their predecessors, sales collapsed. One disgruntled pickle-lover felt that he 'ought to be very much obliged, of course, to those disinterested medical gentlemen' who campaigned for purer food, but for his own part he really liked 'anchovies to be red and pickles green'.

And so the twentieth century saw processing of food taken to new heights. The advent of TV dinners, microwave meals and hydrogenated fats were all intended to increase ease for the eater and profit for the manufacturer rather than provide nutrition. Only with the 1980s rise of the 'foodie', the 1990s fondness for raw fish and sushi, and the 2000s craze for the organic vegetable box has there been an alternative impulse towards unprocessed food. For the very first time in history, simple, raw and seasonal has now become the food of fashion.

42 – Raising Your Elbow

I must not omit the custom of handing round,
after dinner, on the removal of the cloth, a human
skull filled with burgundy.

C. S. Matthews visits Lord Byron
at Newstead Abbey, 1809

'Raising your elbow' is an Italian expression for taking a drink, because the elbow is elevated every time food or drink travels from table to mouth. It's time to explore the way people have raised their elbows throughout the centuries – in other words, to examine table etiquette.

Today, people reading about grand meals in the past are often simply amazed that our ancestors managed to eat so much food. For any period before 1830, though, this is based on a misunderstanding of how food was served. A well-dressed table would contain numerous dishes, like a modern buffet. The diners were not expected to eat it all, but rather to browse among the dishes until they found something they liked. Superfluity was standard for the rich. Indeed, some people's remuneration packages included the 'reversion', or remains, of the meals of more important members of the same household. In the fifteenth-century establishment of the Earl of Northumberland, the earl's two sons must have been watched, hawk-like, as they ate by the five servants who were counting upon the leftovers for their own meal.

Medieval and Tudor people had spoons for their soup, knives for cutting their meat, but no forks. Each possessed his or her own knife. After eating, it was wiped clean on bread and then put away in a tie-on pocket or sheaf hung from the belt. The fingers were equally important eating utensils, so washing them beforehand in a bowl of water was a vital ritual.

A description of the duties of a medieval waiter illustrates how tables were laid. 'Put the salt on the right hand of your lord,' the waiter is told, and 'on his left a trencher or two. On their left a knife, then white rolls, and beside, a spoon folded in a napkin.'

Medieval and Tudor food was sent up to the great hall table in a big dish called a 'mess' (from the Latin *mittere*, to send), and you shared your mess dish with your three 'messmates'. Those of higher status might be served up to fourteen or fifteen dishes, while the lower servants might only get one or two. On grander tables, a 'second remove' would see the table cleared and then laid all over again with another profusion of dishes. Pewter, horn or wooden cups would be filled with beer by the patrolling butler.

In a grand household the dishes would be carried from a service hatch or 'dresser' in the kitchen wall and up to the dining hall by an impressive procession of serving men (plate 33). The parade was masterminded by an officer called the 'usher of the hall'. At Wollaton Hall in Nottingham, instructions from 1572 describe his duty at dinnertime: 'he is with a loud voice to command all gentlemen and yeomen to repair to the dresser. At the nether end of the hall he is to meet the service, saying with a loud voice, "Give place, my masters".'

Up on the dais at the upper end of the hall there were strict rules about which people could sit together. Often you see pictures of kings having dinner all by themselves because there was no one else present of high enough rank with whom they could share a table. The instructions for the training of a medieval page remind the reader of the following rules of rank: a pope, emperor, king, cardinal, archbishop or duke might legitimately share a table, as might a bishop, marquis, viscount and earl. The Archbishop of Canterbury, though, was too senior to eat with the Bishop of York.

In the seventeenth century, you can at least see the royal family seated at the same table in a renowned picture showing Charles I, his wife Henrietta Maria and their son Charles sharing a meal. But the rest of their courtiers, unworthy of even approaching too closely to the royal table, are all standing back and watching respectfully, almost worshipfully, from behind a balustrade.

In the eighteenth century, this curious custom of watching the royal family eat was still occasionally performed at Hampton Court. But now, with the decline of monarchical power, the sight of royal mastication was no longer the treasured treat it had once been, and an element of farce entered the proceedings. Entry was open to any respectably dressed member of the public who joined the queue. This sometimes rowdy audience sat on ranks of seats, and one day the barrier holding them back collapsed. Those leaning upon it fell over and lost their hats and wigs, at which minor calamity 'their Majesties laugh'd heartily'.

Even as the different ranks in society began to mix and share the same table, *placement* still held its sway, and at high-society parties throughout the nineteenth century the procession into dinner was organised according to status as defined by the peerage. It was Edward VII who eventually granted his prime minister the position of precedence immediately after the Archbishop of Canterbury. He did this after observing a dinner where Arthur Balfour, a plain 'mister', was seated below the undergraduate son of a peer. By the twentieth century, that struck even a king as wrong.

The Jacobean traveller Thomas Coryat came back from Italy

with news of a fabulous new implement called the fork. He had noticed how it obviated the need to have everyone's dirty hands in the common dish. Of course, the English treated this novelty with the grave suspicion due to anything foreign: 'we need no little forks to make hay with our mouths, to throw our food into them,' complained Nicholas Breton in 1618. But forks did eventually catch on, and with their adoption the position of the diner's napkin changed as well. Formerly it had been laid over the shoulder to protect clothes from the messy passage of finger-held food from plate to mouth; in the seventeenth century, it moved downwards to be laid on the lap.

Along with more sophisticated eating utensils, behaviour grew increasingly genteel. To 'belch or bulch', wrote Richard Weste in his *Book of Deameanour* (1619) is 'base, most foul and nothing worth'. 'Roll not thy meat within thy mouth that every man may it see,' was how the sixteenth-century Hugh Rhodes put it. He also advised that spitting was just about acceptable, but 'let it not lie upon the ground . . . tread thou it out'.

After the meat course, Tudor or Stuart diners on a grand occasion might expect a 'banquet', the course consisting of sweetmeats and 'subtleties'. Subtleties were feasts for the eyes as well as the mouth, strange confections of nuts, sugar, marzipan and spice formed into wonderful shapes. Other recipes for 'banqueting' food include marmalades of quinces and plums, and a set of instructions describing 'How to Candy all sorts of Flowers, as they grow with their Stalk on'.

Because subtleties really existed for entertainment rather than nourishment, they gave rise to a curiously anarchic form of behaviour. Having admired them, people would smash them up, just as they throw glasses over their shoulders after a toast in some cultures today. The seventeenth-century Robert May described a riotous scene at one banquet of novelty food: 'when lifting first the lid off the one pie, out skip some frogs, which makes the ladies skip and shriek: next after the other pie, when out come some birds'. 'The flying birds and the skipping frogs' caused enjoyable chaos.

Some banqueting food wasn't even edible. When the installation of the Archbishop of Canterbury was celebrated in 1443, the subtlety consisted of 'Saint Andrew sitting on high Altar of estate, with beams of gold'. It seems likely that such extravagant scenes were modelled in wood and plaster rather than sugar.

The Georgian age still saw a buffet-style profusion of dishes being served, albeit in two main courses followed by dessert. A footman's instructions from 1827 describe how the serving dishes should surround a grand centrepiece such as a silver epergne, or 'timesaver', holding candles, fruit and condiments. The footman should arrange the table with military precision, the dishes being 'set in a proper line' or else 'those who sit at the top and bottom will perceive it in an instant'.

Even though the table would be loaded with food, it was rude to reach over and grab. Ravenous guests would sometimes slip the footman a coin to position their favourite dish in front of their own place setting. If you were female, you might even feel forced to remain hungry, because 'eating a great deal is deemed indelicate in a lady . . . her character should be divine rather than sensual'.

The carving of the meat, though, was a task reserved for the hostess, and while she wielded the knife everyone else would have had to conceal their impatience. This was quite a performance, but a necessary part of hospitality. The young Lady Mary Wortley Montagu received lessons in carving three times a week, and practised upon wooden models of 'the different joints of meat'.

Georgian drinking glasses were filled by servants at the wine cooler standing in an alcove at one end of the dining room, and brought to the diner on request. Water glasses stood upon the table. The secret supporters of the Jacobite pretenders to Britain's throne, the exiled, Catholic descendants of James II, would covertly toast 'the king over the water' by picking up their wine glasses and passing them over the water jug. Water glasses were used not just for drinking but also for washing the fingers or teeth, and Tobias Smollett in 1766 complained how even polite people followed the 'beastly' custom of using their glasses to 'spit, squirt and spew the filthy scouring of their gums'.

It was only in the 1830s that the centuries-old habit of buffet-style eating was changed, with the introduction of *service à la Russe*. This supposedly Russian innovation saw each serving dish placed upon the sideboard rather than the table, and the servants helped each diner individually. At first elements of the old ways survived: in the 1850s, a tureen of soup and the fish might still be ready and waiting on the table before the diners were seated. By the 1880s, though, all the food was served in completely separate courses as it is today.

Service à la Russe delighted cutlery-makers, because the more courses you had, the more utensils you needed, and knives and forks began to be laid in thicker and thicker flanks on each side of the plate. But there was something a bit nouveau riche about taking this too far. The fish knife, for example, quickly became an indicator of vulgarity. ('Phone for the fish knives, Norman,' said John Betjeman in his poem parodying typical lower-middle-class sayings.) If you'd been lucky enough to inherit Georgian silver, you probably had little sympathy for the idea of separate courses or the requirement for new cutlery to eat them with. Only the late twentieth century saw a reverse in the general trend for more complicated cutlery: now the knife is on the decline as people eat upon their sofas, and various manufacturers are hoping that the 'spork', a combined spoon and fork for use one-handed, will catch on.

Contrary to first impressions, the change to *service à la Russe* actually made economic sense. If you were presenting a wonderful spread of food as the Georgians had done, you were forced to prepare more food than your guests were actually able to eat.

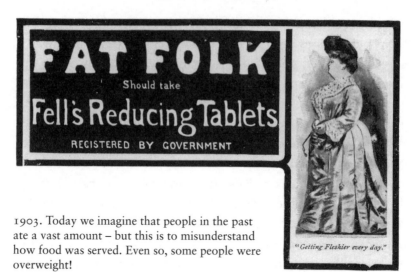

FAT FOLK
Should take
Fell's Reducing Tablets
REGISTERED BY GOVERNMENT

"Getting Fleshier every day."

1903. Today we imagine that people in the past ate a vast amount – but this is to misunderstand how food was served. Even so, some people were overweight!

The abundance and wastage was justified because the leftovers were passed on to those poorer and needier as charity. (The best-known innovation that Consuelo, the new American Duchess of Marlborough, made to life at Blenheim Palace in the 1890s was to separate the meat from the sweet in the cans of spare food distributed to nearby villagers. Everything had previously been jumbled up together.) Serving food in courses, though, meant that you needed to cook only just the right amount.

A dinner party for ten in Edwardian times, the heyday of dining *à la Russe*, might easily have involved five hundred separate pieces of cutlery and crockery. Frederick Gorst, a butler, describes the way well-trained servants would almost dance in the successive courses: 'each footman followed and complemented the others', demonstrating 'the technique which we had all spent years perfecting'.

You might see such a performance in a fine restaurant today, although not usually in a private home. The multicourse meal remains in existence only for special occasions, but it was still a standard, everyday event when, in 1939, the unemployed and upper-class Monica Dickens took a job as a cook. Her very first client presented a daunting request for 'just a small, simple dinner: lobster cocktails, soup, turbot Mornay, pheasants with vegetables, fruit salad, and a savoury'.

Such gourmandising on a daily basis might seem almost obscene, but then portion sizes were much smaller. And indeed, such a meal contains much more protein, and a lot less carbohydrate, than today's bog-standard dinner dish of pasta and tomato sauce. Nutritionally speaking, turbot and pheasant provided a much better balanced meal than today's time-saving middle-class standbys.

43 – The Political Consequences of Sauces

The English had twenty religions and only one sauce.
A French ambassador quoted by
Launcelot Sturgeon, 1822

Launcelot Sturgeon's essay 'On the Physical and Political Consequences of Sauces' was first published in 1822. In it he examined the politics of food and our love–hate relationship with French cooking. He argued that the creation of a carefully blended, delicious sauce was vital to a nation's well-being, as was the cook who made it: 'the importance of an art which thus binds the whole fabric of society must be at once apparent'. Yet in his day, sauce, that ultimate French invention, was feared and derided. The British thought sauce was fashion, not food.

Back in the mists of Norman time, England's rulers spoke French and their downtrodden minions spoke English. The clash of cultures between invader and invaded is clear even in eleventh-century food bills, in which living animals are named in the Anglo-Saxon language of the servants who reared them: cow, sheep, swine, boar and deer. The same creatures appear on the table with the French names used by the Norman masters who ate them: beef, mutton, pork, bacon and venison.

The relationships between nations are expressed and statements of allegiance are made through food. This may be done

306

very simply with visual messages. At Henry VI's Coronation Feast, the first course included dishes decorated with the symbols of his realms of England and France:

A red leach of sliced meats, eggs, fruits and spices, with lions carved therein in white
Custard royal with a leopard of gold sitting therein
Fritter like the sun, with a fleur-de-lis therein.

Attention always has to be paid to the symbolism of royal menus, and the unpopular Hanoverian kings of Britain further damaged their reputations by eating their native German sausages, Rhineland soup and cabbages. ('Kraut' and 'Boche', two derogatory terms for Germans, both come from cabbages which Germans are supposed to love.) Meanwhile, their Jacobite rivals made political capital by ostentatiously consuming even in exile dishes such as Devonshire pie and drinking good old British beer.

Despite Sturgeon's complaints, the English did eat some sauces. An Elizabethan cookbook, for example, contains a 'sauce for a roasted Rabbit' said to have been favoured by Henry VIII containing parsley, butter, sugar, pepper and 'a few crumbs of white bread' to thicken it. But Charles II returned to England from his exile in 1660 with an unprecedented taste for saucy French dishes. For a time sauces came into high fashion: Hannah Woolley's cookbook of 1677 contains seventy-two recipes for them, several described as 'French'.

But these new French sauces failed to become part of the bedrock of British cooking. There persisted a lingering suspicion of 'made' dishes such as casseroles or ragouts. French dishes, as opposed to wholesome English roasts, signified moral degeneration in literature right up to 1813, when Jane Austen in *Pride and Prejudice* made the effete and rude Mr Hurst ignore the heroine from the moment 'he found her prefer a plain dish to a ragout'.

In 1821, *The Cook's Oracle* was among several publications

which attempted to persuade reluctant readers of the benefits of the available 'Receipts for hashes, stews, and ragouts, &c., of these there are a great multitude . . . in the French kitchen they count upwards of 600, and are daily inventing new ones.' The French had a very good reason to invent all these ragouts: in their hotter climate meat perished more quickly, and decay could be delayed or disguised by stewing. In England the more plentiful supply of succulent meat, combined with snobbery about stewing, meant that the roast remains a symbol of solid respectability right up to the present day.

Yet envy also played its part in this hatred of French sauces. The best and highest-paid cooks in Britain were always French, because sometimes, when entertaining to impress, nothing but a sophisticated and complicated sauce will do. Next best to a French chef was a French-trained one, and the Georgian William Verral fell into this category. He was shocked by the primitive kitchens he found in even a fairly well-to-do house in eighteenth-century Sussex: no pans beyond a stew pan and a frying pan, and that as 'black as my hat' with 'a handle long enough to obstruct half the passage of the kitchen'. When he asked for a sieve, he was handed one which had been used for sanding the floor.

The formidable list of implements that Verral considered essential for proper French cooking included eight small stew pans, two very large ones, cake hoops, lemon squeezer, sugar cutters, toasting fork, a larkspit (literally for spitting larks), dripping pans, preserving pots and a 'mustard bullet'. But above all, he needed several 'sauce-pans', pans literally for making sauces. The new kitchen ranges could only accommodate flat-bottomed pans, rather than round-bottomed pots, and in the late eighteenth century the saucepan came of age.

Georgian consumers needed little persuading that saucepans came in 'sets', and that one's set should be complete. Stone and Company, advertising in The Times (1788), informed readers

Saucepans were among a woman's prized possessions: courtship gifts,
everyday household utensils, personal-attack alarms or even weapons

that they had 'greatly improved their sets of Tin Ware, which
renders it the most wholesome and cheapest furniture in use,
and preferable to others offered to the public'. Such adverts
surely created a desire where none had existed before.

These saucepans were usually copper with a tin lining. Copper
could, over time, react with the acid in food to create a poison,
so the tin was vital to keep the copper away from the food. If the
tin lining became worn, it had to be replaced or the pan could

potentially poison. This was the role of the 'tinker' roving from door to kitchen door.

So the possession of a set of saucepans became the goal of many a Georgian housewife. Indeed, a man's gift of a pan to an unmarried woman suggested that matrimony was imminent. In a marital dispute, a woman could lay claim to her saucepans with more chance of success than for any other items from the home except her clothes. She could clash them together to summon aid in cases of domestic violence – or even use them as weapons to strike back.

The idea that French sauces and cuisine should be admired, if not adopted for everyday meals, also found its way across the Atlantic to the New World. Hot summers, plentiful pasture and an outdoor-orientated culture meant that grilled meat and the barbecue became American standards by the 1950s.

But there too fine cooking would become inescapably French. Its greatest proselytiser was Julia Childs, who had an infectious passion for sauce. Her book of 1961, *Mastering the Art of French Cooking*, and her TV show, *The French Chef*, encouraged the 'servantless American cook' to abandon all concern for 'budgets, waistlines, time schedules' and 'children's meals' in order to throw him- or herself into 'producing something wonderful to eat'. Elizabeth Bennet would have been horrified.

44 – Were They All Drunk All the Time?

Would you believe it, though water is to be had
in abundance in London, and of a fairly good quality,
absolutely none is drunk? ... In this country
nothing but beer is drunk.

César de Saussure, 1720s

The alcohol consumption of people in the past often seems prodigious. For a start, everyone drank ale or beer in preference to water. The amounts consumed are impressive. The household of Humphrey Stafford, Duke of Buckingham, for example, consumed more than forty thousand gallons annually, while the monks of Fountains Abbey had a malthouse capable of producing sixty barrels of very strong beer every ten days.

In large households, the 'butler' was originally responsible for serving the beer at mealtimes. There are two theories about where his job title comes from: perhaps from the beer 'butts' which stored the ale, or perhaps from the French *botterlie* for beer cellar. Their proximity to alcohol made many butlers susceptible to 'the butler's complaint': drinking. 'All butlers grumble,' complained one exasperated seventeenth-century employer, 'they're seldom dry, yet still they . . . drink.' In the 1960s, the butler Peter Whiteley found himself fortunate enough to be sent for drying out by his employer: 'she paid for me to be treated by the highest doctor of his kind in the land'.

Apart from butlers, though, most people seemed to avoid dangerous levels of inebriation. The majority of their daily beer was very weak ('smallbeer') and provided a safer drinking choice than water. For working people, too, it also contained calories that were very necessary to their diet.

Many people are aware that the British climate has waxed and waned, and during the 'warm centuries' – the tenth and eleventh – vineyards flourished in England. In 1289, the Bishop of Hereford was still managing to produce 882 gallons of white wine on his estates. But most English grapes were used to make verjuice (a fermented sour juice), and the best wine was imported.

Strong red Gascon wine was the long-time favourite of British drinkers, except during the periods when wars with the French or disputes with the Dutch merchants who transported it disrupted supplies. In the seventeenth century, sweet wines from Portugal and the Canary Islands ousted their French and German predecessors from the top of the wine importers' lists. The volumes consumed are impressive: each member of the garrison of Dover Castle, for example, was given a quart of wine a day in the fourteenth century.

But just like beer, wine wasn't as strong as it is today. Neither were the sharp young wines or 'verjuices' of England as horrid as they sound: they were drunk with sugar or spices added. No one drank mature wine because the casks it was stored in failed to keep out air and it went very bitter very quickly. Only when bottled wine first began to appear in the later Tudor period did maturity and its resultant flavour become appreciated.

Spirits became popular in Ireland before England. They began to seduce Tudor drinkers in the sixteenth century, performing their marvellous work of taking 'away sadness' and of making men 'witty'. Spirits were also known as 'cordial waters', and were thought to stimulate the heart; 'aqua vitae' or 'burning waters' were taken like medicines. But their advertised powers of keeping the plague away were seen sadly to fail during the epidemics of 1593, despite their being widely consumed. The distillers lost much credit as a result.

While alcohol was ubiquitous, and while beer formed an important part of nutrition, that's not to say it wasn't abused. It's been argued that many medieval battles took place between drunken combatants: both to raise their courage and to dull the pain of wounds. Less appropriate was drunkenness at home. 'If any man do perceive that he is drunk,' wrote a Tudor doctor, 'let him take a vomit with water and oil, or with a feather, or a rosemary branch, or else with his finger, or else let him go to his bed to sleep.' In 1552, the first Licensing Act was passed because of the 'intolerable hurts and troubles' caused by the drinkers in alehouses. From then on, landlords had to acquire a licence for their premises from the local Justice of the Peace. Constant complaints about drunkenness followed: in 1576, the poet George Gascoigne described inebriation as 'a monstrous plant, lately crept into the pleasant orchards of England'.

But drinking remained central to social interaction in Britain, and its elites especially liked to overindulge during all-male gatherings. His cistern and wine cooler of silver were among a seventeenth-century nobleman's most prized possessions. He and his friends would be presented with a glass of wine by their servants whenever they called for it throughout a dinner. The servant would hand a full glass to the drinker, who would drain rather than sip it and then hand it back for rinsing and refilling. The ceremonial departure of the ladies from the table to the drawing room marked the start of serious all-male drinking, something that the abstinent John Evelyn described as the 'drink-ordeal'. Whenever he dined at someone else's house, he found it necessary to steel his liver for trial by alcohol, which took place 'whether for the want of better to employ the time,

or affection to the drink, I know not'. There were some aristocrats, he warned, 'whom one could not safely visit after dinner'.
Ladies, though, were not expected to indulge in such antics: the
eighteenth-century Queen Caroline would bawl out a drunken
gentleman, railing 'at him before all the Court upon getting
drunk in her company'.

The convivial gang of all-male drinkers could save time by
having their chamber pots close to hand: hence their often being
located – bizarrely to modern eyes – in the convenient cupboards
of sideboards. But not everyone liked this lazy habit. According
to the seventeenth-century Randle Holme, 'the Jolly crew when
met together over a cup of Ale' should keep the chamber pot
near by 'not for modesty's sake, but that they may see their own
beastliness'. The visiting Frenchman de La Rochefoucauld was
similarly unimpressed in 1784 by drinkers sharing a chamber
pot: 'The sideboard is furnished with a number of chamber pots
and it is a common practice to relieve oneself while the rest
are drinking; one has no kind of concealment and the practice
strikes me as most indecent.' Just as the English have always

The timeless British vice of binge-drinking. The women have withdrawn to
the drawing room to tea, leaving the men to overindulge in the dining room

thought the French effeminate, our neighbours have always thought us boorish in return.

Yet the English remained deeply attached to their ale. The eighteenth-century craze for gin caused consternation not only because of its powerful intoxicating effect, but also because it lacked the ancient, chivalric associations of beer, the drink that 'gave vigour to the arms of our ancestors . . . made them wise in council, and victorious in the field'.

Even the vigorous, religiously inspired teetotal movement of the nineteenth century failed to stamp out the demon drink: 1877 was the year in which more alcohol per head was drunk than before or since. In 1915, the lamp-boy at Longleat House in Wiltshire remembers that still 'beer was allowed regularly . . . it was served in copper jacks, sort of large jugs, and was even drunk at breakfast time'.

In the very same year, the chancellor David Lloyd George, a well-known supporter of the Temperance movement, claimed that alcohol was causing 'more damage in the war than all the submarines put together'. But in fact the two world wars would severely reduce alcohol consumption much more than any government attempts to dictate on the matter.

The production of alcohol had by then moved firmly outside the home, and the brewing industry was severely disrupted in both 1914–18 and 1939–45 by the need to divert resources elsewhere. The amount consumed would remain much lower than the Victorian standard until the end of the 1950s. Then, the return of affluence saw alcohol resume a central position in home life. The cocktail party, the central image of 1950s hospitality, involved plying people with alcohol in one's living room, and Mike Leigh's play *Abigail's Party* (1977) showed the same social occasion remodelled for the 1970s, with the house-proud but crass Beverley forcing her guests to drink themselves sick. Meanwhile, off-stage, the fifteen-year-old Abigail holds a raucous party of her own. The focus of the drinks industry during the 1980s and 1990s would be upon young people, who might otherwise have turned to the readily available drugs instead for their intoxicants.

Drinking at home remains the bugbear of the nation's landlords, and middle-aged, middle-class professionals casually having wine with their dinner every night are the group in society that consumes the most alcohol. A new awareness of the health problems it brings may have lowered consumption levels from their Victorian high. What still exists, though, in all its messy glory, is the ageless and very British concept of the binge.

45 – The Wretched Washing-Up

I hate discussions of feminism that end up with
    who does the dishes . . .
But at the end, there are always the damned dishes.
                    Marilyn French, 1978

Before the dishwasher, any grand house – and indeed many modest dwellings too – had a special room for washing up. The scullery takes its name from the Norman-French *escuelerie*, meaning dish room. The 1677 *Directions for Scullery Maids* lists their duties as follows: 'you must wash and scour all the plates and dishes that are used in the kitchen . . . also all kettles, pots, pans, chamberpots'.

The scullery wasn't just for washing dishes, but also for rinsing food, and even for plucking or removing the entrails of fowl or flesh on their way into the kitchen. Big stone sinks were complemented by wooden kitchen units (you can see some surviving medieval ones at Haddon Hall in Derbyshire), and salting or preserving might also take place here.

In medieval sculleries, people washed the dishes with a nasty black soap made out of sand, ashes and linseed oil. At least it shifted grease. Their seventeenth-century descendants used a 'soap jelly', made by mixing grated soap with water and soda. The cunning scullery maid knew that copper pans could be brightened with lemon and salt (I've tried this and it really works). Mrs Black, in her book *Household Cookery* (1882), was still recommending 'warm water in which is a little soda. Once a week the sauce-pans ought to be well scoured inside. Rub the inside of tinned sauce-pans well over with soap and a little fine sand or bath-brick till they become quite bright.'

Washing up was always one of the very worst jobs in the kitchen. Albert Thomas, who'd done it many times himself, recalled that even a modest dinner party for ten in a wealthy household of the 1920s required no less than 324 items of silver, china and glass to be washed, in addition to the saucepans. Monica Dickens described the depressing state of her 1930s kitchen after dinner, when 'every saucepan in the place was dirty; the sink was piled high with them. On the floor lay the plates and dishes that couldn't be squeezed on to the table or dresser.' She sobbed over many a late-night encounter with the Vim tin.

But many hands could make light work of the task. Indeed, in remote country houses, where entertainment was in short supply, washing up was even a mild form of fun: Eric Horne, the butler, recalled 'a goodly company of us in the servant's hall at night, as the grooms and under gardeners would come in and wash up . . . more for company than anything else'.

Washing dishes and cleaning plates is hard on the hands, and an off-duty footman could still be identified by the state of his thumbs. Unless a household employed a specialist plate-maid, it was he who would blister his digits rubbing jeweller's rouge into silver. 'Cleaning plate is hell,' wrote Ernest King, another butler. 'The hardest job in the house . . . the blisters burst and you kept on despite the pain and you developed a pair of plate hands that never blistered again.' Cleaning knives was a similarly dark art. According to *The Footman's Directory*, it was best done with a mixture of hot melted mutton suet and powder rubbed from a brick.

Like all other domestic duties, washing up could be used to express social hierarchy. In Princess Marina's twentieth-century household at Kensington Palace, the princess herself washed her decorative and ornamental china collection twice a year. The butler washed the best china after family meals, and the 'odd man' did the ordinary china after the other servants had used it.

Only when the people who'd formerly employed servants began to have to do their own washing up did they realise how bad their kitchens had been for their servants' backs. Lesley Lewis, recalling a country-house childhood in pre-war Essex, described the 'two wide shallow sinks under the window . . . it was not until I washed up here myself, in the 1939 war, that I realised how inconvenient the equipment was'. The explanation for many inconveniently low sinks is rather depressing: often they were intended for use by the young, and children were the dishwashing machines of choice in many kitchens.

The first patent for a mechanical dishwasher was taken out in the US by one Joel Houghton in 1850. He designed a wooden tub with a handle at one side: you turned this to spray water

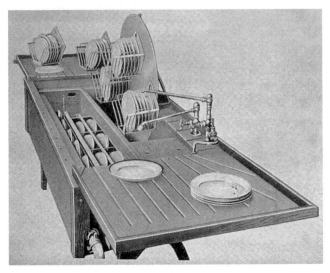

An early mechanical crockery washer from c.1930

somewhat ineffectually onto the dishes. Like so many other contraptions, it was only really made practical in the 1920s when both piped water and electrical power could be readily employed. The dishwasher, though, belongs with the extractor fan and the electric mixer, rather than the cooker or the refrigerator: it did not become a widespread commercial success until well after the Second World War.

Conclusion: What We Can Learn from the Past

The palsy increases on my hand so that I am forced
to leave off my diary – my phrase now is farewell for ever.
Last written words of Lady Sarah Cowper, 1716

This is the end of one story, but the beginning of another.

Today's homes are warmer, more comfortable and easier to clean than ever before. But I believe that the next step in their evolutionary journey will be a strangely backward-seeming one, and that we still have much to learn from our ancestors' houses. In a world where oil supplies are running out, the future of the home will be guided by lessons from the low-technology, pre-industrial past.

In Britain today, the current 'Lifetime Homes' legislation governing the design of new houses is curiously medieval in tone. It insists that, once again, rooms should be able to multitask. The living room must have space for a double bed in case its owner becomes incapacitated and can't climb upstairs to bed. There must be room downstairs to install a lift to reach the bathroom if necessary. The age of specialised rooms, which reached its height in the nineteenth century, is long since over, and adaptability is returning to prominence.

When the oil runs out, we'll see a return of the chimney (plate

41). The only truly sustainable sources of energy are the wind (hard to harness in urban areas), the sun and wood. Forests, if carefully cherished, could provide us with fuel for ever. 'Biomass', or wood-burning, stoves are already making a welcome return, and will grow increasingly popular as sources of domestic heat. The sun is also becoming more important in house design. Once upon a time, people selected sites with good 'air'; now, well-thought-out houses are situated to minimise solar gain in summer, and to maximise it in winter. Most houses will need to face south, to accommodate heat-buffering conservatories and solar panels on sloping roofs, a change that will destroy our now-conventional street arrangements.

The return of the chimney serves another purpose as well, and examples can now be found even in modern buildings without fireplaces. It allows natural ventilation. It lifts stale air out of the house, just like the funnel does on a ship. Mechanical air conditioning uses valuable energy and will soon become simply unaffordable, but a simple chimney containing a heat-recovery unit allows fresh air in while retaining the heat from stale air going out.

Upon the medieval model, walls are getting thicker, for insulation – to keep warmth in – and, increasingly importantly, to keep heat out in a warming world. Windows will grow smaller once again, and houses will contain much less glass: not only because of the intrinsically high energy cost of the glass itself, but because it's such a thermally inefficient material. I myself live in a tall glass tower, built in 1998, and must agree with Francis Bacon, who condemned the great glass-filled palaces of the Jacobean age. In a house 'full of Glass', he wrote, 'one cannot tell where to become to be out of the Sun or Cold'.

We'll also experience the return of the shutter: it's the best way of keeping heat out of a house. Along with a hotter climate, we'll also experience water shortages. Many homes have been put onto meters already, but the daily water consumption per person still runs in Britain today at an average of 160 litres. The government expects us to get down to eighty litres – the contents of just one deep bath – by the end of the decade, and that amount is to include toilet-flushing, cooking and cleaning, as well as washing the body. The simple earth or midden toilet has already been revived in the form of the ecologically sound composting loo. The reuse of 'grey water' (slightly dirty water) for jobs like flushing toilets will become standard, and water will become a much more valuable resource, just as it once was when you had to carry every drop into your house by hand. We'll be growing as water-thrifty as the Victorians were with their average use of twenty litres a day.

There has already been a revival in the natural building materials of the past, breathable substances with low environmental footprints, like wood, wool insulation and lime mortar. In the last ten years, timber-framed houses have once again started to sprout up across Britain. We'll likewise become more medieval in reusing, adapting and making additions to our houses. On an island short of space, it's been calculated that we need to build 200,000 new homes each year to cope with population growth and family breakdown, and that's not even taking possible net immigration into account. According to the Empty Homes Agency, there are currently 700,000 homes standing unused. One simple, indeed obvious, course of action would be to bring them up to date and get them back into occupation, just as people did in the past when resources were scarcer. Buildings today are seen almost as disposable and are not built to last. In the future much more importance will rightly be attached to the materials and energy invested in them.

Inside these new – or indeed old – homes, more time and effort will be spent on getting and keeping them clean. When antibiotics finally become ineffective, as seems likely in the next few decades, minor and indeed major illnesses could once again become things to be tolerated rather than avoided, and we won't be able to rely upon detergents to destroy dirt. Elbow grease will be more highly valued, the skills of growing and preparing food will have to be relearned, and old-fashioned housewifery like Mrs Panton's will return to prominence. The Victorian cook was a terrific recycler and wasted nothing.

Today's builders and town planners are also interested in the notion that people don't just inhabit houses, they live in 'places'. Tudor towns were perfect examples of what planners seek: densely populated, walkable communities, in which rich and poor live in close proximity. In their markets local, seasonal food was available, just as it is in the phenomenon of the farmer's market today.

Many argue that the twentieth century's council estates have had disastrous social consequences. People in poverty feel, and indeed actually grow, poorer if forced to live in a sink estate, while the middle classes flee to their own leafy ghettoes outside city centres. A successful 'place' mixes up the different groups in society, forcing them to mingle and to look out for each other. In this sense, a great mansion like Hardwick Hall was successful social housing: in it Bess of Hardwick lived within metres of the dozens of people under her care. It was a life of huge inequality, but people were part of a common endeavour.

This sounds conservative, but it's radically so. Today we live lives of vastly varying levels of luxury without really being aware of the alternative experiences of those above and below us in terms of wealth. We've spent too long inside our own snug homes, looking smugly out through the window at the world. There's a sense in which children are now prisoners of the home, kept indoors by distrustful parents. We don't know enough about our neighbours, and the dwindling of the natural resources which have fuelled our way of life since the eighteenth century will force us to change and to share more fairly both the work and the reward.

But change should not be a frightening thing. Throughout

all the periods of history, people have thought their own age wildly novel, deeply violent and to be sinking into the utmost depravity; likely, in short, to herald the end of the world. It's comforting to think that the world has not yet ended, and that the pleasures of home life are perennial:

To be happy at home is the ultimate result of all ambition.
(Dr Johnson)

Acknowledgements

Although my name is on the cover of this book, I've written it as a mere dwarf standing on the shoulders of giants. Not only must I acknowledge the historians who have gone before me, but also the researchers on the accompanying BBC TV series and the many experts I had the privilege of interviewing. As the work is based so much upon secondary sources, it seemed wiser to free the text of footnotes, yet it would be wrong to omit mentioning the works of other people upon which I have drawn. I wholeheartedly recommend the following books, of which full details are given in the bibliography below.

For medieval England, Ian Mortimer's *The Time Traveller's Guide* (2008) was incredibly handy; equally so for the Tudor period was Alison Weir's *Henry VIII: King and Court* (2002). For early modern women's lives in the seventeenth century, I relied heavily upon Laura Gowing's *Common Bodies* (2003) and Laurel Thatcher Ulrich's *Good Wives* (1983). Lisa Picard's various books on the early modern period were vital; Don Herzog's *Poisoning the Minds of the Lower Orders* was revelatory for the eighteenth century, as was Amanda Vickery's *Behind Closed Doors*; and Judith Flanders's excellent *The Victorian House* was absolutely essential.

For servants across all periods, Jeremy Musson's *Up and Down Stairs* (2009) is the place to go, and for the topics of beds, bathrooms and heating you need Lawrence Wright's three books first published in the 1960s. Emily Cockayne's *Hubbub* (2007) is full of enjoyably disgusting details on dirt, and Julie Peakman on sex is to be highly recommended (*Lascivious Bodies*, 2004).

For particular chapters, Amanda Carson Banks on *Birth Chairs, Midwives and Medicine* (1999) was just as useful as Valerie Fildes on *Wet Nursing* (1988). A. Roger Ekirch's 2001 theory about sleep, published in the *American Historical Review*, was entirely new to me. Keith Thomas's 1994 essay on cleanliness was essential, as was Mark Blackwell's 2004 article on tooth transplantation. David Eveleigh's was the most reliable book on toilets (*Bogs, Baths and Basins*, 2002). Of the many books I consulted, Sarah Paston-Williams's *The Art of Dining* (1993) was perhaps the most useful on food, and James Nicholls's article 'Drink, the British Disease?' (2010) deserves special mention. Details were provided by all the other books in the bibliography as well.

I must also thank everyone who provided interviews for the book or films, or shared their expertise in other ways: Amanda Vickery, Adrian Tinniswood, Judith Flanders, Jane Pettigrew, David Adshead, Sally Dixon-Smith, Leila Mauro, Issidora Petrovich, Professor David Morgan, Alison Sim, Lesley Parker, Hannah Tiplady, Cathy Flower Bond, Victoria Bradley, Phil Banner, Dr Lesley Hall, Deirdre Murphy, Ray Tye, Ann Lawton, Joanna Marschner, Beryl Evans, Kris Gough, Jean Alden, Val Sambrook, Joanne and Kevin Massey, Angela Lee, Dominic Sandbrook, Andrew Barber, Andy Swain, Patricia Whittington Farrell, Sebastian Edwards, David Milne, Richard Hewlings, Peter Yorke, Sparkle Moore, Jasia Boelhouwer, Ivan Day, Peter Brears, Reena Suleman, Dr John Goodall, Maureen Dillon, Clive Aslet, Alex Jones, Charlotte Woodman, Janet Bradshaw, Mick Ricketts, Simon McCormack, Helen Bratt-Wyton, Tom Betteridge and Katherine Ibbett.

At Silver River, I'm ever so grateful to Daisy Goodwin, Deborah O'Conner, Sam Lawrence and Beccy Green in the office, and then to the *If Walls Could Talk* team itself: Caterina Turroni, Eleanor Scoones, James Greig, Harry Garne, Brendan Easton, Adam Toy, Huw Martin, Simon Mitchell, Adam Jackson, Fred Hart, James Cooper, and above all, Emma Hindley and Hugo MacGregor, series producer and director respectively. At the BBC, Martin Davidson and Cassian Harrison saw us through stalwartly from start to finish. At Faber, Julian Loose (my much-valued three-time editor), Anne Owen, Rebecca Pearson and all their colleagues have done me proud.

At home, my dearest Mark's expertise as an architect helped make this book better. Finally, I dedicate my work to Ned Worsley. Not only did she bring me up to be interested in history and houses, but she also did the picture research. Thanks, Mum.

ACKNOWLEDGEMENTS

PICTURE CREDITS

In-text Illustrations

Pages 9, 52, 60, 79, 81, 87, 108, 126, 143, 147, 155, 164, 197, 200, 223, 240, 244, 263, 265, 267, 288, 304, 319: Private collection; page 23: Royal College of Obstetricians and Gynaecologists; reproduced with permission; pages 24, 30, 34: Wellcome Library, London; page 46: From *English Women's Clothing in the Nineteenth Century*, C. Willett Cunnington (1937), Faber and Faber, London; page 49: V&A Images/ Victoria and Albert Museum, London; pages 61, 152: Weidenfeld archives; page 89: © The British Library Board (7743.d.29); page 118: © Historic Royal Palaces; page 120: By courtesy of the Trustees of Sir John Soane's Museum; page 134: Library of Congress; page 161: Museum of London; page 170: Museum of Menstruation and Women's Health; page 193: Ceredigion Museum, Aberystwyth; page 213: © The British Library Board (1607/1716); pages 237, 314: © The British Museum; page 309: The British Library Board (1509/1462).

Colour Plates

1: © NTPL/Dennis Gilbert; 2, 4, 6, 10, 14, 34: © Historic Royal Palaces; 3: Bibliothèque Nationale de France; 5: By kind permission of the Trustees of the Wallace Collection, London; 7, 13, 30, 32, 38: Private collection; 8: Wellcome Library, London; 9: Tate, London, 2009; 11, 18: © NTPL/Robert Morris; 12, 15, 17, 24, 26, 39: Silver River Productions UK; 16: Tate, London, 2009; 19: Beamish Museum Limited, Photographic Library; 20: By kind permission of the Laramie Plains Museum, Wyoming, USA; 21: © The British Library Board (Royal 16 F.II, f. 73); 22: Museumlandschaft Hessen Kassel, Graphische Sammlung; 23: Ref. 67944 © NTPL/Andreas von Einsiedel; 25: Ref. 143462 © NTPL/Nadia Mackenzie; 27: Ref. 20869 © NTPL/Andreas von Einsiedel; 28: Ref. 5597 © NTPL/Michael Boys; 29: Norfolk Record Office, ref. MC 2105/1/1, PH3; 31: Science and Society Picture Library; 33: The Bodleian Libraries, University of Oxford (MS Douce 383, fol. 17r); 35: Reproduced by permission of York Civic Trust, Fairfax House, York; 36: Abergavenny Museum; 37: Ref. 151480 © NTPL/Nadia Mackenzie; 40: Centre for Local Studies at Darlington Library; 41: www.bioregional.com

329

Bibliography

Addy, S. O., *The Evolution of the English House* (n.p., 1898)

Airs, Malcolm, *The Tudor and Jacobean Country House* (Stroud, 1995)

Allen, Valerie, *On Farting, Language and Laughter in the Middle Ages* (Basingstoke, 2007)

Angeloglou, Maggie, *A History of Make-Up* (London, 1970)

Anon., *Advice to Governesses* (London, 1727)

—— *Ordinances for the Royal Household Edward III to William and Mary* (London, 1787)

Arnold, Janet, *Queen Elizabeth's Wardrobe Unlock'd* (Leeds, 1988)

Aronson, A., 'The Anatomy of Taste', *Modern Language Notes*, vol. 61, no. 4 (April, 1946), pp. 228–36

Banks, Amanda Carson, *Birth Chairs, Midwives and Medicine* (Jackson, Mississippi, 1999)

Barclay, Andrew, 'The Inventories of the English Royal Collection, *temp.* James II', *Journal of the History of Collections*, vol. 22, no. 1 (2010), pp. 1–13

Blackwell, Mark, '"Extraneous Bodies": The Contagion of Live-Tooth Transplantation in Late-Eighteenth-Century England', *Eighteenth-Century Life*, vol. 28.1 (winter 2004), pp. 21–68

Blume, Judy, *Are You There God? It's Me, Margaret* (London, 1978)

Booy, David (Ed.), *The Notebooks of Nehemiah Wallington, 1618–1654* (Aldershot, 2007)

Boswell, J., *Same-Sex Unions in Premodern Europe* (New York, 1994)

Bowle, John, *John Evelyn and His World* (London, 1981)

Breton, Nicholas, *The Courtier and the Countryman* (1618)

Brown, Julia Prewitt, *The Bourgeois Interior* (Charlottesville and London, 2008)

Campbell, Richard, *The London Tradesman* (London, 1747)

Case, Elizabeth, *Cook's Away* (New York, 1943)

Cawthorne, Nigel, *Robin Hood* (London, 2010)

Chalmers, Leona W., *The Intimate Side of a Woman's Life* (New York, 1937)

Chavasse, Pye H., *Advice to a Wife* (Birmingham, third edn, 1853)

Cheyne, G., *An Essay on Health and Long Life* (London, 1724)

Clarke, Norma, *Queen of the Wits* (London, 2008)

Clifford, Colin, *The Asquiths* (London, 2002)

Cockayne, Emily, *Hubbub, Filth, Noise and Stench in England* (New Haven and London, 2007)

Conran, Terence, *The House Book* (London, 1974)

Corfield, Penelope, 'Walking the City Streets, the Urban Odyssey in Eighteenth-Century England', *Journal of Urban History*, vol. 16, no. 2 (1990), pp. 132–74

Cosnett, Thomas, *The Footman's Directory* (London, 1825)

Cox, Margaret, *Life and Death in Spitalfields, 1700–1850* (York, 1996)

Cram, David, Jeffrey L. Forgeng and Dorothy Johnston (Eds), *Francis Willoughby's Book of Games* (Aldershot, 2003)

Cregan, Kate, *The Theatre of the Body, Staging Death and Embodying Life in Early-Modern London* (Turnhout, Belgium, 2009)

Cuddy, Neil, 'The Revival of the Entourage', in David Starkey (Ed.), *The English Court, from the Wars of the Roses to the Civil War* (London, 1987)

Delaney, Janice, Mary Jane Lupton and Emily Toth, *The Curse: A Cultural History of Menstruation* (Urbana and Chicago, 1974, 1988)

Dillon, Maureen, *Artificial Sunshine: A Social History of Domestic Lighting* (London, 2002)

Drummond, J. C., and Anne Wilbraham, *The Englishman's Food: A History of Five Centuries of English Diet*, revised Dorothy Hollingsworth (London, 1939, 1994)

Duby, Georges (Ed.), *A History of Private Life*, vol. 2, *Revelations of the Medieval World* (Harvard, 1988)

Duchess of Devonshire, The, *The House, A Portrait of Chatsworth* (London, 1982)

Duffy, Eamon, *Marking the Hours* (New Haven and London, 2006)

Ekirch, A. Roger, *At Day's Close: A History of Nighttime* (London, 2005)

—— 'Sleep We Have Lost: Pre-Industrial Slumber in the British Isles', *The American Historical Review*, vol. 1, no. 2 (April, 2001)

Elias, Norbert, *The Civilizing Process, State Formation and Civilization* (Oxford, 1982)

Eveleigh, David J., *Bogs, Baths and Basins* (Stroud, 2002)

Evelyn, John, *The Miscellaneous Writings of John Evelyn*, Ed. William Upcott (London, 1825)

Fildes, Valerie, *Wet Nursing, a History* (Oxford, 1988)

Flanders, Judith, *The Victorian House* (London, 2004)

Floyer, Sir John, and Edward Baynard, *Psychrolousia: Or, The History of Cold Bathing* (1674)

French, Marilyn, *The Women's Room* (London, 1978, 1997)

Furnivall, Frederick J. (Ed.), *The Babees Book, etc.*, Early English Text Society (London, 1868)

Gerard, Alexander, *An Essay on Taste* (Edinburgh, 1780)

Gere, Charlotte, with Lesley Hoskins, *The House Beautiful: Oscar Wilde and the Aesthetic Interior* (London, 2000)

Girouard, Mark, *A Country House Companion* (London, 1987)

—— *Elizabethan Architecture* (London, 2009)

—— *Life in the English Country House* (London and New Haven, 1978)

Gorst, Frederick John, *Of Carriages and Kings* (London, 1956)

Gouge, William, *Of Domesticall Duties* (London, 1622)

Gowing, Laura, *Common Bodies: Women, Touch and Power in Seventeenth-Century England* (New Haven and London, 2003)

Greco, Gina L., and Christine M. Rose (Eds), *The Good Wife's Guide, Le Ménagier de Paris* (Ithaca and London, 2009)

Greed, Clara, *Inclusive Urban Design: Public Toilets* (Oxford, 2003)

Grundy, Isobel, *Lady Mary Wortley Montagu* (Oxford, 1999)

Hagglund, Elizabeth, 'Cassandra Willoughby's Visits to Country Houses', *The Georgian Group Journal*, vol. xi (2001), pp. 185–99

Halford, Sir Henry, *An Account of what Appeared on Opening the Coffin of King Charles I* (London, 1813)

Halliday, Stephen, *The Great Stink of London* (Stroud, 1999)

Hammond, P. W., *Food and Feast in Medieval England* (Stroud, 1993)

Handlin, David P., *The American Home* (Boston and Toronto, 1979)

Hardyment, Christina, *Home Comforts, a History of Domestic Arrangements* (London, 1992)

Harrison, Molly, *The Kitchen in History* (Reading, 1972)

Harrison, Rosina (Ed.), *Gentlemen's Gentlemen* (London, 1976)

Hart-Davis, Adam, *Thunder, Flush and Thomas Crapper* (London, 1997)

Hartley, Dorothy, *Food in England* (London, 1954)

Hartley, L. P., *The Go-Between* (London, 1953)

Hawthorne, Rosemary, *Knickers, An Intimate Appraisal* (London, 1985)

Herzog, Don, *Poisoning the Minds of the Lower Orders* (Princeton, 1998)

Hole, Christina, *The English Housewife in the Seventeenth Century* (London, 1953)

Holme, Randle, *The Academy of Armory* (1688)

Hoock, Holger, *Empires of the Imagination* (London, 2010)

Horn, Pamela, *Flunkeys and Scullions* (Stroud, 2004), p. 155

Horner, Craig (Ed.), *The Diary of Edmund Harrold, Wigmaker of Manchester, 1712–15* (Aldershot, 2008)

Hussey, David, and Margaret Ponsonby, *Buying for the Home* (Aldershot, 2008)

James, Henry, *The Europeans* (1878; Harmondsworth, Middlesex, 1964)

—— *The Portrait of a Lady* (London, 1881)

James, Thomas Beaumont, *The Palaces of Medieval England* (London, 1990)

Kerr, Robert, *The Gentleman's House* (London, 1864)

Klapthor, Margaret Brown, and Allida M. Black, *The First Ladies of the United States of America* (Washington, 2006)

Kugler, Anne, '"I feel myself decay apace": Old Age in the Diary of Lady Sarah Kugler (1644–1720)', in Lynn Botello and Pat Thane (Eds), *Women and Aging in British Society since 1500* (Harlow, Essex, 2001), pp. 43–65

Kynaston, David, *Family Britain 1951–57* (London, 2009)

Laqueur, Thomas, *Making Sex, Body and Gender from the Greeks to Freud* (Cambridge, Massachusetts, and London, 1990)

Lawson-Dick, Oliver (Ed.), *Aubrey's Brief Lives* (1949; London, 1992)

Lees-Milne, James, *Ancestral Voices and Prophesying Peace, Diaries 1942–1945* (1975; London, 1995)

Light, Alison, *Mrs Woolf and the Servants* (London, 2007)

Lindsay, Philip, *Hampton Court, A History* (London, 1948)

Marriage Guidance Booklets, no. 1, *Sex in Marriage* (n.d.)

Miller, William Ian, *The Anatomy of Disgust* (Harvard, 1997)

Mortimer, Ian, *The Time Traveller's Guide to Medieval England* (London, 2008)

Mullins, Samuel, and Gareth Griffiths, *Cap and Apron: An Oral History of Domestic Service in the Shires, 1880–1950* (Leicestershire Museums, Harborough Series, No. 8, 1986)

Musson, Jeremy, *Up and Down Stairs, The History of the Country House Servant* (London, 2009)

Muthesius, Hermann, *The English House* (1904; Oxford, 1979)

Myers, A. R. (Ed.), *The Household of Edward IV* (Manchester, 1959)

National Trust, The, *Kedleston Hall* (1998)

Nicholls, James, 'Drink, the British Disease?' *History Today* (January 2010), pp. 10–17

Nicolson, Harold, *Monarchy* (London, 1962)

Nicolson, Juliet, *The Great Silence, 1918–1920, Living in the Shadow of the Great War* (London, 2009)

Niesewand, Nonie, *Contemporary Details* (London, 1992)

Norton, Mary Beth, *Founding Mothers and Fathers, Gendered Power and the Forming of American Society* (New York, 1996)

Novy, Priscilla, *Housework Without Tears* (London, 1945)

O'Connell, Sheila, *London, 1753* (British Museum, London, 2003)

Palmer, Marilyn, 'Comfort and Convenience in the English Country House', in *The Edwardian Great House*, Ed. Malcolm Airs (Oxford, 2000)

Palmer, R., *The Water Closet* (Newton Abbot, 1973)

Partridge, John, *The Treasurie of Commodious Conceites, and Hidden Secrets* (London, 1584)

Paston-Williams, Sara, *The Art of Dining* (National Trust, London, 1993)

Peakman, Julie, *Lascivious Bodies, a Sexual History of the Eighteenth Century* (London, 2004)

Pettigrew, Jane, *A Social History of Tea* (London, 2001)

Plante, Ellen M., *The American Kitchen, 1700 to the Present* (New York, 1995)

Pollard, Justin, *Alfred the Great* (London, 2005)

Purcell, Sarah J., and L. Edward Purcell, *The Life and Work of Eleanor Roosevelt* (Indianapolis, 2002)

Pym, Barbara, *Jane and Prudence* (London, 1953)

Reynolds, Helen, *A Fashionable History of Make-up* (London, 2003)

Riley, Terence, *The Un-Private House* (The Museum of Modern Art, New York, 1999)

Russell, Dr Richard, *Dissertation on the Use of Seawater* (1752)

Rybczynski, Witold, *Home, a Short History of an Idea* (London, 1988)

Sambrook, Pamela, *A Country House at Work: Three Centuries of Dunham Massey* (National Trust, 2003)

—— 'Strategies for Survival: The Servant Problem in the First Half of the Twentieth Century', in *The Twentieth Century Great House*, Ed. Malcolm Airs (Oxford, 2002)

—— *The Country House Servant* (Stroud, 1999)

Sandbrook, Dominic, *Never Had It So Good: A History of Britain from Suez to the Beatles* (London, 2005)

Sayers, Dorothy L., *Busman's Honeymoon* (Harmondsworth, 1937)

Scott, Margaret, *Medieval Dress and Fashion* (The British Library, n.d., *c.*2003)

Shawcross, William, *Queen Elizabeth, The Queen Mother* (London, 2009)

Slack, Paul, *The Impact of Plague in Tudor and Stuart England* (London, 1985)

Smith, Eliza, *The Complete Housewife*, seventeenth edn (London, 1766)

Starkey, David, 'Representation through Intimacy', in Ioan Lewis (Ed.), *Symbols and Sentiments, Cross-Cultural Currents in Symbolism* (London, 1977), pp. 187–224

Stone, Lawrence, *The Family, Sex, and Marriage in England, 1500–1800* (London, 1977)

Sturgeon, Launcelot, *Essays, Moral, Philosophical and Stomachical, on the important science of Good-Living* (London, 1822)

Symons, Michael, *A History of Cooks and Cooking* (Totnes, 2001)

Thane, Pat, *Old Age in English History* (Oxford, 2000)

Thomas, Keith, 'Cleanliness and godliness in early modern England', in Anthony Fletcher and Peter Roberts, eds., *Religion, Culture and Society in early modern England* (Cambridge, 1994) pp. 56–83

Tinniswood, Adrian, *The Arts and Crafts House* (London, 1999)

Tomalin, Claire, *Samuel Pepys, The Unequalled Self* (London, 2002)

Trusler, John, *The Honours of the Table* (1788; Cambridge, 1931)

Tyron, Thomas, *A Treatise of Cleanliness* (London, 1682)

—— *Some Memoirs of the Life of Mr Thomas Tryon* (London, 1705)

—— *Wisdom Dictates* (London, 1691)

Ulrich, Laurel Thatcher, *Good Wives* (Oxford, 1983)

Verral, William, *A Complete System of Cookery* (London, 1759)

Vickery, Amanda, *Behind Closed Doors* (London, 2009)

Waller, Maureen, *1700, Scenes from London Life* (London, 2000)

—— *Ungrateful Daughters* (London, 2002)

Ward, W. R., 'The Administration of the Window and Assessed Taxes, 1696–1798', *English Historical Review,* vol. 67 (1952), pp. 522–42

Warner, Jessica, *Craze, Gin and Debauchery in an Age of Reason* (London, 2003)

Wecker, Johann Jacob, *Cosmeticks* (London, 1660)

Weir, Alison, *Henry VIII, King and Court* (London, 2002)

Wharton, Edith, *The Buccaneers* (1938; Harmondsworth, 1994)

Willett, C., and Philip Cunnington, *The History of Underclothes* (London, 1951)

Williams, Neville, *Powder and Paint* (London, 1957)

Wilson, Philip K., *Surgery, Skin and Syphilis: Daniel Turner's London (1667–1741)* (Atlanta, 1999)

Wood, J. G., *The Illustrated Natural History* (London, 1853)

Woodforde, John, *The Strange Story of False Teeth* (London, 1968)

Woolley, Hannah, *The Gentlewoman's Companion; or A Guide to the Female Sex* (London, third edn, 1682)

Wright, Lawrence, *Clean and Decent* (London, 1960, 1980)

—— *Home Fires Burning* (1964)

—— *Warm and Snug* (1962)

Wright, T., *A History of Domestic Manners and Sentiments in England During the Middle Ages* (London, 1862)

Yorke, F. R. S., *The Modern Flat* (London, 1937)

—— *The Modern House* (London, 1934)

Index

INDEX

Faulkner, William, 171
Felbrigg, Norfolk, 167
Female Medical Society, 25
fertility, 67, 73, 76
Fielding, Henry: *Enquiry into the Causes of the late Increase of Robbers*, 285
Fiennes, Celia, 92–3
fireplaces: chimneys, 192, 322; Hampton Court, 191; hearth tax, 196; heating, 191, 192, 198, 199–200; kitchen, 3, 241; stoves, 198, 199; used as toilets, 153–4
firewood, 95
fish, 279
fleas, 112, 152
floor coverings, 176–7, 192
Floyer, Sir John: *The History of Cold Bathing*, 118
foie gras, 286–7
food: poisoning, 297; storage, 250, 270–3; tinned, 296, 297
food mixer, electric, 273, 320
foodies, 256, 269, 297
Footman's Directory, The, 103, 201, 215, 231, 247, 263, 318
footmen: distances covered daily, 262; duties, 103, 199, 210–11, 251, 318; hierarchy of, 208; livery, 207, 211; powdered hair, 142; replaced, 247; serving meals, 251, 304; sodomised, 77; table setting, 302; wife's demands for, 231
forceps, 22–3
forks, 299, 301
Foundling Hospital, London, 33
Francis I, 39, 82, 138–9
Frankfurt Kitchens, 267–8
French, Marilyn: *The Women's Room*, 27, 215, 273, 317
French: cuisine, 307–8, 310; language, 306
fridges, 271–3
fruit, 294–5
frumenty, 280
Fuller, Thomas: *Gnomologia*, 254
funerals, 236–40

Galen, Claudius, 58, 117
games, 226–7, 229
Garbo, Greta, 149
garderobes, 152, 154, 166, 216
Garter, Order of the, 39, 39, 108
gas: cooking, 241, 264–6; lighting, 201–3
Gas Light and Coke Company, 201–2
Gaskell, Elizabeth: *Cranford*, 193
Gay, John, 260
Gayety's Medicated Paper, 167
Gentleman's Magazine, The, 26, 132
George II, 26–7
George III, 76, 156, 201
George IV, 45, 47
George VI, 22
germs, 15, 25, 172
ghosts, 101–2
Gillette, King C., 144
Gillray, James, 34
gin, 285–6, 315
Girls' Own Paper, The, 271
Glasse, Hannah, 29, 208
glasses, 302–3
Glyn, Elinor, 63
Go-Between, The, 277
Goldsmith, Oliver, 12
gonorrhoea, 80, 81, 83
Good Housekeeping, 257
Gorst, Frederick, 304
Great Bed of Ware, 9
great chamber, 41, 178, 220, 227
Great Exhibition (1851), 163, 185, 264
great hall: architecture, 245–6; entertainment, 229, 280; fireplace, 191; floor covering, 176–7; Hampton Court, 191; meals, 245–7, 275, 280, 299; sleeping, 3, 6, 177; storage, 38; Victorian, 247
Great House of Easement, 153–4
Great Stink (1858), 162
greenhouses, 199
Grey, Lady Jane, 77
Grimesthorpe Castle, Lincolnshire, 167
Grimmett, Gordon, 211
guests, 219, 225–9
Gulliver, Lemuel: *The Pleasures and Felicities of Marriage*, 183

342

Horne, Eric, 142, 209, 210, 318
hospitals, 18, 20, 27–8, 61–2
hotels, 217
Houghton Hall, Norfolk, 194
House of Commons, 74
house parties, 227–8
household size, 217–18
housemaids: advice to young, 208;
    cleaning tasks, 200; duties, 15, 98–9,
    199–200; emptying chamber pots, 15,
    115, 126–7; hair, 144
housework, 215–18, 323–4
Howard, Henrietta, 140
Howard, Katherine, 153
Howard, Thomas, 178
Humberstone, M.: *The Absurdity and
    Injustice of the Window Tax*, 196
humours, four, 58, 59, 82, 117–18, 134,
    236
Hunter, John, 135, 239

ice cream, 270, 271
ice house, 270–1
Ideal Home Exhibition, 273
illegitimate babies, 74, 75–6
impotence, 64, 73
Infant Life Protection Bill (1872), 35
infanticide, 74
Ironmonger, The, 128
ITV, 229
Izal, 168

Jacobites, 302–3, 307
James I, 92, 226, 239; *The Counterblast
    to Tobacco*, 281
James II, 21, 302
James, Henry, 187
Jennings, George, 158, 165
Joan of Kent, 100–1
John Bull, 235
Johnson, Samuel, 10, 181, 325
Johnson and Johnson, 170
Jones, Dr John: *The Mysteries of Opium
    Reveal'd*, 25
Joubert, Laurent, 96

Katherine of Aragon, 68–9, 138–9, 238

Kedleston Hall, Derbyshire, 119, 180–2,
    185, 250–1
Kensington Palace, 42, 47, 94, 319
Kenwood Chef food mixer, 273
Kerr, Robert, 208, 261
kettles, electric, 272
keys, 90, 131
kibbutz, 218
King, Ernest, 115, 318
Kingsley, Charles: *The Water Babies*, 123
kissing, 78, 223, 230
kitchen: all-male, 243–4; basement, 251;
    brazier, 261; cottage, 249; design,
    257, 264, 267–8; distance from din-
    ing room, 249–51; electric cookers,
    265–6; extractor fans, 256, 268; fire
    dangers, 249; fitted, 267–8; food
    storage, 250, 270–3; fridges, 271–3;
    gas cookers, 241, 264–6; history, 241,
    268–9; medieval, 261; oven, 241,
    258–9, 262, 265, 268, 291; range,
    127, 241, 255, 262–3; royal, 243–4;
    servants, 247–8, 251–2, 264; smells,
    253, 255–6, 270; spit roasting, 258,
    260–1, 291; stewing stove, 261;
    stoves, 198, 262; twentieth-century,
    248, 252–3; utensils, 278; washing up,
    317–20
kitchen gardens, 199
knickers, 43, 45
Knight, Charles, 141
knives, 299

La Rochefoucauld, François de, 151,
    225, 314
Ladies Dispensatory, The, 23, 79
Ladies' Home Journal, 263
Ladies' Temperance Society, 44
Lancet, The, 25
Larkin, Philip, 63
Lauderdale, Elizabeth Dysart, Duchess
    of, 54, 284
Lawrence, D. H.: *Lady Chatterley's
    Lover*, 72
laxatives, 59, 60, 119, 295
*Learned Dissertation on a Dumpling,
    A*, 241

parlour, 173, 177, 184, 192, 230, 280
Parr, Katherine, 139
parties, 225–8
Partridge, John: *The Treasurie of Commodious Conceites*, 25, 55
Pawson, John, 131
Peasants' Revolt, 100–1
Peirce, Melusina Fay, 216–17
Penny (royal barber), 138–9
Penshurst Place, Kent, 6
Pepys, Samuel: bedroom, 10, 61; bowel movements, 156; chocolate drinking, 285; hairdressing, 139–40, 141; maidservants, 75, 139–40; sex life, 65; surgery, 61; tea drinking, 283; use of tobacco, 281–2; view of rouge, 146; wakefulness, 97, 100; wife's bowel movements, 154; wig, 140–1
petticoats, 43–4
Petworth House, Sussex, 279–80
Philip, King of Spain, 216
Philip, Prince, 94
Philippa, wife of Edward III, 176
pillow cases, 14
pillows, 8, 14
piped water, 109, 119–22
pockets, 49–50
Poison Detected, 296
pornography, 20, 54, 72, 77, 127
porridge, 277
potatoes, 282–3, 293–4
pottage, 258, 292–3
Powys, Mrs Lybbe, 182
prayer books, 53, 54
praying, 51
precedence, 300
pregnancy, 18–19, 26, 27, 254
presence chamber, 177
Princes in the Tower, 100
privacy, 4, 8, 11–12, 101, 157, 208
privy chamber, 177
privy parlour, 245
prostitutes, 47, 63, 81–2, 145, 148–9, 202
Prynne, William, 137
Pückler-Muskau, Prince, 227
puerperal fever, 20, 25

purge, 60
Puritans, 30, 53, 130–1, 137, 146, 233
pyjamas, 86–7
Pym, Barbara: *Jane and Prudence*, 148

Queen magazine, 272
Queen's Closet Opened, The, 55

Radio Times, 229
ragouts, 307–8
Raleigh, Sir Walter, 281
Ramazzini, Bernardino, 31
rape, 65
Rational Dress Society, 44
razors, 144
reading, 51, 152
reception room, 178–9
recipes: beauty treatments, 138, 148, 149; books, 55, 266, 289; cookery, 271, 283, 289, 294, 301, 307; household management, 112, 263; medical, 25, 57, 59, 73–4; standardised, 263, 289
refrigerator, 271–3
Regulo thermostat, 264–5
Rhodes, Hugh, 301
Richard II, 100
Richard III, 100
Robin Hood, 291
Robin starch, 257
Roland the Farter, 293
Romance of the Rose, 64, 110
Roosevelt, Eleanor, 225
rouge, 146, 149
Rousseau, Jean-Jacques, 33–4
Rowlandson, Thomas, 97
Royal College of Physicians, 57
Royal College of Surgeons, 136
Royal Naval Dockyard, Portsmouth, 139
Royal Society, 216
Rules to be Observed in Walking with Persons of Honour, 221
Rumford, Count, 198, 262
rushes, 176–7, 192
Russell, John: *Book of Nurture*, 5, 166, 246

Russell, Richard: *Dissertation on the Use of Seawater*, 119
Rutland, Duke of, 201

St James's Palace, 76, 202, 270
Saki, 243
salads, 294
Salisbury, Countess of, 39
saloon, 178, 181, 194
salt, 278–9, 289, 299
Saltram House, Devon, 286
Sambourne, Linley, 127, 162
Sanctorius, physician, 118
Sanderson Company, 186, 189
Sandringham House, 163
Sanitary Reform Movement, 15
sanitary towels, 170–2
saucepans, 308–10, 318
sauces, 306–10
Saussure, César de, 88, 311
scullery, 317–18
scullery maids, 317–18
Sealed Knot, 54
seawater, 119
servants: beds, 6, 14–15; chamber servants, 41–2; cleanliness, 128; disappearance of, 205; employers' sexual relations with, 74–5, 77, 139–40; kitchen, 247–8, 251–2; liveries, 206–7; manners, 220–1; relations between family and servants, 208–12; relations between mistress and servants, 212–14; royal bed-making, 89–90; status of domestic service, 206–8; table etiquette, 299; timekeeping, 98–9; washing up, 317–19; water carrying, 125–7
service à la Russe, 303–4
sex: bathhouses, 110–11; bundling, 66–7; conception, 73–6; eighteenth-century attitudes, 26–7, 63–4; female sexuality, 64–6; frigidity, 59; homosexuality, 20, 77–8; impotence, 64, 73; marriage, 70–2; masturbation, 64, 77, 78–9; medication for lust, 78; nineteenth-century attitudes, 12, 26, 63; orgasm, 64, 65–6; pornography, 20, 54, 72, 77, 127; pre-marital, 67; twentieth-century attitudes, 70–2; venereal disease, 80–3; wedding rituals, 67–70
Sex and the City, 56
Seymour, Jane, 238
Shakespeare, William, 295; *King Lear*, 107; *Richard III*, 100
shampoo, 143
shaving, 138–9, 144
sheets: bathing, 108–9, 111; bed-making, 13, 14, 15, 88, 89; childbed linen, 19; cleaning, 17, 115, 167; four-poster beds, 9; royal, 89; servants' beds, 6; top, 13, 14, 16; warming, 22
Shelley, Percy Bysshe, 70
shower, stand-up, 130
Shrewsbury, Bess of Hardwick, Countess of, 178, 324
Shugborough Hall, 264
shutters, 322
sinks, 319
skin: make-up, 145–50; pale, 145–6; spots and sores, 147–8
sleeping: bundling, 6–7; daytime, 96–7; patterns, 95–9; sharing sleeping space, 3–4, 8–9, 12–13
Smellie, William, 22–3
smells: chamber pots, 153; communal toilet, 153; extractor fan, 256, 268; flushing toilet, 159, 160; Great Stink, 162; kitchen, 250, 253, 255–6, 270; lower classes, 128; miasma theory of sickness, 254; perfumes, 123, 254; personal odour, 113, 122, 254; pregnancy, 254; sanitary towel disposal, 171–2; smoking, 281–2; soap-making, 115; sweat, 122, 123; tainted meat, 270; tallow candles, 194–5
Smith, Eliza, 148
Smithfield Market, 287, 288
smoking, 281–2
smoking room, 173, 178, 282
Smollett, Tobias, 122, 303
Snow, Dr John, 162
snuff, 282
soap, 115, 317

sofas, 179, 181–2, 185
solar, 6, 177, 230
solitude, 51–2
Sophia, Princess, 76
Southey, Robert, 175
SPAN houses, 204
Spectator, The, 146, 213
Spencer, Elizabeth, 41, 231
spices, 279–80
spirits, 312–13
spit roasting, 258, 260–1, 291
spoons, 299
Starck, Philippe, 131
Statute of Artificers, The, 97
stays, 47–8, 223
Steele, Richard, 97, 275
Stone and Company, 308–9
storage: closets, 51, 53–4; clothes, 37–8; food, 250, 270–3
Stowe, Harriet Beecher, 264; *American Woman's Home*, 262
Stratfield Saye House, Hampshire, 199
studio apartment, 179
Sturgeon, Launcelot, 306, 307
subtleties, 132, 280, 281, 301–2
Sudeley Castle, 139
suffragettes, 149
sugar, 280–1, 289
supper, 275
surgeons, 61
sweat, 118, 122, 123
sweet potatoes, 282–3
Swift, Jonathan, 75, 211, 295
Syon Abbey, 238
syphilis, 55, 80, 82, 83, 148

table etiquette, 298–304; top table, 245–6
takeaways, 248, 259
Tallow Chandlers, Worshipful Company of, 195
tampons, 171
tapestries, 175, 176, 192, 200
tapeworm, 294
taps, 109, 118
taste, 180
Tatton Old Hall, Cheshire, 14

tea (drink), 276, 283–5
tea (meal), 274, 275–6
teenagers, 35–6
teeth: cleaning, 132–3; false, 133–4, 135; live tooth transplantation, 135, 136; removing, 132
television, 228–9, 245
Temperance movement, 44, 315
Thomas, Keith, 123
Thompson, Flora: *Lark Rise to Candleford*, 258
Tiffin, Mr (bug-destroyer), 213
timber-framed houses, 323
time: measurement, 98–9; telling the, 95; timetables, 98–9
Times, The, 50, 308
toast, 276
toaster, electric, 273
tobacco, 281–2
toilet paper, 166–8
toilets: carriage pots, 157; chamber pots, 43, 126–7, 151, 153, 157; close stool, 27, 59, 60, 90, 152–3, 156–7, 167; communal, 153–4; composting, 323; D-bend, 159, 164–5; earth closets, 160, 323; fixed-position indoor, 152; flushing, 157, 158–60, 323; royal, 156, 167; S-bend, 159, 165; stool ducketts, 167; terminology, 165; Wesley's insistence on, 122–3
tomatoes, 282
toothache, 133
toothbrushes, 133
top table, 245–6
Tower of London: executions, 77; garderobes, 152; Medieval Palace, 6; Peasants' Revolt, 100; prisoners, 51, 175, 286; ritual bath, 108; royal bedchamber, 53, 176
Treatise of Ghosts, A, 96
trenchers, 246
turtle soup, 286

Ulrich, Laurel Thatcher, 66
Uncumber, St, 64
undertakers, 236–8
underwear, 38–9, 42–5, 114, 116